ERASTUS CORNING
Merchant and Financier
1794-1872

Erastus Corning

ERASTUS CORNING

Merchant and Financier

1794-1872

IRENE D. NEU

CORNELL UNIVERSITY PRESS

Ithaca, New York

This work has been brought to publication with the assistance of a grant from the Ford Foundation.

CORNELL UNIVERSITY PRESS

First published 1960

First printing, Fall Creek Books, 2010

Fall Creek Books is an imprint of Cornell University Press dedicated to making available again classic books that document the history, culture, natural history, and folkways of New York State. Presented in new paperback editions that faithfully reproduce the contents of the original editions, Fall Creek Books titles will appeal to all readers interested in New York and the state's rich past. For a complete listing of titles published under the Fall Creek Books imprint, please visit www.cornellpress.cornell.edu.

To

ARTHUR H. COLE

Preface

IN the middle of the last century Erastus Corning of Albany,
New York, had a nationwide reputation. Known in the East as
a merchant, railroad president, financier, and politician, he
was recognized in the West as a railroad promoter and land
speculator. His career stretched backward for more than three
decades and was to stretch ahead for another two.

Beginning as a clerk in a hardware store at the age of thirteen,
Corning at twenty-one had acquired a partnership in a firm engaged in the same business. By 1825, when he was just over
thirty, he was already established as one of the leading merchants
of Albany, New York's second city. By that time, also, he was
branching into the diversified activities which were to char-
acterize his later career. In the mid-1830's he launched the Utica
and Schenectady Rail-Road Company and the Albany City
Bank, assuming the presidency of both. In the thirties, too, he
made his first large investments in land, becoming a member
of no less than five land companies. By the end of the 1840's he
had become what the nineteenth century called a "monied
man." He was, in addition, something of a politician, having
served several terms as mayor of Albany and being recognized
as a member of the powerful Albany Regency, the Democratic
oligarchy of New York State.

In the fifties Corning brought about the New York Central
consolidation and served as first president of the consolidated
road. In the same decade he headed the company which built
the Sault Canal. As time went on he added to his land and rail-

road holdings, and on the eve of the Civil War he was the richest man in Albany. In the course of the war he was to grow richer.

Active till the end of a long life, Corning was for half a century an outstanding figure on the American business scene. This book is an attempt to tell the story of his career and thereby to contribute to an understanding of the role of the merchant capitalist in early and mid nineteenth-century America. The fact that little attention is given to Corning as a politician is not to imply his unimportance in the political arena, nor is it to ignore the connection between business and politics; it is merely to bow to the limitations of time and space.

Other limitations have been imposed by the nature of the sources. The Corning Papers in the Albany Institute of History and Art are excellent in that they cover Corning's entire career, but the Papers consist almost wholly of letters received. Copies of outgoing correspondence, as well as account books, were reportedly the victims of a storage accident before the collection came into the possession of the Institute. New York Central records that might have helped to fill the gap—records such as letter books for the period of Corning's presidency of the road —are also apparently lacking. It has been necessary, therefore, to try to reconstruct Corning's activities without access to adequate "inside" information.

I am grateful to the Albany Institute for permission to use and to quote from the Corning Papers and to the editors of the *Mississippi Valley Historical Review* for permission to reprint some of the material in Chapter IX which appeared originally in that review in an article entitled "The Building of the Sault Canal: 1852–1855," vol. XL (June, 1953), pp. 25–46. The frontispiece, a copy of a portrait that is in the possession of the Corning family, appears through the gracious courtesy of Mrs. Edwin Corning and the Honorable Erastus Corning of Albany.

From the generous suggestions of Professor Lewis E. Atherton, Mr. Bray Hammond, and Dr. Fritz Redlich, all of whom read parts of the manuscript, I have benefited greatly. To Professor Paul Wallace Gates of Cornell University I am especially indebted, for through many years his interest in Erastus Corning has matched my own. My enjoyment of the Gertrude A. Gilmore Fellowship at Cornell in 1956 made possible the revision of part of the manuscript. Finally, the cheerful forbearance of the staff of the Albany Institute of History and Art during my months-long searching of the Corning Papers is as much a part of this work as the words I have written. Only for the shortcomings of the volume do I take full credit.

I. D. N.

Cape Girardeau, Missouri
April 1960

Contents

· I ·

"Cash in a/c with Trunk"

ONE sunny day in December, 1869, when the sleighing was especially enjoyable, a traveler on his way from Albany to Troy happened to notice Erastus Corning, then one of the grand old men of New York's capital city, riding along behind a team of fine bay horses. Proceeding at a leisurely pace, Corning viewed his surroundings with mild, kindly eyes and bowed pleasantly to those who passed him on the road.

"I know of no man past middle age," the traveler later remarked, "with the single exception, perhaps, of Cornelius Vanderbilt, who has so handsome a face as Mr. Corning. More than half a century ago he came into Albany a crippled boy friendless and penniless. By an industry marvelous to me . . . this poor boy grew to be a very rich man." [1]

When the traveler described the young Corning as "friendless and penniless," he was hardly stating the facts of the case. For this he must be forgiven, since Corning himself seems to have fostered the legend, perhaps in a conscious effort to conform to the stereotype of the self-made American—a species rather rarer, as recent scholarly probings have shown, than was once thought to be the case. But if Corning was not a "self-made" man—that is, one who had pulled himself up from poverty to wealth by his own bootstraps—he would seem to have been very much in the pattern of the businessman of his period.

[1] Anonymous letter in *New York Leader,* Dec. 6, 1869, quoted in Joel Munsell, *Collections on the History of Albany,* IV (Albany, 1871), 79.

American by birth, of a New England father, English in national origin . . . . urban in early environment, he [the "typical" American industrial leader of Corning's day] was . . . born and bred in an atmosphere in which business and a relatively high social standing were intimately associated with his family life.[2]

These words might have been written of Corning himself. Born in Norwich, Connecticut, on December 14, 1794, he was of the sixth generation of Cornings in America, being a descendant of Ensign Samuel Corning, a Puritan, who settled in Beverly, Massachusetts, at least as early as 1641. The father of Erastus, Bliss Corning, had served in the Revolution; his mother, Lucinda Smith, was also of an old American family. At the time of their marriage Bliss and Lucinda Corning were living in Preston, Connecticut, but shortly thereafter, they moved to Norwich. Erastus was their fourth child and third son.[3]

There is reason to believe that when Erastus was young his family was somewhat hard up for money, in part because of the apparent shiftlessness of the father and in part because of the number of children. (In time there were eleven.) But that one of the young Cornings, at least, enjoyed the best that the community had to offer in the way of educational opportunities would seem to be clear. During the winter of 1802–1803, when Erastus was eight years old, he was a member of the "select circle of twenty-five students" who attended the school of Pelatiah Perit, a young man just graduated from Yale.[4] One of Corning's classmates at that time was Lydia Huntley, who

[2] Frances W. Gregory and Irene D. Neu, "The American Industrial Elite in the 1870's: Their Social Origins," in William Miller, ed., *Men in Business: Essays in the History of Entrepreneurship* (Cambridge, Mass., 1952), 204.

[3] Thomas P. Hughes, *American Ancestry*, I: *The City of Albany* (Albany, 1887), 17; Cuyler Reynolds, *Hudson-Mohawk Genealogical and Family Memoirs* (New York, 1911), II, 770–771.

[4] *Encyclopedia of Contemporary Biography of New York* (New York, 1882), I, 108. Pelatiah Perit was afterward a member of the firm of Goodhue and Company of New York City and president of the Chamber of Commerce of that place. For a sketch of Perit, see "Pelatiah Perit, Lately President of the Chamber of Commerce, and of the Seamen's Saving Bank, New York," *Merchants' Magazine and Commercial Review*, L (April, 1864), 245–253.

later, as Mrs. Sigourney, was to be a prolific writer. The following description of Perit's school is from her *Letters of Life:*

The order of the school was perfect. The classics were excellently well taught, as were also the English studies. . . . I recollect geography was quite a favorite. . . . The reputation of this school transcending aught of the kind which had preceded it in that region, caused numerous applications to obtain its privileges. But as the number was limited . . . the aspirants were doomed to disappointment.[5]

Even allowing for Lydia Sigourney's hyperbole (she was greatly given to it), one must concede that this was no poor, backward school. When Perit left to enter business the following year, his place was taken by the Reverend Daniel Haskell, also a graduate of Yale.

About 1805 or 1806 Bliss Corning, emulating the example of many of his fellow citizens of Connecticut, moved with his family to New York, where he settled at Chatham, in Columbia County. Erastus seems to have continued his education in that place, attending school there for a short period, until just after his thirteenth birthday.[6]

It is doubtful if the other children of Bliss and Lucinda Corning enjoyed as much schooling as Erastus. Undeniably the father seemed in no position to pay for it. In the case of Erastus, the tuition almost certainly came from Benjamin Smith, his mother's brother, who early took an interest in this child of his sister. Years later the *Albany Evening Journal* was to state that Smith, a successful merchant of Troy, New York, "discerned a peculiar intelligence" in his nephew and for that reason became interested in him.[7] Perhaps a closer approxmation to the truth is that the uncle, a bachelor, was moved by motives of affection for his sister and kindness toward her son, as Erastus was a cripple. At the age of two he had fallen from his crib and injured his hip.[8] Doubtless he was picked up, soothed, and

[5] *Letters of Life* (New York, 1866), 62, 64.
[6] Cuyler Reynolds, *Albany Chronicles* (Albany, 1906), 508.
[7] *Albany Evening Journal,* April 9, 1872.
[8] *Albany Evening Times,* April 9, 1872.

tucked in again—the extent of "treatment" in those days before the X-ray. The result was that for much of his life he walked with the aid of crutches. It takes but little imagination to understand why this nephew, rather than one of his brothers, was singled out for his uncle's special attention.

Smith's interest in Erastus was to continue as long as the uncle lived. Indeed, it was Smith who launched the boy upon his business career, for when, sometime in 1807, Erastus left his parents' home in Chatham, it was not to seek his fortune alone in a hostile world but to go to Troy to work in the hardware and iron store of Heartt and Smith, in which his uncle was a partner.

Smith had the distinction of being one of the first settlers in the village of Troy, which dated from 1789. According to a contemporary, he was very highly regarded in the community. He was a man of simple and unobtrusive manners, industrious but not especially ambitious. Of moderate means, he was noted for his charity. He seems to have been known and liked by the majority of his fellow townsmen, who from time to time expressed their appreciation of his merits by appointing or electing him to local political office.[9] A young man making his way in the world could hardly have found a more useful protector.

Troy in the first decade of the nineteenth century was a village of some 3,000 inhabitants, 400 dwellings, and 80 stores "finely seated on a handsome gravelly plain, on the E. bank of the Hudson, 6 miles N. of Albany." River Street, the principal thoroughfare, extended a short distance along the waterfront, and all the other streets of the village branched from it.[10] Troy at this period, as is apparent from the ratio of stores to dwellings, was a place of considerable trade with outsiders. The supplies which came up the Hudson by sloop or smaller vessel passed in great part through the mercantile establishments of the village into the hands of western storekeepers, who moved

[9] John Woodworth, *Reminiscences of Troy* (Albany, 1860), 66–67.

[10] Horatio Gates Spafford, *A Gazetteer of the State of New-York* (Albany, 1813), 314–315.

their merchandise by river or wagon road to their stores in the interior. The hardware and iron store of Heartt and Smith was a typical Troy mercantile house. Here, as a boy of thirteen, Erastus Corning began the career which was to make him a millionaire eight times over.

When Corning first entered the employ of the concern of Heartt and Smith, it was his duty to clean the lamps, sweep the store, remove and replace the shutters, and do the other chores about the place.[11] Doubtless he hopped about cheerfully and quickly enough on his crutches, and doubtless, too, he was observant, readily picking up knowledge of the details of the business and making himself more and more useful to Messrs. Heartt and Smith.

As early as 1809 young Corning, then fifteen years old, went into business for himself. His new occupation was a side line, carried on through the indulgence of Heartt and Smith, who permitted the boy to engage in small buying and selling operations on his own. The first indication of this new activity is found in a letter of January 6, 1810, from N. B. Bassett, of Albany, to Corning: "Mr. Peter Sharpe of New York informs me that he forwarded to you some time Since a bundle of Whips & wishes you to . . . inform him . . . if they have come to hand." [12]

About this time Erastus started a new page in his personal account book, labeling it "Cash in a/c with Trunk." [13] "Trunk" was concerned, for the most part, with the young man's commercial transactions, but it also included small loans to and payments from friends. Perhaps the account was so named

[11] George Rogers Howell and Jonathan Tenney, eds., *Bi-centennial History of Albany* (New York, 1886), II, 536.

[12] Corning Papers, Albany Institute of History and Art, Albany, N.Y.; hereafter cited as CP.

[13] Among the Corning Papers are two small account books kept by Corning during his years in Troy. One includes entries from Sept. 2, 1809, to Dec. 1, 1815; the other from June 1, 1812, to Feb. 23, 1813. It appears that the second book was used while the first was temporarily mislaid. Corning was at this time obviously a novice at bookkeeping, so the books are no index to his over-all financial condition; they simply include a number of apparently unrelated items.

because the boy kept his stock in a box or chest, a frequent practice among small western merchants.[14] Or perhaps "trunk" merely referred to the cashbox in which Erastus kept his working capital.

"Cash in a/c with Trunk" continues for several years and shows that, in addition to whips, Corning was buying and selling tobacco, "segars," pipes, brushes, needles, pins, bedcord, sugar, lemons, and oranges—all on a small scale. In February and March, 1810, he was attempting to sell on commission forty-nine pamphlets entitled *Abbe Salernaukis* for J. W. Gazely of Norwich. But this apparently did not turn out well, for by the end of March the pamphlets had been returned to Gazely.

From "Cash in a/c with Trunk" it is possible to reconstruct other details of the boy's activities at this time. He seldom made an attempt to show the profits on a particular item or to record the gains for a given period, but it is clear that the volume of his sales, though never large, was steady, so that over a period of three or four years he could have accumulated a small sum, and doubtless did.

His usual course was to buy a small quantity of an article— whips, pipes, citrus fruit, etc.—and then dispose of his stock by the piece or in small lots, at a moderate advance in price. If he was unable to finance a given purchase and the seller was unwilling to extend credit, money was borrowed from Heartt and Smith or from Benjamin Smith personally. These sums were always repaid. (Even at this early date young Corning had learned the value of keeping his credit good—a lesson he never forgot.)

The transaction involving the whips, which was referred to above, was probably typical. In late 1809 Erastus contracted for their purchase from Peter Sharpe of Maiden Lane in New York City. In all probability letters from Benjamin Smith and other merchants of Troy and perhaps also of Albany, vouching for the boy, accompanied the request for the whips. The mer-

[14] Fred Mitchell Jones, *Middlemen in the Domestic Trade of the United States, 1800–1860* (Urbana, Ill., 1937), 33.

chandise was doubtless purchased on a six months' or longer
credit, which was customary at the time. When Corning failed
to acknowledge the receipt of the whips, Sharpe wrote to N. B.
Bassett of Albany asking him to look into the matter. Bassett
was probably an acquaintance of Sharpe and may have been
one of the merchants who recommended Corning to the New
Yorker. In any case, in November, 1811, when Sharpe was
anticipating a change in his business, he wrote direct to
Corning pressing a settlement of his account.[15]

In addition to buying and selling on his own, Corning sometimes acted as agent for others. The attempted sale of Gazely's
pamphlets was a case in point. A more successful venture took
place in the summer of 1811 when the boy disposed of "10
Boxes Lemons left with me to Sell by Capt Charles Tupper
18th June 1811 on his account." The first week the young
merchant sold three boxes for cash and three boxes at thirty
days, grossing $67. Then there were no sales for three days, but
on June 27 he sold "A. Frost 1 Box and counted 200 @ 4.50."
The remaining boxes he sold to himself. The total of the sales
amounted to exactly $100. Of this, $90 was entered under
"Cash & Rects"; 37½ cents was paid for carting (presumably
from the river to the store); $1.87½ went for freight; and $7.75
was Corning's commission.[16] The boy seems also to have acted
as agent in disposing of fruit for William Williams of New
York and A. M. W. Merrill, a ship's master.[17]

While Corning was acting for others in Troy, acquaintances
in various places were acting for him. J. K. Horton of Union
Village on December 6, 1811, forwarded to him $9.12 "which
is the amount of whips I have sold." [18] That same year Corning
entered in his account book "Memo of Corn Bought & Shiped

---

[15] Peter Sharpe to Corning, New York, Nov. 2, 1811, CP. Doubtless the 1809
purchase was the first of several, for the bill presented by Sharpe amounted to
$87. A note on the letter in Corning's hand states: "Sent $87 by S. Sellick 6 or
7th Novr 1811."

[16] Account book, 1809–1815, CP.

[17] William Williams to Corning, New York, June 26, 1810; A. M. W. Merrill
to Corning, Boston, April 18, 1811: CP.

[18] J. K. Horton to Corning, CP.

on Board the Sloop Atlantic N. Negus & A. M. W. Merrill
masters Bound to Boston 3rd April 1811. . . . (to Sell on my
account.)." The corn (seventy bushels of it) was purchased by
Corning in Troy for $44.94. On May 20 a "Balance" (profit?)
of $12.11 was recorded, and the account closed.[19] If one judges
from his records, grain speculation was a somewhat unusual
activity for the young man. He must have been more than
mildly interested in the commodity market at this time, however, for on April 18 Captain Merrill had written him from
Boston quoting the prices of yellow corn, white corn, rye, and
white beans.[20]

But Corning's chief side-line activity consisted in the buying
and selling of lemons and oranges. This was the one he later
remembered and talked about, and it is the only one which
found its way into contemporary accounts when he was a
famous man.[21] The fruit was bought through William Williams of New York (the same man for whom Erastus sometimes
acted as agent) or from the master of a river boat. In the latter
case, the purchase was probably a cash transaction, and if the
boy was short of money, it was here that the convenient till of
Heartt and Smith or the willing pocket of Benjamin Smith
came in. On one occasion, at least, Erastus commissioned William Peirce, his landlord, to survey the New York market
during a trip to the city, for Peirce wrote to him from the
metropolis:

I have made inquiry as to Lemons and can get those that appear
to be fresh at Eleven Dollars by the single box and ten dollars by
the ten boxes of W Trappan a frenchman at Fly Market and should
you conclude to buy you can send by next steamboat.[22]

The boxes of citrus fruit were displayed on the front steps
of Heartt and Smith's store, where Corning could attend to
their sale along with his other duties.[23] In June and early July

[19] Account book, 1809–1815, CP.   [20] Merrill to Corning, April 18, 1811, CP.
[21] See Howell and Tenney, *History of Albany*, II, 536; *Albany Ev. Times*, April
9, 1872.
[22] Letter dated April 24, 1811, CP.
[23] Howell and Tenney, *History of Albany*, II, 536.

of 1811 he disposed of ten boxes of lemons; during a comparable period the following year he records that he paid for nine and a half boxes.

Corning spent seven years in Troy—years which, it seems certain, passed quickly for him. From early in the morning until night he worked in the store. Occasionally he probably was seen swinging down to the wharf on his crutches to claim merchandise consigned to him or to haggle with a river captain over the purchase of a box of fruit. In the evenings he was out with the other boys and in the course of time found himself something of a favorite with the Troy girls.[24] (He was to marry one of them.) On Saturday nights, it is said, he posted the books of a Mr. Filer, a tailor, to aid in paying for clothes and mending.[25] From time to time he hired a horse and buggy and went off for a day or two to visit his parents in Chatham—not half so often as his sister Clarissa urged him to come, but probably quite as often as he was willing to lend his father money.

Bliss Corning seems to have been somewhat shiftless. In any event, Erastus' account books for the Troy period contain evidence of numerous small loans which the boy made to his father. In addition, among the Corning Papers there are many letters from Clarissa, giving details of the family's life and begging Erastus to send home various articles for her and their mother's use. On one occasion Clarissa wrote that their mother would be glad to have him come home to see the new baby, and especially glad if he brought the baby a shirt.

In a small way, young Erastus was becoming something of a capitalist. One source says that by 1814 the youth was worth $500, the sum of the profits from his private ventures plus the "slight savings" from his salary.[26] It might be remarked in passing that if any of his capital represented savings from wages Heartt and Smith were more generous with their clerks than was Corning himself at a later date, when he took it for granted that the useful information a young man acquired in his service "would be fully equivalent to any pecuniary sacrifice he

[24] Gardner R. Brown to Corning, Troy, March 23, 1814, CP.
[25] *Albany Ev. Times*, April 9, 1872.   [26] *Ibid.*

might be compelled to make beyond the amount of his salary." [27] But even assuming that Heartt and Smith paid Smith's nephew a wage in excess of that paid to the ordinary clerk, it is not likely that there was much, if anything, left over after necessary expenses were paid. On the other hand, Corning was engaged in his private ventures as early as January, 1810, and, according to his account books, continued in them at least until March, 1814—a period slightly in excess of four years. If the $500 which he is said to have had by the end of that time is prorated, it is found that the youth would have had to save approximately $125 a year, or $10 a month. That he could have done so from the profits of his side-line activities seems entirely possible.

When Erastus came to Troy in 1807 as a boy of thirteen, Benjamin Smith found lodging for him at the public house of William Peirce, which was across the street from Heartt and Smith's store. Here Corning lived as a member of the Peirce family during the whole of his stay in Troy,[28] and here he met other young men who lived with the Peirces. One was William L. Marcy, who later became governor of New York. From scattered bits of evidence it may be assumed that the Peirce boarders and their friends were a gay lot.[29] When, with the outbreak of the War of 1812, the boys formed themselves into a military unit, the crippled Erastus was permitted to keep the records, and years later he boasted that he was a veteran of the second war with England.[30]

In addition to Marcy, Corning in his Troy days made other potentially influential acquaintances. One was Jonas C. Heartt, the son of his employer, who, in the 1830's and 1840's, came

[27] J. Broderick to Corning, Schenectady, Sept. 10, 1831; see also Daniel Campbell to James Horner, Albany, March 14, 1837: CP.

[28] *Albany Ev. Journal*, April 9, 1872; Corning to Martin Van Buren, Albany, April 9, 1829, CP.

[29] See Brown to Corning, Troy, March 23, 1814; New York, Sept. 21, 1814: CP; Corning to T. Apoleon Cheney, Albany, Nov. 16, 1857, Miscellaneous Papers no. 58, Collection of Regional History, Cornell University, Ithaca, N.Y.

[30] "I think I have heard you say you were a warrior in 1812 to 1815." John F. Winslow to Corning, Washington, Feb. 27, 1855, CP.

to be mayor of Troy and a businessman in his own right.[31] Dating from the years in Troy, also, was Corning's friendship with Jacob S. Platt, then a clerk in a store in nearby Waterford, but later a member of the firm of Platt, Stout and Ingoldsby, the largest hardware merchants in New York City.[32]

It was during his Troy period that many of Corning's ideas concerning politics took shape. Benjamin Smith was a strong Jeffersonian Republican. Guided and influenced by him, Erastus early and very understandably acquired a strong bias for his uncle's party.[33] William Peirce was of the same political persuasion and doubtless influenced the ideas of Corning as well as those of the other young men who boarded at his house. Although Corning left Troy before he came of age politically, his future course was already set. He never found occasion to change it. In the late 1820's and in the 1830's he will be found supporting the program of Andrew Jackson [34]—one of the group of eastern businessmen who formed a citadel of Jacksonian Democracy that has been too often overlooked.[35] Not even the Civil War was to shake Corning's allegiance to his party.

During the War of 1812 the firm of Heartt and Smith of Troy was dissolved, a member of the Heartt family buying the one-third interest which had belonged to Benjamin Smith.[36]

[31] Arthur James Weise, *Troy's One Hundred Years, 1789–1889* (Troy, 1891), 45, 209, 326.

[32] Jacob S. Platt to Walter Barrett [i.e., Joseph Scoville], Philadelphia, May 31, 1862, in Scoville, *The Old Merchants of New York City* (New York, 1865), IV, 57.

[33] Corning to Van Buren, Albany, April 9, 1829, CP.

[34] See, for instance, *Albany Argus*, Feb. 1, 1833, in which Corning appears as a signer of a resolution upholding Jackson's stand on nullification.

[35] Bray Hammond, "Public Policy and National Banks," a review of Arthur M. Schlesinger, Jr., *Age of Jackson*, in *Journal of Economic History*, IV (May, 1946), 82; Hammond, *Banks and Politics in America from the Revolution to the Civil War* (Princeton, N.J., 1957), 329–330.

[36] Philip Heartt to Corning, Troy, Sept. 16, 1828, CP. At this period the dissolving of a partnership meant the end of a business concern. The new partnership was a new concern. Only the stock of the old concern was sold to the new—not the other assets or the liabilities. The assets were liquidated and the liabilities discharged by the members of the old firm. As late as 1845 litigation

For a time Erastus Corning continued in the employ of the Heartts,[37] but early in 1814, when he was just over nineteen years of age, he left them, apparently under friendly circumstances, to go to work for John Spencer and Company of nearby Albany.

---

was still taking place in connection with the settlement between Heartt and Smith—litigation in which Erastus Corning was involved by reason of his being executor of Smith's estate (Jonas C. Heartt to Corning, Troy, Nov. 21, 1845, CP).

[37] *Contemporary Biography of New York*, I, 108.

· II ·

Erastus Corning, Merchant

THE Albany to which Erastus Corning came on a March day in 1814 not only was the capital of New York, but was in wealth, population, and trade the second city of the state and the sixth or seventh in rank among the cities of the United States. Lying on the west bank of the Hudson 160 miles north of New York City, it was at that time the focal point of "more extensive intercourse . . . than . . . any other place between the Eastern and Western sections of the Union."[1] In 1813 an observer had remarked that "it is doubted if there be a place on this continent which is daily visited by so many teams."[2] Here, then, on a larger scale was the commerical scene with which Corning had become familiar in Troy.

But Albany, unlike Troy, was not merely a commercial center. Dating from 1624, it went back to the days when the Dutch controlled the Hudson Valley. When young Corning arrived there, he found an old, established society dominated by such ancient, proud families as the Gansevoorts, the Ten Broecks, and the Van Rensselaers. And because the city was the capital of the state, a distinguished group of lawyers had gathered there, among them James Kent, chief justice of the State Supreme Court; Ambrose Spencer, then at the high point of his career of "almost undisputed dictatorship of politics in

[1] Horatio Gates Spafford, *A Gazetteer of the State of New-York* (Albany, 1813), 118.
[2] *Ibid.*

13

New York"; [3] and Harmanus Bleecker, just back from a term in Congress. Two years later, in 1816, Martin Van Buren and Benjamin F. Butler were to set up law practice in the city.[4]

In the streets of the town were to be found many evidences of the former Dutch occupancy—houses with Dutch doors and gable ends, Dutch names on signs over the entrances of shops, and, occasionally, the sound of the Dutch language.[5] But overlying all this was the bustle of the newer Albany, the commercial center which was to spawn the city's new leaders—men who, with their ladies, were to storm the entrenched position of the old aristocracy and who were to make the lawyers and politicians subservient to their ends.

During the early decades of the nineteenth century the Hudson River was the life line of Albany. Quays stretched for a mile along the waterfront, and there were usually to be found from 80 to 200 sloops and schooners loading and unloading. In 1812 it had been estimated that at least 356 boats were serving the city. By March, 1814, when young Corning arrived in the capital, four steamboats were carrying passengers (those, at least, who were willing to risk their lives when the boilers burst) between New York City and Albany in the average time of 30 to 36 hours, at a fare of $10 a person.[6]

Slightly back from the Hudson and paralleling it lay old Court Street (subsequently called South Market Street and now South Broadway). The east side of Court, just south of State, was known as "Hardware Row," and it was here that John Spencer and Company had its store.[7]

---

[3] Julian P. Boyd in Dumas Malone, ed., *Dictionary of American Biography* (New York, 1928–1936), XVII, 444.

[4] Harriet L. P. Rice, *Harmanus Bleecker, an Albany Dutchman, 1779–1849* (Albany, 1924), 60–61.

[5] *Ibid.*, 1; Glyndon G. Van Deusen, *Thurlow Weed, Wizard of the Lobby* (Boston, 1947), 53.

[6] Spafford, *Gazetteer of New-York* (1813), 118, 122; *Albany Argus*, Sept. 23, 1814.

[7] "On this small frontage on the east side of South Broadway, between State and Beaver streets, long known as the Hardware Row, the heaviest business in this line, north and west of New York, was transacted for a series of years" (Joel Munsell, *Collections on the History of Albany*, III [Albany, 1870], 449).

We have concluded to have you come down and stay with us a short time [the senior member of the firm wrote to Erastus Corning on March 3, 1814]. If you meet our expectations and it should prove agreeable to you we would like you to continue with us—We wish you to come down on Monday next— [8]

It is almost certain that Corning was not a stranger to John Spencer,[9] for, as hardware merchants in adjacent cities, Spencer and Benjamin Smith were acquainted with each other. As early as 1810, to cite but one episode, Heartt and Smith and John Spencer and Company had been engaged in a common effort to settle their affairs with the firm of Petrie and Carter of Little Falls, New York, western merchants who had quitted business owing for goods sold them on credit by the Troy and Albany hardware houses.[10] Through his connection with Smith, Spencer was doubtless aware of Smith's nephew and clerk. However, young Corning was apparently brought to Spencer's particular attention by Joseph Weld, another Troy hardware merchant who would seem to have had a benevolent interest in the youth. Perhaps Erastus was already at that time courting Weld's daughter, Harriet, whom he subsequently married.[11] In any event, when Weld was solicited by Spencer to find him a promising clerk, the Troy merchant recommended Corning. It is reported that Spencer at first objected to hiring a crippled youth, but his initial reluctance soon gave way to a genuine respect for his new associate.[12]

When Corning went to Albany he was in his twentieth year. Behind him was seven years' experience in the iron and hard-

[8] John Spencer and Company to Erastus Corning, CP.

[9] John Spencer was born in 1780 and died in 1824. The firm of John Spencer and Company was formed about 1808 and at that time consisted of Spencer and Thomas Gould (Gorham A. Worth, *Random Recollections of Albany from 1800 to 1808*, 3d ed. [Albany, 1866], 48).

[10] Richard Petrie to Corning, Little Falls, N.Y., May 20, 1810, CP.

[11] Scholars have recently become aware of the importance in the career of a young businessman of the position of his father and of the help which the father could often give the son. Of equal importance, perhaps, was help from uncles—often maternal uncles—and fathers-in-law or prospective fathers-in-law. This was a point which was quite clear to Horatio Alger.

[12] *Albany Ev. Times*, April 9, 1872.

ware business and in his pocket was the money he had accumulated during the term of his apprenticeship—perhaps
$500. In one way or another he continued to increase his
capital, for in a little more than two years, on June 19, 1816,
he bought a partnership in John Spencer and Company. In addition to the money which the new partner had at his command, Spencer took a note for a substantial sum (certainly in
excess of $4,000, perhaps in excess of $6,000),[13] and it may
have been that Benjamin Smith, who never lost interest in his
nephew, also lent the young man money or signed his note.

At the time that Corning bought into the firm of John
Spencer and Company, William Humphrey was a third
partner.[14] Two years later, in 1818, Humphrey withdrew. Perhaps it was in anticipation of his withdrawal that the new member of the firm had been accepted. In any case, for the next
six years Spencer and Corning carried on the business, seemingly in the greatest amicability and with marked success.
When Spencer died in August, 1824, Corning purchased from
the heirs his former partner's share and thus became sole
owner of the concern. A few months later he took John T.
Norton, formerly of the firm of Henry W. Delavan and Company of "Hardware Row," into partnership with him—a
partnership which lasted for several years.[15]

Corning's reason for acquiring a new partner was not the
necessity of sharing the financial burden of the concern. At
this point in his career his credit was well established. Even if
it is assumed that he was in debt for the sum he had paid to
Spencer's heirs, it is unlikely that he was being pushed for
payment or that he would be. The reason for his preferring to
operate on a partnership basis must be sought elsewhere, but

[13] Receipt for interest payment made by Corning, signed by John Spencer, Jan.
20, 1819, and referring to articles of agreement executed June 19, 1816, CP.

[14] William Humphrey, born about 1786, died in Kasoag, Oswego County, N.Y.,
in March, 1866. During most of his long life he was in the hardware trade and
was reported to be "a gentleman of great integrity and excellence of character"
(Munsell, *Collections on Albany*, III, 295).

[15] *Albany Argus*, March 1, March 15, 1825; Munsell, *Collections on Albany*, III,
295, 449.

it is not hard to find. The mercantile and commercial pattern of his day, requiring as it did the personal attention of the merchant to all the details of his business and very often his presence in remote places, made it imperative that a person in whom complete trust could be placed must be always available, either to remain in charge at home or to act with authority at a distance. How better to fill this need than by enlarging the membership of the firm, so that the representative of the concern would be acting in his own interest? This was a principle that had been employed by the Medici in fifteenth-century Europe, and it was no less valid in nineteenth-century America. Therefore, the overwhelming majority of mercantile houses were set up as partnerships. Corning was merely following the practice of the day.

What were the nature and extent of the business with which Corning had identified himself? Like most other mercantile houses in Albany during the early decades of the nineteenth century, John Spencer and Company (and later Corning and Norton), was both a wholesale and a retail concern—the retail trade dependent upon the city of Albany and its environs, the much more important wholesale trade drawing its customers in the persons of western storekeepers from as far away as Buffalo, if not beyond. The latter circumstance gave a highly seasonal "flavor" to trade, the eastern trips of the storekeepers being confined to the spring and fall, with preference given to the former season by those who made but one trip a year. As a consequence, Corning's firm annually experienced two brief periods of great activity and long months during Albany's hot, uncomfortable summer and its cold, bleak winter when there was barely enough doing to keep the clerks occupied.[16]

This periodic torpor gave the owners opportunity to care for two most important aspects of their business. First, a member

---

[16] John T. Norton to Corning, Albany, April 6, May 21, 1827, CP. For general remarks on the American mercantile pattern at this period see Lewis E. Atherton, *The Pioneer Merchant in Mid-America* (Columbia, Mo., 1939); Norman Sydney Buck, *The Development of the Organization of Anglo-American Trade, 1800–1850* (New Haven, Conn., 1925); Fred Mitchell Jones, *Middlemen in the Domestic Trade of the United States, 1800–1860* (Urbana, Ill., 1937), 33.

of the firm was free to go to New York, Philadelphia, and Boston to buy stock. Second, and hardly less important, Corning or a partner had opportunity to make a trip to the West in an effort to collect money owed to the firm by western merchants.

So long as Spencer was a member of the concern, he took care of the "down river" purchasing. In April, 1819, for instance, he made a trip to New York and Philadelphia, buying iron in the first city and hardware in the second. The iron, at least, was not a domestic product but had been imported from Sweden. At this period John Spencer and Company was also buying English and Russian iron and German steel. Indeed, imported iron, purchased in New York, formed the bulk of their stock, but some New Jersey iron was contracted for from Albany. The Swedish iron which Spencer bought in New York in the spring of 1819 was acquired through a wholesaler or agent, C. B. S. Richmond. This seems to have been the usual procedure. There is reason to believe, however, that as early as 1820 John Spencer and Company was importing iron direct from England, thereby eliminating the services of the American middleman. This practice increased in importance as time went on.[17] By 1829 Corning and Norton had a resident agent in New York City, a James H. Whitney, who was paid $700 a year "at all times to attend to their Business in preference to any other engagement."[18] Goods, whether purchased by a member of the firm or through its agent, were customarily bought on a six months' or longer credit, the usual interest rate being 6 or 7 per cent.[19]

Although Albany in the 1820's and 1830's was considered a seaport (being at the head of navigation on the Hudson), imports from abroad were usually transshipped at New York for

[17] John Spencer to Corning, New York, April 20, 1819; Philadelphia, April 28, 1819; Corning to Spencer, Albany, Sept. 23, Nov. 11, Nov. 14, 1820; Norton to Corning, Albany, Sept. 9, 1828: CP. For Erastus Corning and Company's importations from England in the 1830's, see *Albany Argus* (e.g., Nov. 19, 1833).

[18] Corning to James H. Whitney, Albany, Jan. 21, 1829, CP.

[19] See, for instance, Spencer to Corning, New York, April 20, 1819; Norton to Corning, New York, Nov. 3, 1828: CP.

the trip to the capital, inasmuch as square-rigged vessels had difficulty navigating the length of the river. It was the custom to insure the merchandise during both the passage on the high seas and the trip up the Hudson—the insurance being arranged by the consignee. As early as September 23, 1820, Corning wrote to Spencer, who was then in New York:

The sheet iron from Scholefield & Taylor was the most of it rec^d in Store last evening. There is say ¼ of it mutch damaged. . . . Can there be any thing recovered from the underwriters? [20]

A decade later John T. Norton was writing from New York to Corning in Albany:

I have effected insurance on the 140 Tons Iron from Boston to Albany at ½ perct except on such as may be on board the sloop that cleared on Saturday—if she sailed on that day the premium is to be one per ct, but if not ½ per ct— [21]

The reference to the higher premium "on such as may be on board the sloop that cleared on Saturday" no doubt indicates that news of heavy weather on that day or the next had reached the New York underwriters.

Not infrequently a shipment from overseas arrived in New York in badly damaged condition, a circumstance which tells much about the primitive "packaging" of the day. In such an event the consignee could look for redress not only from the insurers, but also from the customs officials. It was the rule to appraise the damaged goods on the dock and to grant an allowance off the duties then and there. In August, 1831, some English sheet iron destined for the Corning firm was found upon its arrival in port to have been damaged during the voyage. In this case the reduction in the duties was set at 20 per cent.[22] Since this occasioned no surprise on the part of the member of the concern who reported it, it may be assumed that the figure was neither extraordinarily low nor unusually high.

[20] Corning Papers.   [21] Letter dated Oct. 14, 1831, CP.
[22] Norton to Corning, Albany, Sept. 9, 1828; James Horner to Corning, Albany, Aug. 8, 1831: CP.

As has been remarked, when Corning arrived in Albany in 1814, all freight, with the exception of a small amount that may have been carried on the passenger steamboats, was conveyed up the Hudson by sailboat. In 1824 this was still the case,[23] but by the middle of the next decade there were "12 steamboats employed in the transportation of passengers and light freight between this city and New York. . . . and . . . 7 steamboats engaged in towing barges between Albany and New York." [24]

By sail, then, or steam, the stock purchased in New York or elsewhere by Corning or his partner was transported up the Hudson and was unloaded on the hardware firm's pier. It was placed under cover in the nearby store or in the warehouse on the quay, and all was in readiness for the season's business.

In the meantime, one of the partners would have been on a western collecting trip. As credit was extended to the Albany merchants by the New York and English firms from which they purchased their stocks, so the merchants of the river town, in turn, extended credit to the western storekeepers. The westerners were expected to settle their accounts on their next trip east, if not before, but proof that they frequently failed to do so is abundant. In the season of slack trade, therefore, a member of the firm would set out for the West to collect as many as he could of the outstanding debts. A letter of February, 1832, written to Corning by his junior partner who that winter made the western trip is revealing not only of the young man's activities, but also of the lack of financial exchange facilities at the time:

I sent a package [of money] . . . by Mr Porter from Buffalo and another yesterday by Mr Loomis from Buffalo. I do not expect to get much money hear [Batavia, N.Y.], as they are all complaining of the scarcity of that very necessary article. I shall go South from

---

[23] Horatio Gates Spafford, *Gazetteer of the State of New-York* (Albany, 1824), 14.

[24] Thomas F. Gordon, *Gazetteer of the State of New York* (Philadelphia, 1836), 344.

here to day and shall be at Canandaigua about the 20 at Auburn the 22 yours acknowledging the receipt of the package by Mr McKnight is recd. . . . I sent a package from Geneva by a Mr Smith which you do not mention.[25]

Sometimes, on such a trip, the partner found it necessary to deal with a bankruptcy, of which there were many in the western country. The approved method of handling such a situation was to reach the failing merchant before his other creditors could do so and make a private settlement with him. John T. Norton carried out such a maneuver in December, 1827.

I reached here last evening [he wrote to Corning from Geneva, N.Y.] & this morning [Christmas Day] laid siege to Chapin & have succeeded in obtaining sundry notes . . . amounting to something more than our claim, all guaranteed by him. . . . It must not be mentioned that he has secured us in any way, as I promised him, it should not.[26]

When a visit from a collector, or perhaps in some cases two or three such visits, failed to induce a western merchant to settle his debt with Corning's concern, accounts were put in suit.[27] Frequently the debtor sought to clear himself by offering something less—usually a good deal less—than the full amount that he owed. "Mr W Stanley of the firm of C & W Stanley is down to compromise," Corning was informed from the store while he was vacationing in Canaan, New York, in the summer of 1832. "Our demand is about $1100 his offer is 10/ [per cent?] —but no security." [28] In 1834 a Henry Chapin of Canandaigua (perhaps the same Chapin who had failed in business in Geneva and whose debt Norton attempted to collect on Christmas Day in 1827) addressed a petition to Corning and other merchants of Albany and New York City:

Many years have passed away since I became indebted to you. . . . No means of escape from my unhapy thrauldom are with in my

[25] Horner to Corning, Feb. 8, 1832, CP.   [26] Letter of Dec. 25, 1827, CP.
[27] Norton to Corning, Albany, July 21, 1829, CP.
[28] Horner to Corning, Albany, Aug. 29, 1832, CP.

reach, so long as I remain a resident of this place. . . . I have decided . . . to seek a new abode, an untried home in the wiles [*sic*] of Michigan. . . . I present my request to you with great confidence . . . that you shall discharge me from all previous claims, on my giving to you my note payable in three years, for 10 per cent of the debt originally contracted without interest.[29]

Sometimes it was impossible to realize anything from a bad debt without the creditor's taking over a parcel of real estate. This accounts for Corning's being interested at an early date in land and other property in many of the cities and towns of western New York, in Ohio, and in Vermont. At a later period, scattered holdings in Michigan and Wisconsin were acquired in the same way. Among Corning's papers are almost countless letters, summonses, and other documents concerned with this aspect of mercantile life in early nineteenth-century America.

The sums which the western merchants were permitted to owe were surprisingly large. As has been seen, C. & W. Stanley was indebted to the Corning firm alone for approximately $1,100, and it is likely that smaller or perhaps similar amounts were owed to other eastern merchants. Henry Chapin addressed his petition to fifteen creditors. A western merchant who failed in July, 1829, owed Corning and his partner some $2,200.[30]

These examples of probable loss notwithstanding, the hardware and iron trade as carried on in Albany by John Spencer and Company and by Corning and Norton (as well as by Corning and other partners at a later date) was a profitable one. If some customers failed to settle their accounts, others did not. During a week in September, 1828, which was characterized by Norton as "shockingly slow," the firm chalked up receipts of $4,153. Later that same month a single day's receipts totaled $2,000.[31]

Not the least of the problems of the early nineteenth-century Albany merchants were those concerned with currency and

[29] Petition of Henry Chapin, Canandaigua, May 17, 1834, CP.
[30] Horner to Corning, Albany, July 27, 1829, CP.
[31] Norton to Corning, Albany, Sept. 13, Sept. 30, 1828, CP.

exchange. Much of the currency issued by the western country banks was almost worthless, and specie in the hinterland was almost unknown. What was more, if a country storekeeper managed to collect sufficient money for the settlement of a debt in the East, there were few commercial channels through which the funds could be transferred. As already noted, when one of the Corning partners was on a western collecting trip in 1832 he was forced to entrust packages of money to travelers (one of whom, at least, was a stranger) for delivery to Corning in Albany.

In point of fact, however, most financial transactions took the form of drafts and notes, which, if endorsed with "good" names, circulated as currency. John Spencer and Company and Corning and Norton were good names, for the partners were careful to keep their credit sound. Westerners who purchased goods of the concern gave their notes. The notes were endorsed by a member of the firm and were discounted by the Albany banks. Drafts on the company were everywhere accepted. In turn, the firm accepted and discounted drafts on other concerns that were considered "good." [32]

Notwithstanding that the firm of Corning and Norton was obviously flourishing, in the summer of 1828 Norton decided to withdraw from it.

As the period is near when arrangements should be made for the next year's business [he wrote to his partner in August], it will be well to give the matter . . . attention. . . . I do not for myself now see any way by which it can be continued on its present scale . . . in case I realize what I may now reasonably calculate upon, I shall have as much as I shall want.[33]

When he implied that the firm was overextended (that is, that it was operating on a larger scale than the partners' capital justified), Norton was doubtless right, since a tendency

---

[32] Among the Corning Papers are scores of documents—notes, drafts, letters, etc.—concerned with these transactions. See, for instance, Whitney to Corning, New York, May 27, 1830, and John McArthur, Jr., to Corning, Johnstown, Sept. 1, 1830.

[33] Letter dated at Albany, Aug. 1, 1828, CP.

to overextend was a characteristic of Corning at almost any period of his career. It might be argued (as it was by Norton) that this was an entrepreneurial weakness, but from the long view it probably was not, for Corning's temerity in operating on slim reserves permitted him to go ahead when a more timid man might have faltered. Only when he was old and sick did he show a disposition to make himself "snug." In 1828 he was but thirty-four, and old age was a long way off. On May 13, 1829, he gave Norton his bond, payable in two years, for $42,405.07, with interest, "being in full of [Norton's] half of the Stock on hand in the concern of Corning & Norton as per Inventory 1st March 1829." [34]

Corning had then been in Albany fifteen years.

[34] Receipt of bond signed by John T. Norton, dated at Albany, May 13, 1829, CP.

· III ·

Citizen of Albany

DURING the time that he was assuming his place as one of Albany's foremost merchants, Erastus Corning was also becoming a figure of importance in the city's social, civic, and political life. He seems always to have been a gregarious person; it is therefore not surprising that when he first went to live in Albany he missed the gay times he had known in Troy. Writing to one of his upriver friends during his first autumn in the capital city, he remarked more than a little wistfully: "I last winter [in Troy] enjoyed myself as well as could be expected for a person in my situation." For this he was scolded. Asked his correspondent:

Why will you consider yourself unhappy! You certainly have no reason too [sic], your prospects in life are good, you are blessed with talents, health, and notwithstanding what you refer too [his lameness], very great activity. You are surrounded with friends by whom you are esteemed.[1]

On another occasion the same correspondent wrote:

Three or four very pretty Girls last evening enquired very particularly about you. You therefore must not get so much enamoured of your Albany Girls as to forget them, but preserve a foot hold in both places.[2]

Corning evidently acted on this advice, for on March 10, 1819, when he was twenty-five, he married a Troy girl—Har-

[1] Gardner R. Brown to Erastus Corning, New York, Sept. 21, 1814, CP.
[2] Brown to Corning, Troy, N.Y., March 23, 1814, CP.

riet Weld, whose father, some five years before, had brought him to the attention of John Spencer. Harriet Weld Corning was a native New Englander, having been born in Roxbury, Massachusetts. Hers was the eighth generation of her family in America. Sometime before her marriage, her brother had wed one of the daughters of Gilbert Cummings, an Albany merchant.[3] Therefore, when Harriet and Erastus set up housekeeping in rented quarters on Beaver Street, they immediately began to move in a circle which included not only the husband's friends and business associates, but also the wife's family connections. As was so often the case in those days, the two categories overlapped, business relationships being reinforced by family ties.

By 1825, six years after his marriage, the name of Erastus Corning commanded sufficient prestige in Albany to appear among the members of a committee "to devise measures . . . for carrying into effect the celebration of the completion of the Grand Erie Canal," and the young capitalist contributed $10 to help "defray the expenses attending the celebration of the meeting of the waters of the Erie and Hudson."[4] In March, 1827, when he went South to convalesce after a serious illness, one of the letters of introduction which he carried with him described him as "a gentleman of the very first respectability."[5] In 1828 he was elected an alderman.[6]

In that year the Cornings moved from Beaver Street into a fashionable house at 102 State Street, halfway up the hill to the Capitol, and there they were to live for the rest of their lives. Corning was reported to have bought the house for $18,000, part of the sum being a legacy from Benjamin Smith, who had died in 1826.[7] The marriage of Erastus and Harriet Corning

[3] Charles F. Robinson, *Weld Collections* (Ann Arbor, 1938), *passim;* Arthur James Weise, *History of the City of Troy* (Troy, 1876), 119.

[4] Joel Munsell, *Collections on the History of Albany,* II (Albany, 1867), 450–451, 474.

[5] Samuel Hicks and Sons to William Gaston, New York, March 26, 1827, CP.

[6] Amasa J. Parker, *Landmarks of Albany County, New York* (Syracuse, N.Y., 1897), I, 324.

[7] Corning to Messrs. Goddard and Bibby, Albany, Jan. 17, 1828, CP; *Albany Ev. Times,* April 9, 1872.

was a happy one, marred only by constant demands upon the husband by the wife's impecunious relatives (especially Thomas Turner, the husband of Harriet's sister, Mary) and by the early deaths of three of their sons. Between the years 1820 and 1836 the Cornings had five children, all boys, only two of whom —Erastus, Jr., and Edwin—were to live to maturity.[8] In the course of time Erastus and Harriet were to take into their home the four daughters of Thomas and Mary Turner, provide for their education, and arrange good marriages for them. The many letters of these girls to "Dearest Auntie and Uncle" afford delightful glimpses of nineteenth-century manners and customs, and their marriages to business associates of their uncle provide another illustration of the reaffirming of business relationships through personal unions.[9]

As he made his way to his place of business each morning during the last years of the 1820's, Alderman Corning could well be proud of himself and of the position he had attained. Still in his early thirties, he was one of Albany's outstanding merchants, known as a man of affairs not only in his home city but also in New York, Philadelphia, Boston, and, through the country storekeepers, as far west as the very edges of the frontier. He had married well and had established a family. He was respected by his fellow citizens. And he had conquered his lameness to the point at which it was possible for him to walk with the aid of only a cane.

His days were crowded. There was the excitement of arriving at the store, setting the clerks to work, reading his letters, conferring with his partners. Then there was the trip home for the big midday meal. Afterward, he was back at the store, with perhaps a stop at the bank or a neighbor's counting room and,

[8] "Memorandum of the ages of the family" (in unidentified handwriting and of unknown date), CP.

[9] The letters are to be found among the Corning Papers. The eldest niece, Sarah Turner, married Watts Sherman, cashier of the Albany City Bank; Harriet Turner became the wife of John V. L. Pruyn, who was Corning's attorney and was for many years secretary of the New York Central Railroad; Mary (or Marie) Turner married Isaac Burch, a Chicago banker and railroad promoter; and Emma Turner became the wife of General Robert Lenox Banks, treasurer of the New York Central.

late in the evening, home again for supper. This routine was
sometimes varied by trips to New York or to the West. When he
went down river, he enjoyed the sail in the company of other
men bent on business in the metropolis. The bustle of the
port city pleased him, and it was pleasant to be deferred to
by the wholesalers and brokers. When he went west, traveling
up the Erie Canal or journeying overland by stagecoach or
hired rig, he kept an interested eye on the growing towns and
villages which would one day be cities, and he marked the
strategic points on rivers and lakes which he thought a develop-
ing commerce might make valuable. Beyond New York he
glimpsed the rich lands of the Great Lakes country, a vast, almost untapped treasure awaiting exploitation.

During the whole of his business career Corning was primarily a merchant. This was what he called himself, and this
he was considered by his contemporaries. Even in later years,
when he was widely known as a financier, a person seeking an
interview with him was most likely to find him in the counting
room at the back of the store on Broadway. Yet, as early as the
1820's, he became involved in several outside interests that were
to claim an increasing amount of his time and attention. One of
these interests was iron manufacturing.

When Corning went to Albany in 1814 to enter the employ
of John Spencer and Company, Spencer was one of the proprietors of a small iron furnace and foundry at 84 Beaver Street,
just around the corner and up the hill from "Hardware Row."
This establishment, known as the Eagle Air Furnace, had been
erected about 1809 by Spencer and Warner Daniels, who seems
to have been a practical ironmaster. When Corning bought a
partnership in John Spencer and Company in 1816, he probably also acquired an interest in the Eagle Air Furnace. In any
case, by 1825 the firm of Corning and Norton was the sole
owner of that enterprise. But as a money-making concern, the
Eagle Air Furnace was not an outstanding success, and in January, 1829, an attempt was made to sell it. It was not until 1833,
however, that it was disposed of to William V. Many and

Robert E. Ward. Subsequently the establishment was operated as the Albany Eagle Air Furnace Machine Shop. Erastus Corning and Company (successor to Corning and Norton) continued to serve as merchandising agent.[10]

Of more lasting importance than his investment in the Eagle Air Furnace was Corning's interest in the Albany Nail Factory, situated on Wynants Kill or Creek, just south of Troy. This concern was successor to the Albany Rolling and Slitting Mill, built in 1807 by John Brinckerhoff and Company. Corning purchased the mill at auction in 1826, at a reported price of $5,280, and renamed it the Albany Nail Factory. About 1830 the 34 workmen employed there were annually producing some 825 tons of rolled iron, rather more than half of which was cut into nails. This was the nucleus of a business which subsequently took rank among the foremost iron and steel concerns in the country.[11]

In the mid-1820's Corning invested in at least one bank, the New-York State, of Albany,[12] and as early as 1824 he started to invest in insurance companies. In the spring of that year he put $125 into the stock of the United States Insurance Company.[13] The following year he was listed as a director of the Merchants' Insurance Company of Albany, a concern incorporated with a capital of $250,000 and authorized "to make all kinds of insurance against fire, and all kinds of insurance upon vessels, goods, wares and merchandise on the inland waters of this state and the adjoining states" and on vessels in the coastal trade.[14] In 1833 he was a director of the Albany Insurance Company, and about 1835 he was president of the Mutual, one of the three

[10] *Albany Argus*, Jan. 6, 1829, Sept. 6, 1833; Joel Munsell, *The Annals of Albany*, VIII (Albany, 1857), 357, and *Collections on Albany*, III (Albany, 1870), 449; John T. Norton to Corning, Albany, March 30, 1827, CP.

[11] John Leander Bishop, *A History of American Manufactures from 1608 to 1860* (Philadelphia, 1864), II, 632; Arthur James Weise, *Troy's One Hundred Years, 1789–1889* (Troy, 1891), 264.

[12] He was elected a director of the bank on June 6, 1826 (Munsell, *Annals of Albany*, VIII, 152).

[13] Receipt signed by J. L. Brown, April 7, 1824, CP.

[14] *Albany Argus*, March 8, 1825.

fire insurance companies then having headquarters in Albany.[15]
By that time, also, he was president of the Albany City Bank
and owned stock in at least six other banks in the state.[16]

Beginning in the early 1830's some of Corning's money went
into railroads. His initial investment in this area was in the
Mohawk and Hudson, a 14-mile line between Albany and
Schenectady—the first railroad in New York state and the first
link in today's New York Central system. On October 27, 1831,
he entered into the joint purchase of 130 shares of this stock
with Edwin Croswell, editor of the *Albany Argus;* James Porter, a director of the Canal Bank of Albany; William G. Bucknor, a New York City broker; and Churchill C. Cambreling, a
New York City businessman and member of Congress.[17] Over
a period of seventeen months, from January, 1832, to May,
1834, three New York brokers were buying and selling Mohawk
and Hudson stock for Corning. The number of shares involved
was never very great, but Corning seems to have been playing
the market, buying when the stock was low and selling when
he could do so at a profit.[18]

In June, 1833, Corning was elected a director and vice-president of the Mohawk and Hudson, a position which he filled
for two years.[19] Also in 1833 he began his association with the
Utica and Schenectady, a railroad which was incorporated in
April of that year. At the first stockholders' meeting in August,
1833, Corning was elected to the board of directors; on the
same day he was chosen president of the company.[20] In that
position he was to continue for the twenty years that the Utica
and Schenectady enjoyed corporate entity; from that position
he was to step into the presidency of the New York Central.

[15] *Ibid.*, Jan. 11, 1833; John J. Hill, *Reminiscences of Albany* (New York, 1884),
40.

[16] See below, p. 101.   [17] Statement of purchase, CP.

[18] William G. Bucknor to Corning, New York, Jan. 6. 1832; Prime, Ward, King
and Company to Corning, New York, April 24, 1833; Gilbert Allen to Corning,
New York, May 30, 1834: CP.

[19] Alvin F. Harlow, *The Road of the Century: The Story of the New York
Central* (New York, 1947), 19; *Albany Argus*, June 24, 1834.

[20] *Laws of the State of New York*, 1833, 462–468; *Albany Argus*, Aug. 17, Aug.
19, 1833.

Meanwhile Corning was becoming deeply enmeshed in politics and was working his way into the inner councils of his party. By 1833 he was a prominent member of the Albany Regency, the Democratic organization of the capital city. At the end of that year his party came into control of the Board of Aldermen and proposed to elect Corning mayor. The wave of vituperation set off in the opposition press served to show the position of importance which Corning already held in the affairs of the city. The editor of the *Microscope*, a Whig paper, referred to the Democratic choice as "the wealthy nabob of State Street" and accused him of attempting to deprive the city's laborers and cartmen of their livelihoods by exerting "all his powers" to run the tracks of the Mohawk and Hudson Railroad along the docks, thereby greatly simplifying the transfer of goods from the cars to the river boats.[21] Edwin Croswell, editor of the *Albany Argus*—a paper that in a later day would have been called the "mouthpiece" of the Regency—was ready with a pious rejoinder:

We cannot follow the opposition papers in their personalities. It is not necessary to allude to the wealth or the private character of either of the candidates. . . . [Francis Bloodgood, a prominent lawyer, was Corning's opponent.] We trust that both have sufficient [means] to discharge the duties and maintain the respectability of the office.[22]

Corning was elected by a vote of twelve to eight and assumed his new position on the first of January, 1834. Thrice more, in 1835, 1836, and 1837, he was the choice of the Board of Aldermen to head the city government.[23] Later he was to serve in other distinguished political offices—as a state senator from 1842 to 1845 and as a representative in Congress from 1857 to 1859 and from 1861 to 1863—but the role of public servant was never so important to him as the role of behind-the-scenes political manipulator. In the latter capacity he was to spare neither time nor money to accomplish his ends.

[21] Quoted in the *Albany Argus*, Dec. 24, 1833. [22] *Ibid.*
[23] Cuyler Reynolds, *Albany Chronicles* (Albany, 1906), 508.

On New Year's Day, 1835, Mayor Corning and his wife received the calls—"numerous beyond example"—of the townspeople. The *Argus* reported that the house on State Street was "literally thronged." [24] On January 2 the same paper noted among the names of a list of gentlemen who had contributed "towards the support of the Press, the efficient agent under Divine Providence, in the great cause of temperance" that of Erastus Corning. He was down for $1,000.

The money for Corning's subsidization of the political press as well as for his various investments came almost wholly from the profits of his iron and hardware store. It is possible that the legacy from Benjamin Smith helped finance the purchase of the Albany Nail Factory and the State Street residence, but Smith, although he was a person of influence, was hardly rich, and the sum that he could leave his favorite nephew was not large. Be that as it may, Corning's buying of the ironworks and the house on State Street went far to enhance his prestige. And even though the house was an expensive luxury, there is every reason to believe that the young merchant could afford it, for by the end of the decade of the twenties the firm of Corning and Norton was no longer a small enterprise. As already noted, in the spring of 1829 the inventory of the concern was valued at some $85,000.

The withdrawal of Norton from the hardware firm in that year made it necessary for Corning to find a new partner. This he did in the person of James Horner, a young man who had been with Corning and Norton for several years as a clerk. At this time the firm's name was changed to Erastus Corning and Company. Horner's initial investment was probably quite small, with Corning holding his note, the expectation being that it would be paid off with Horner's share of the profits of the business. In this way Corning not only assured himself of a trustworthy partner, but also retained the services of a good man, for Horner had threatened to leave the firm rather than continue as a clerk. Horner was to remain a partner for some eighteen years. In 1833, Daniel Sparhawk, another former clerk, was accepted as a third partner, but he withdrew in 1837.[25]

In 1844 Gilbert C. Davidson joined the firm, which then became Corning, Horner & Co. Davidson was the son of Alexander Davidson, an Albany merchant who died in 1825. As executor of the elder Davidson's will, Corning assumed an interest in the children, at least two of whom—Gilbert and John McBain—became his protégés. Gilbert, who was a clerk in Corning's store in 1839 and perhaps earlier, trod the same road to partnership as had been taken by Horner and Sparhawk.[26]

The firm of Corning, Horner & Co. continued until June 20, 1848, when Horner withdrew. It was at that time that Corning's elder son, Erastus, Jr., joined his father and Davidson in the concern, which continued business "under the partnership name of Erastus Corning & Co." [27]

The elder Corning retained one-half interest in the firm; Davidson took a two-sixths share, and the remaining one-sixth fell to the younger Corning. In March, 1854, John F. Winslow, who was then a partner in the ironworks at Troy, also joined the Albany firm, continuing as a member until 1860. When, a year or two later, Davidson retired because of poor health, the Cornings, father and son, carried on alone.[28]

During all these changes in partnership the business of the firm continued in substantially the pattern of the twenties and thirties. To be sure, the financial and geographic scope of operations increased, but these were differences in degree rather

[25] *Ibid.*, March 10, 1829, March 5, 1833; Daniel Campbell to James Horner, Albany, March 14, 1837, CP; *Hoffman's Albany Directory and City Register for the Years 1837-8* (Albany, 1837).

[26] *Albany Argus*, March 7, 1845; Berthold Fernow, ed., *Calendar of Wills on File and Recorded in the Offices of the Clerk of the Court of Appeals, of the County Clerk at Albany, and of the Secretary of State, 1626-1836* (New York, 1896), 131; Gilbert C. Davidson to Corning, Albany, Dec. 13, 1839; Kasoag, N.Y., Feb. 5, 1864: CP.

[27] Articles of Copartnership, dated June 20, 1848, signed by Erastus Corning, Gilbert C. Davidson, and Erastus Corning, Jr., CP.

[28] Erastus Corning & Co. to S. C. Hall and Company, Albany, Oct. 31, 1854; Corning to M. A. Neef, Albany, Dec. 14, 1861; John F. Winslow to Corning, Troy, Aug. 25, 1863: CP; *Albany City Directory*, 1853-1854, 1854, 1861, 1862.

than in method. It will be remembered that when Norton withdrew from the firm in 1829, an inventory revealed the stock on hand to be worth some $85,000. In the early 1860's the company's inventories ranged between $180,000 and $260,000, but the old rules of partnership still obtained. When Davidson left Erastus Corning & Co. in 1862, the settlement between him and the Cornings followed the lines of the settlement between Norton and Corning in 1829.[29]

With improved transportation and communication, the western territory from which the firm drew its customers expanded greatly. In the 1820's the bulk of the trade of John Spencer and Company and of Corning and Norton was drawn from the region east of Buffalo. By 1837 Ohio and Michigan merchants were becoming of increasing importance to Erastus Corning & Co. In the 1850's and 1860's, if not before, "Corning territory" included Indiana, Wisconsin, and Illinois—but, as in the twenties, many westerners were not paying their bills without the promptings of a collector, and most of the earlier problems concerned with money and exchange were still very much in evidence.[30]

During the first two decades of Corning's residence in Albany he devoted almost all his time to the affairs of the hardware house. It was then that he earned for himself a place among the "widely-known" merchants of "conceded ability" who dominated the city.[31] As late as 1835 his chief interest remained the store, but beginning with the 1840's he gave increasing attention to the other activities in which he was becoming ever more deeply involved. When articles of copartnership were drawn up at the time that Gilbert C. Davidson and Erastus Corning, Jr., entered the hardware concern, the elder Corning was careful to stipulate that, although

[29] Davidson to Corning, Albany, March 25, 1862; Kasoag, Feb. 5, 1864: CP.

[30] Watts Sherman to Corning, Albany, July 21, 1837; Horner to Corning, Albany, April 15, 1838, April 11, 1840, Aug. 10, 1844; Winslow to Corning, Albany, Jan. 26, 1856; Troy, Jan. 16, 1863: CP.

[31] Harriet A. Weed, ed., *Autobiography of Thurlow Weed*, in Thurlow Weed, *Life of Thurlow Weed, Including His Autobiography and a Memoir* (Boston, 1884), I, 447.

the said Gilbert C. Davidson & Erastus Corning Jr are to devote all their time and services, & apply their best energies . . . to the business. . . . Erastus Corning is only to devote so much of his time & services to the partnership . . . as he may find convenient.[32]

Although Corning continued to supervise the firm and in periods of emergency devoted a great deal of time and attention to its affairs, for the most part the details of the business were handled by his partners and clerks, and there were entire years when Corning gave the store—though not the firm's important connections—very little attention. In choosing trustworthy, able partners Corning showed rare judgment. This was remarked upon by his contemporaries,[33] and it is well supported by evidence to be found in his papers. He seems also to have been a man who held the esteem of his associates. Certain it is that he inspired in some of them (for instance, John T. Norton, James Horner, and Gilbert C. Davidson) a degree of devotion to him and to his interests which is not to be explained in terms of mere favor-currying.

In mid-century Erastus Corning & Co. was one of the most extensive enterprises of its kind in the state of New York, if not in the United States.[34] Receipts during what was probably a typical month of 1866 totaled $110,000.[35] It was about this time that Corning chose to retire from the firm, the concern being taken over by a group of younger men, including Erastus Corning, Jr.[36] The senior Corning was then a venerable seventy, the richest man in Albany and easily his city's first citizen.

[32] Articles of Copartnership, June 20, 1848, CP.

[33] John J. Hill, *Reminiscences of Albany* (New York, 1884), 13; George R. Howell and Jonathan Tenney, eds., *Bi-centennial History of Albany* (New York, 1886), II, 537; Munsell, *Collections on Albany*, IV, 4.

[34] Corning to S. A. Goddard, Albany, Nov. 17, 1861, CP; Howell and Tenney, *History of Albany*, II, 537, 540; Gorham A. Worth, *Random Recollections of Albany from 1800 to 1808*, 3d ed. (Albany, 1866), 49.

[35] Corning, Jr., to Corning, Albany, July 21, 1866, CP.

[36] Corning to A. Tuedley, Albany, June 13, 1870, CP. The firm continued as Corning and Company until 1886 or 1887, when it was succeeded by Ward and Byrne (Albany City Directory, 1886, 1887). This concern ceased operations about 1890. (It was not listed in the *Albany Directory* of 1891 or in subsequent directories.)

The following chapters, except the last, relate in detail Corning's activities in various fields of investment—in iron manufacturing, in banking, in railroading, and in land speculation. As has been noted, he became interested in these endeavors early in his career; he was to retain his interest in each of them to the end. Most chapters, therefore, will span the half-century of his business life.

· IV ·

Man of Iron

IN the early 1830's and for a number of years to come Corning's Albany Nail Factory, purchased in 1826, bore more than a slight resemblance to the American "iron plantations" of colonial days. Situated on Wynants Kill, just south of Troy, New York, the complex of buildings included not only a water-powered rolling mill, nail and spike factories, and sheds and warehouses, but also houses for the company's agent and employees and a company store in which were sold staple foods, beer, dry goods, and other household necessities.[1]

About the beginning of the decade of the thirties the annual product of the mill was some 825 tons of rolled iron. This was converted into "every description of band iron, nail plates, hoops and rods, &c." A little more than half of the iron that was processed in the mill was machine-cut into nails, which were headed by hand. In the summer of 1833 twenty-six nail-cutting machines were in operation; during the year 1834 the number of employees of the factory ranged from thirty-seven to forty-two. Their average pay seems to have been about a dollar a day, with the blacksmiths at the top of the scale and the nail-cutting machine operatives at the bottom.[2]

[1] *Albany Argus*, July 9, 1833; Thomas Turner to Erastus Corning, Troy, N.Y., Feb. 3, 1830, July 3, 1834, Oct. 25, 1837, CP. Corning himself bought many articles, including food and dry goods, through the store at the nail factory. See bill for April 10 to Sept. 30, 1834, CP. For a description of the colonial iron plantations see Arthur Cecil Bining, *Pennsylvania Iron Manufacture in the Eighteenth Century* (Harrisburg, 1938), 30–33.

[2] *Albany Argus*, July 9, 1833; Turner to Corning, Troy, April 5, 1834; list of men employed in the Albany Nail Factory, Dec., 1834: CP; Arthur James Weise,

Raw material for the mill at this period consisted chiefly of Russian and Swedish bar iron. As early as 1826, however, horse nail rods were being manufactured from "O. Sable Iron." [3] This was iron from the Ausable region of New York's Champlain Valley, then in the early stages of its development as an iron-producing area. The importance of domestic ore increased as time went on, but through the 1830's, at least, the mill's sources of raw material remained largely foreign. On the other hand, the Albany Nail Factory's market was wholly local. One outlet, of course, was the store of Erastus Corning & Co. in Albany. In addition, other Troy and Albany hardware merchants who supplied western storekeepers were steady customers, for there was an almost constant demand from the frontier for the products of the ironworks, especially nails. In 1833 it was stated that "the nails and iron manufactured at these works have always found a ready sale . . . in Albany and Troy and vicinity without the payment of commission to agents." [4]

The fact that there was a good market in the immediate vicinity goes far to explain the growth and expansion of the Albany Nail Factory, for in its early history the quality of its management was not such as to augur well for the success of the enterprise. For more than a decade subsequent to his purchase of the mill in 1826, it remained as a stepchild among the other interests of Erastus Corning. So taken up was he with his business in Albany and with the launching of his career as politician, banker, and railroad promoter that he had little time to devote to his affairs in Troy. Local management of the concern over a period of a dozen years was left to Harriet Corning's ineffectual brother-in-law, Thomas Turner. Turner's position was a sinecure, for he was lacking in both managerial ability and practical experience in iron manufacturing. Moreover, he was inefficient, irascible, and given to constant complaining.[5]

Troy's One Hundred Years, 1789–1899 (Troy, 1891), 264; *Encyclopedia of Contemporary Biography of New York* (New York, 1878–1884), II, 353.

[3] *Albany Argus,* April 28, 1826; *Contemporary Biography of New York,* II, 353.

[4] *Albany Argus,* July 9, 1833.

[5] See especially Turner to Corning, Troy, April 8, 1832, Sept. 11, 1837, CP.

About the time that John T. Norton joined Corning in partnership in the Albany hardware house, that is, late in 1826 or early in 1827, the two also became partners in the Albany Nail Factory under the firm name of Norton and Corning.[6] So financially unrewarding was the concern in the late 1820's that in 1829 the owners considered selling it. In Norton's opinion, "the money safely on interest, would in the end be much better." [7] In late 1833, however, the factory was still in the possession of Norton and Corning. At that time James Horner (who since 1829 had been a partner in Erastus Corning & Co. of Albany) took over Norton's share in the Troy concern. When Horner entered the firm, Corning was meeting the payroll only with difficulty, but in the course of the 1830's large sums of money must have gone into new buildings and equipment, for by 1837 the establishment in Troy, purchased a decade earlier for a little more than $5,000, was valued at $52,500, exclusive of inventory. An inventory of 1843 showed a stock of manufactured and unmanufactured goods worth $105,000.[8]

In 1837 Corning had finally been driven to relieving Thomas Turner of his managerial duties and replacing him with a resident partner, John Flack Winslow. Born in Bennington, Vermont, in 1810, Winslow was the son of an ironmaster. In his early youth he had served a two-year clerkship with W. and A. Marvin, merchants of Albany, and later he had worked in other mercantile houses in New York City and in New Orleans. In 1831 or 1832, however, he returned to the trade of his father, going in that year to Boonton, New Jersey, to become agent and manager of the New Jersey Iron Company's works. There he had an opportunity to observe skilled workmen operating the best in machinery, for both men and machines had been brought from England. In 1834 Winslow purchased the Clinton iron property in Bergen County, New Jersey, which he ran on his own account. When, therefore, he agreed to take over the man-

[6] Weise, *Troy's One Hundred Years*, 264.

[7] John T. Norton to Corning, Farmington, Conn., Aug. 10, 1829, CP.

[8] Turner to Corning, Troy, April 5, 1834; "Proposition" of John F. Winslow, dated at Troy, Sept., 1837; Winslow to Corning, Troy, April 10, 1843: CP.

agement of the Albany Nail Factory, it was with a background
of five or six years' experience in iron manufacturing.[9]

In response to Corning's overtures Winslow proposed to take
a one-third interest in the establishment at Troy, then valued
at $52,500, planning to pay by far the larger part of the $17,500
for which he would be obligated out of his share of the profits
after he had joined the concern. Only some $3,500 was to repre-
sent new investment, and $2,200 of that amount was to be paid
in iron—presumably from Winslow's New Jersey works—
which was then in the hands of Erastus Corning & Co. For the
balance Winslow offered collateral in the form of real estate
in Auburn, New York, and in New York City. This security
was to be "redeemed" as quickly as possible by Winslow's earnings from the business, those earnings to be based on the one-
third interest. Moreover, according to the terms of the proposed
agreement with Corning, Winslow as manager of the ironworks was to receive a living allowance for himself and his
family and was not to be charged interest on that part of his
purchase which remained unpaid.[10] Thus Winslow was to acquire a partnership in the Albany Nail Factory in much the
same way that Corning himself, more than twenty years earlier,
had moved into a partnership in the mercantile house of John
Spencer and Company.

Other clauses in the agreement which Winslow proposed
stipulated that any iron which was bought by the Albany Nail
Factory through Erastus Corning & Co. of Albany was to be
charged to the ironworks at cost price, but all goods furnished
by the works to the Albany concern were to be sold on as favorable, but no better, terms as like articles could be obtained elsewhere.[11]

Winslow took up his residence in Troy in the summer or
fall of 1837 and seems to have managed the works from that
time, but Corning was slow about coming to a definite agree-

[9] Charles S. Boyer, *Early Forges and Furnaces in New Jersey* (Philadelphia,
1931), 45; David Parsons Holton and Frances K. Holton, *Winslow Memorial*
(New York, 1877–1888), II, 821–822; Henry Hall, ed., *America's Successful Men of
Affairs* (New York, 1895–1896), II, 885–886.

[10] "Proposition" of Winslow, dated at Troy, Sept., 1837, CP.   [11] *Ibid.*

ment with him. By May, 1838, Winslow's patience was wearing thin.

If you intend being up here in a day or two please bring along our papers [he wrote to Corning on May 22]. I have in the course of the business enough to perplex & annoy me, & I am about tired of remaining here any longer, hanging by the Eye lids. . . . There are circumstances enough to make me feel sufficiently uncomfortable without having this added to the rest.[12]

It was not that Corning objected to the general terms of the agreement as it had been drawn by Winslow, but the fact that there were two particular points of contention between the men. One was the amount to be allowed Winslow for expenses. Corning stipulated $1,000 a year, but Winslow said that he intended "in this matter . . . to feel & act, independently. It is a poorer business than I think it is if it will not afford me a respectable support & more than that I dont think I desire." [13] The other point under discussion was the length of the term of copartnership. Corning wished to limit it to three years, but Winslow felt that such a short-term contract was prejudicial to his interests.[14] On both counts Winslow's views seem to have prevailed. For thirty years he and Corning were to be not only business partners but also friends—two highly individualistic men who respected each other.

When Winslow in the spring of 1838 maintained that he had "in the course of the business enough to perplex & annoy" him, he was doubtless alluding in part to the machinations of Thomas Turner, who was still on the scene. Not only did Turner attempt to interfere with Winslow's management, but he also spied on his movements and reported them to Corning.[15] It appears that Turner had some slight financial interest in the Albany Nail Factory,[16] and the liquidation of this may have presented difficulties. In any event, he remained in Troy at least until 1839. He should have been dealt with earlier, of course,

[12] Winslow to Corning, Troy, May 22, 1838, CP.
[13] Winslow to Corning, Troy, Sept. 11, 1837, CP.   [14] *Ibid.*
[15] Turner to Corning, Troy, Oct. 25, 1837, Jan. 30, 1839, CP.
[16] Turner to Corning, Troy, Sept. 18, 1837, CP.

as soon as Winslow assumed charge, but whereas Corning could
be stern toward men with whom he was personally unacquainted
or who were at a distance, he was softhearted to the point of
foolishness toward those whom he knew and who were in the
immediate vicinity. When Turner finally left Troy, it was to
take up a position in the new village of Corning, in Steuben
County, New York, which his benefactor was then promoting
and which had the advantage of being some little distance
away.

At the time that Winslow came into the Albany Nail Factory
in 1837, the name of the concern was changed to the Albany
Iron Works, a name that it was to retain until 1875. Through
the years the membership of the firm was to change—James
Horner was to drop out and Gilbert C. Davidson and Erastus
Corning, Jr., were to become partners [17]—but the elder Corning always remained in a position of authority, and all major
decisions were made with his concurrence. Under Winslow's
management, which covered a period of three decades, the Albany Iron Works expanded steadily. The number of employees
increased from an average of forty in the mid-thirties to 750
by 1860, and the monthly payroll, which had been $1,400 in
1834, was in excess of $23,000 in 1867.[18]

In 1849 and again in 1852 disastrous fires swept the works.
The first destroyed the spike factory at a reported loss of
$40,000 above insurance, and the second carried away "the new
& old mills" at a loss of $50,000. In both cases improved build-
ings were immediately erected on the sites of those which had
been destroyed.[19]

By 1864 the Albany Iron Works included three rolling mills
—two driven by steam and one by water power—an axle fac-

[17] Weise, *Troy's One Hundred Years*, 264–265.
[18] Turner to Corning, Troy, April 5, 1834; Robert Bainbridge to Corning,
Troy, July 11, 1867: CP; John Leander Bishop, *A History of American Manufactures from 1608 to 1860* (Philadelphia, 1864), II, 633.
[19] Bishop, *History of American Manufactures*, II, 633; Winslow to Corning,
Troy, Oct. 30, 1849; Gilbert C. Davidson to Corning, Albany, June 28, 1852: CP;
Joel Munsell, *The Annals of Albany*, 2d ed., I (Albany, 1869), 376; IV (Albany,
1871), 348.

tory, a spike factory, and a nail factory. According to a contemporary observer, the establishment covered some forty or fifty acres, on which there were "numerous buildings, constituting a small village in itself." [20] At that time the investment of the concern in real estate and machinery was said to be about half a million dollars, an estimate which was probably exaggerated, for three years later, in 1867, Winslow valued his one-third interest at $120,000.[21]

As time went on, the market reached by the Albany Iron Works expanded greatly. In 1833, on the eve of the railroad era, the entire product of the Albany Nail Factory passed into the hands of hardware merchants in Troy and Albany. The coming of the railroad offered new opportunities and was directly responsible for the rather phenomenal growth of the works under Winslow's direction. In all probability as early as 1835 or 1836 spikes from the Albany Nail Factory had been used in the building of the Utica and Schenectady Railroad, of which Erastus Corning was president. A decade later Winslow was aggressively urging the products of the Albany Iron Works on railroad builders throughout the country and had become something of a traveling salesman in the process. Following his usual practice of keeping Corning informed of his activities, he wrote to the senior partner on August 24, 1846:

I go down the river this Evg. [to New York City] and may return via Boston &c, [as] there are several Rl Roads about laying down Iron in that region, & we must look to supplying them with spikes. I shall get such letters in N Yk tomorrow as will further my object.[22]

In November, 1848, Winslow was prodding Corning to call on the officers of the New York and Albany Railroad (he meant the New York and Harlem, with which the New York and Albany had been consolidated two years before) and make application for their order of spikes. A year later Winslow noted the shipment of an order of spikes "pr tow Bts" to the Harlem's rival, the Hudson River Railroad. While in New York City in

[20] Bishop, *History of American Manufactures*, II, 632–633.
[21] *Ibid.;* Winslow to Corning, Troy, April 4, 1867, CP.   [22] Corning Papers.

July, 1850, he negotiated for a contract to supply 150 to 175 tons of spikes to the Alton and Sangamon Railroad in Illinois. In December, 1852, he was in Ohio soliciting orders for spikes and axles from the Cleveland, Columbus and Cincinnati and the Little Miami railroads. From Cincinnati he reported that "all say our spikes & axles are the best they know of." [23]

During the winter of 1855–1856 Corning was in Europe, but Winslow's careful reports continued to reach him. In January, 1856, Winslow was assuring his partner that the Albany Iron Works would show a handsome profit for the preceding year. He further reported that he had recently added the Great Western of Canada to its list of railroad customers.[24] A decade later, in 1866, the works was supplying the "Pacific Railroad" with railroad chairs, spikes, and axles and was "pretty well known on the Pacific Side as Manufacturers." All the California trade came through an agent, G. M. T. Davis, of New City City.[25]

Through the years Erastus Corning & Co. of Albany continued to be a principal outlet for the products of the Albany Iron Works. It was expected, in fact, that the Albany house would absorb the daily output in excess of orders. For a long period this system worked well, but in 1864 the surplus from the ironworks began to pile up in the warehouse. In Winslow's opinion the reason for this was that prices, "based upon NY cost of Importation," were too high. "We shd rather be governed," he advised, "by Pittsburgh & other Western manufacturing points & they are below NY rates from 10 to 20 dolls pr ton." [26]

The chief competitor of the Albany Iron Works through the whole of its history was the Troy Iron and Nail Factory, of which Henry Burden and Sons were proprietors. In the 1860's the Burden establishment was at least as large as that of Corning and Winslow, if not larger. Between the two concerns

[23] Winslow to Corning, Troy, Nov. 21, 1848, Oct. 30, 1849; Mount Savage, Md., July 26, 1850; Cincinnati, Ohio, Dec. 16, 1852: CP.

[24] Winslow to Corning, Albany, Jan. 26, 1856, CP.

[25] Winslow to Corning, Troy, Jan. 4, 1866, CP.

[26] Winslow to Corning, Troy, July 22, 1864, CP.

a certain amount of ill will was probably to be expected, but the situation was aggravated by the unpleasant personality of Henry Burden and, in the 1820's and 1830's, by the equally unpleasant personality of Thomas Turner, the manager of the Albany Nail Factory. Nonetheless, as early as 1832 there seems to have been an attempt on the part of Burden and Turner to come to an understanding where common interests, such as prices and markets, were concerned.[27]

When John F. Winslow took over the management of the Albany Iron Works in 1837, he made honest efforts to meet Henry Burden halfway in the settlement of difficulties. This was not easy, but Winslow persevered. In December, 1846, he reported to Corning: "Burden & myself had a 'sitting' last Evg. according to appointment & contrary to our usual custom in like cases recently we parted in very good humor with one another." [28] The good humor was only temporary, however, and the usual bad relations between the two firms were soon reinstated, but by 1868, and perhaps earlier, the fixing of prices by agreement between the Albany Iron Works and the Burdens was a settled practice.[29]

In addition to the local day-by-day difficulties between the Burdens and the manager of the Albany Iron Works, a series of lawsuits in which Henry Burden accused his competitor of infringement of patent rights was fought in the courts over a period of three decades. There was scarcely a year's peace between 1839 and the 1870's.[30] The most famous of the suits were those involving the right of Corning, as chief proprietor of the Albany Iron Works, to use a spike machine which Burden claimed violated a patent held by him. In October, 1849, the Circuit Court of the Northern District of New York decided in

[27] Turner to Corning, Troy, April 8, 1832, CP.

[28] Letter dated at Troy, Dec. 14, 1846, CP.

[29] Henry Burden and Sons to Corning, Troy, Nov. 18, 1868, CP.

[30] Turner to Corning, Troy, April 8, 1832; James Horner to Corning, Albany, Oct. 17, 1839; John V. L. Pruyn to Corning, New York, July 8, 1843; Erastus Corning, Jr., to Corning, Berlin, Germany, June 22, 1851: CP; 4 *Federal Cases*, 701–712; 24 *Federal Cases*, 223–241; 14 Howard, 193–218; 15 Howard, 252–272. Comments on these cases are to be found in the John V. L. Pruyn Journals, Manuscripts Division, State Library, Albany, N.Y.

favor of Corning, but three years later the Supreme Court of the United States reversed the decision, remanded the case to the lower court, and ordered that a master be appointed to compute the amount of damages Corning was to pay Burden for the illegal use of the spike machine.[31] This by no means ended the matter, for the master proved to be Reuben H. Walworth, a friend of Corning's since his boyhood days in Troy.[32] Walworth began hearings on the Burden case on April 5, 1854. The proceedings rapidly deteriorated into a farce that has been amusingly described by one of Burden's lawyers:

Now began a series of interminable delays which threw Jarndyce *vs.* Jarndyce, of Bleak House fame, quite into the shade. Burden, an ardent man, believed the proceedings would be closed in three months, and that, as the defendants had made an enormous amount of spikes, the plaintiffs would be awarded at least $250,000 damages. Alas! Burden had not carefully studied Jarndyce or Walworth.

The case went on . . . till all the original counsel were frozen out of it or had died. But the tough ex-chancellor [Walworth], who was drawing heavy fees as he went along, was like Jefferson's Federalist office-holders—he neither died nor resigned. And so the years rolled away.[33]

Walworth's final report to the court was not made until May, 1866, twelve years after the hearings had begun. In March, 1869, the report was finally confirmed, and Burden was awarded a mere $8,475.09, with interest from 1849. In a subsequent suit he failed to force Corning to pay the costs of the long litigation, and he himself was ordered to pay half the master's fees.[34]

[31] 24 *Federal Cases*, 223, 226–227; 14 Howard, 218.

[32] Walworth had studied law in the office of John Russell while Corning was clerking for Heartt and Smith. He had been admitted to the bar in 1809 and in the course of time had become chancellor, that is, head of the courts of equity, of New York State. The merger of the courts of law and equity, as provided in the New York constitution of 1846, abolished Walworth's position. In 1848 he was an unsuccessful candidate for governor, after which he retired from political life. He died in 1867 (Richard B. Morris in Dumas Malone, ed., *Dictionary of American Biography* [New York, 1928–1936], XIX, 406–407).

[33] Henry B. Stanton, *Random Recollections*, 3d ed. (New York, 1887), 142.

[34] 24 *Federal Cases*, 227, 236, 237, 239.

Other suits, not so long drawn out or so well known, were concerned with alleged infringements by Corning and his partners of Burden's patents on a horseshoe machine and on a machine for rolling puddle balls—the so-called "squeezer case." Burden won a technical victory in the first, and Corning, by reason of a writ of error, was triumphant in the second. There was also a prolonged controversy concerning the distribution of the waters of Wynants Kill, the stream which turned "the vast and complicated machinery" of both the Albany Iron Works and the Troy Iron and Nail Factory.[35] Thus, during the thirty years that Winslow managed the Albany Iron Works, trouble with the Burdens was almost constant.

Another area in which frequent difficulties arose was that of labor relations. In both the 1850's and the 1860's there was considerable dissatisfaction among the workers, no doubt due in part to Winslow's practice of meeting rising production costs by cutting wages. In 1853, 1864, 1868, and perhaps other years there were serious disturbances which resulted in strikes. For dealing with this eventuality Winslow's formula (almost certainly approved by Corning) was to let the factory stand idle until the workmen "came too." [36]

In addition to the Albany Iron Works and the Burdens' Troy Iron and Nail Factory, there was after 1846 a third iron manufactory in Troy. In that year a rolling mill was erected by the Troy Vulcan Company. This was the beginning of the concern that later became the Rensselaer Iron Works, which was purchased about 1854 by John A. Griswold and Company. Like Erastus Corning, John A. Griswold had begun his career as a clerk in a Troy hardware house. Subsequently he worked as a bookkeeper for a cotton manufacturer and later established a wholesale and retail drug business. In 1855 he was mayor of Troy. Prior to April of that year Corning and Winslow bought a half interest in the Rensselaer Iron Works, John A. Gris-

[35] 4 *Federal Cases*, 701, 711; 15 Howard, *Supreme Court Reports*, 252; Henry Burden to Corning, Woodside, N.Y., March 18, 1868, CP.

[36] Davidson to Corning, Albany, Nov. 12, 1850; Winslow to Corning, undated, but probably written at Troy in 1850; same to same, undated, but endorsed in Corning's hand, "1853"; same to same, Troy, March 17, 1864; James E. Walker to Corning, Albany, Aug. 15, 1868: CP.

wold and Company retaining ownership of the other half. According to Winslow, the concern was at that time "going to the bugs at Locomotive speed." Nonetheless during the last nine months of 1855 the mill produced over 10,000 tons of iron, 8,500 tons of which were made into rails.[37]

In the middle of the 1860's the three ironworks at Troy accounted for more than one-sixth of the capital investment in industry in that city. Almost one-quarter of the employed men of the city were engaged in iron manufacturing.[38]

Another ironworks in which Corning invested was in Allegany County, Maryland. His interest there went back to 1847, when he became a member of a company that was formed to purchase the works at Mount Savage. John F. Winslow was also a member of the company, as was John Murray Forbes of Boston, with whom Corning was already associated in a number of railroad ventures and through whom he and Winslow seem to have become interested in the Mount Savage concern.[39]

The Mount Savage ironworks dated from 1840, when two blast furnaces for the making of pig iron had been erected by the Mount Savage Iron Company. Three years later the Maryland and New York Iron and Coal Company built a rolling mill at the same site. Here in 1844 were turned out the first heavy iron rails to be produced in the United States. Sometime prior to 1847 the Mount Savage interests—that is, the blast furnaces of the Mount Savage Iron Company and the rolling mill of the Maryland and New York Iron and Coal Company— were consolidated and acquired by an English concern.[40] Be-

[37] Roy Palmer Baker in *Dictionary of American Biography*, VIII, 8–9; Weise, *Troy's One Hundred Years,* 265; Winslow to Corning, Albany, Jan. 26, 1856, CP.

[38] Bishop, *History of American Manufactures*, II, 631. In 1860 only Pennsylvania exceeded New York in the number of hands employed in the manufacture of "bar, sheet, and railroad iron, &c.," the former state claiming 10,177, the latter 1,473. The value of the annual product of the Pennsylvania ironworks was placed at $10,974,013, that of New York's at $2,251,250. Pittsburgh accounted for more than one-third of Pennsylvania's product, Troy for more than one-half of New York's. Other large iron-manufacturing centers of the period were in Ohio, New Jersey, Virginia, Kentucky, and Tennessee (United States, *Eighth Census, 1860*, III, *Manufactures*, clxxxi, clxxxiii, 395).

[39] Winslow to Corning, Cumberland, Md., Oct. 4, 1847; Troy, Nov. 22, 1847: CP.

[40] Joseph T. Singewald, Jr., "Report on the Iron Ores of Maryland, with an

sides the furnaces and rolling mill, the establishment in the mid-1840's consisted of "a monster steam engine" erected at a cost of $72,000, a puddling furnace, a foundry, a firebrick yard, a store, 320 houses for workmen, a nine-mile railroad, and iron and coal mines. In other words, it was a typical "iron plantation." "From the balance sheets of the company," it was stated in 1849, "the works appear to have cost $1,600,000." [41] Yet in 1847, as the result of poor management and perhaps of intensified competition with foreign iron due to a revision of the tariff, the works had closed down and had been sold by the sheriff. John Murray Forbes (who had a financial interest in the defunct English company), Erastus Corning, John F. Winslow, and others purchased the entire establishment for a reported price of $200,000.[42]

Winslow, who supplied the necessary practical knowledge for running the ironworks, was elected president of the new Mount Savage Iron Company and made strenuous efforts to get the plant into operation. During the early part of 1848 he negotiated with the officers of the Baltimore and Ohio Railroad, which was being extended to the Ohio River, for their contract for rails. In February of that year he reported to Corning that "one of the Furnaces is finished & in tip top order for commencing work," but the following year the plant was again idle.[43]

One of Winslow's difficulties at Mount Savage, as at Troy, was labor trouble. From the outset he conflicted with the Irish

Account of the Iron Industry," *Maryland Geological Survey,* IX (Baltimore, 1911), 139–140; James M. Swank, *History of the Manufacture of Iron in All Ages* (Philadelphia, 1892), 434.

[41] *Merchant's Magazine and Commercial Review,* XXI (Oct., 1849), 460.

[42] *Ibid.;* Winslow to Corning, Cumberland, Md., Oct. 4, 1847, CP. Corning held 550 shares of the company's stock. In 1851 Watts Sherman, New York banker and former cashier of the Albany City Bank (of which Corning was president), was a stockholder to the extent of $11,050.41. Several Englishmen also had an interest in the new company (Winslow to Corning, Troy, June 17, 1848; Watts Sherman to Corning, New York, Dec. 25, 1851; John Murray Forbes to Corning, Boston, Dec. 27, 1860: CP).

[43] Winslow to Louis McLane, probably written at Troy, Jan. 23, 1848; Winslow to Corning, Mount Savage, Feb. 25, 1848; same to same, Troy, March 28, June 16, 1848: CP; *Merchant's Magazine and Commercial Review,* XXI (Oct., 1849), 461.

and English workmen who constituted the bulk of the force of 4,000 employed at Mount Savage when the works was in full operation.[44] Applying his old formula (that is, reducing wages in order to lower operating costs), Winslow met the determined opposition of the men, who, it was reported,

> are so banded together amongst themselves, and with the workmen in other establishments, that they will remain idle, or work at other business for one-half what the Company could afford to give them, rather than abate one cent from their wages. Puddlers, for instance, who formerly received $3 to $5 per ton, could now earn $2 50 per ton, but prefer to work in mines, or on the canal, for one-half that amount.[45]

Nor was labor trouble the only difficulty. The revolutions in Europe, causing a suspension of internal improvements on the continent, led English manufacturers of railroad iron to send most of their product to America, a practice in which they were encouraged (so American manufacturers believed) by a very low tariff.[46]

> It is to be hoped [the *Merchant's Magazine and Commercial Review* of October, 1849, observed] that ere long a peace in Europe, and alteration of the tariff, or a return to reason on the part of the workmen, will bring the superior article made at Mount Savage into general use on our railroads.

By July, 1850, that hope was partly realized, for the works was busy turning out 1,000 tons of rails for the Utica and Schenectady (of which, it will be remembered, Erastus Corning was president). [47] After that, however, there seems to have been another shutdown, as in the summer of 1852 Winslow was pressing upon Corning the necessity of raising $250,000 for Mount Savage, because, he urged, "when we *again* start it shd be with a determination to do all the works are capable of doing." [48] In November, Winslow was quoting a price on 2,000

---

[44] *Merchant's Magazine and Commercial Review*, XXI (Oct., 1849), 461; Winslow to Corning, Troy, July 20, 1848, CP; Writers' Program of the Works Projects Administration, *Maryland: A Guide to the Old Line State* (New York, 1940), 518.
[45] *Merchant's Magazine and Commercial Review*, XXI (Oct., 1849), 461.
[46] *Ibid.*   [47] Winslow to Corning, Mount Savage, July 26, 1850, CP.
[48] Winslow to Corning, Troy, July 17, 1852, CP. Italics supplied.

tons of compound rail for John W. Brooks of the Michigan Central Railroad (in which Corning was also deeply interested financially). About this time there was an upsurge in the rail market, partly because American railroads continued to expand rapidly and partly because the older eastern roads were replacing their original "strap" rails with the heavier "U" and "T" rails. Winslow was jubilant. "I have applications for rails by the score," he wrote to Corning, "but we intend to serve our friends first." [49]

In 1855 the Mount Savage works produced some 8,300 tons of rails. Yet the following year the mill shut down, never to reopen. In 1875 it was dismantled. About the same time that the mill was closed, the furnaces, too, went out of blast. They were put into operation again during the Civil War, but after that were finally abandoned.[50]

The failure of the ironworks at Mount Savage despite the best efforts of the competent Winslow was caused principally by the lack of a convenient supply of raw material. The furnaces were built with the intention of using the iron ore of the immediate vicinity, but it was found to contain too much carbon.[51] The necessity of hauling ore to the works from a distance militated against efficient production, an insurmountable handicap when combined with a highly competitive market.[52]

Corning's investments in iron manufacturing dictated an interest on his part in a high tariff on imported iron products. But in addition to being an iron manufacturer he was also

[49] Letter dated at Troy, Nov. 8, 1852, CP.
[50] Singewald, "Report on the Iron Ores of Maryland," 140.   [51] *Ibid.*
[52] About the close of the Civil War the Mount Savage Iron Company and the Frostburg Coal Company merged to form the Consolidation Coal Company. (It will be remembered that there were coal mines on the Mount Savage property.) Early in 1870 the last-named company purchased the coal and railroad interests of the Cumberland Coal and Iron Company (Horace Turner to Corning, Wheeling, W.Va., April 27, 1864; Forbes to Corning, Boston, Oct. 21, 1867; circular signed by H. C. Hicks, Treasurer, Consolidation Coal Company, March 4, 1870: CP). In 1870, also, there was formed at Mount Savage the Mount Savage Fire Brick and Mining Company, of which, in the 1880's, James Roosevelt, father of Franklin D. Roosevelt, was head (Writers' Program, *Maryland*, 518).

president of the New York Central Railroad, which imported each year through his Albany mercantile house thousands of tons of iron rails. Other railroads throughout the country were also customers of Erastus Corning & Co. On the roads' purchases the Albany concern of course received a commission. If high duties had to be paid, fewer tons of rails might be bought. Therefore, as an ironmaster on the one hand and a merchant and railroad president on the other, Corning was not always consistent in his attitude toward the tariff.[53]

In 1849, when the iron manufacturers of the country were feeling the effects of British competition, due in large measure, they claimed, to the low tariff of 1846, Corning accepted the presidency of an association formed by some of the ironmasters of New York "to take into consideration the tariff on iron." But six years later, in January and February of 1855, when Congress was considering a proposal to remit to the railroads of the country the duty they had paid on imported iron during the preceding three years and John F. Winslow was in Washington arguing against the measure, Corning was paying David Hamilton, a lobbyist, to act on behalf of the New York Central in favor of the proposal—this at a time when Corning's financial investment in two rail mills was very large.[54]

As iron manufacturers during the Civil War, Corning and Winslow helped supply the Union Army. A Democrat and a merchant, Corning at first opposed the war and later gave it only lukewarm support, his criticism of the Lincoln administration at times being extreme.[55] But on the outbreak of hostili-

[53] For a discussion of the tariff on rails and other railroad iron from 1847 to 1860 and of the interindustrial conflict over the matter, see Alfred D. Chandler, Jr., *Henry Varnum Poor, Business Editor, Analyst, and Reformer* (Cambridge, Mass., 1956), 181–186.

[54] Munsell, *Annals of Albany*, 2d ed., II (Albany, 1870), 325; F. W. Taussig, *The Tariff History of the United States*, 8th ed. (New York, 1931), 130–131; David Hamilton to Corning, Washington, Feb. 26, 1855, CP. One of the rail mills in which Corning was at this time interested was that of the Rensselaer Iron Works at Troy; the other was that of the Mount Savage Iron Company in Maryland.

[55] During part of the war Corning was in Congress. On Jan. 21, 1862, O. H. Browning, a Senator from Illinois, recorded in his diary: "At night called to

ties John F. Winslow hurried to Washington to obtain a share of the war contracts for the Albany Iron Works. By September, 1861, he could report to Corning: "We have . . . propositions before the War & Navy Depts, & with attention, we shall secure a fair proportion of what is wanted." [56] All during the war large quantities of steel from the Albany Iron Works, perhaps as much as eight tons a day, went into the manufacture of cannon. Solid-lip railroad chairs (iron blocks forming a kind of socket for supporting a rail and securing it to a tie), which had been invented at the works, were turned out by the thousands for use by the army as it took over and began to restore the ruined railroads of the border states and the upper South.[57]

The most famous war project in which the Troy ironworks were concerned was the building of the *Monitor,* the ironclad that was victorious over the Confederate *Merrimac* at Hampton Roads in the spring of 1862. The gunboat, which featured a revolving turret, was the invention of John Ericsson, a Swede by birth who had lived and worked in England for a number of years before coming to America in 1839. He was a first-class engineer and designer and was responsible for a number of inventions, most noteworthy of which was the successful application of the principle of the screw propeller to an ocean-

---

see Mr & Mrs Corning, and had a talk with him on the State of the Country. He is very dispondent [sic] and thinks the radical and extreme policy of the administration has made the restoration of the Union impossible in any other way than by the North Western States forming an alliance with the States of the lower Mississippi. If this were done he thinks Pennsylvania, New York, New Jersey &c would soon join, and ultimately the remaining states, and that thus we might become again one people" (Orville Hickman Browning, *Diary,* ed. with introduction and notes by Theodore Calvin Pease and James G. Randall [Springfield, Ill., 1925-1933], I, 617-618). In May, 1863, Corning headed a committee which forwarded to Lincoln the resolutions drawn up at a Democratic meeting in Albany protesting the arrest of Vallandigham. Lincoln's courteous but uncompromising reply, addressed to Erastus Corning and others, was "one of the President's most remarkable political letters" (Lincoln, *Complete Works,* ed. by John G. Nicolay and John Hay [New York, 1905], VIII, 298-314).

[56] Letter dated at Troy, Sept. 10, 1861, CP.

[57] George Rogers Howell and Jonathan Tenney, eds., *Bi-centennial History of Albany* (New York, 1886), II, 540; Arthur James Weise, *History of the City of Troy* (Troy, 1876), 234; Winslow to Corning, Troy, Sept. 3, 1861, CP.

going vessel. He also designed an ironclad warship in which
Napoleon III showed some interest.[58] In 1861, with the help
of C. S. Bushnell, a railroad president from Connecticut who
acted as promoter, the design of the ironclad was submitted to
the Navy Department. After some delay a contract for the
building of the *Monitor* was let, Ericsson, Bushnell, John F.
Winslow, and John A. Griswold each taking a one-quarter
interest.[59] The last two men were valuable partners not only
because they furnished the operating capital for the project but
also because their rolling mills at Troy could supply the armor
plate for the vessel.

Within six months the *Monitor* venture paid a net profit of
$79,857.40—almost $20,000 for each investor.[60] The name of
Erastus Corning is notably absent from the contract. He was
at the time a member of Congress and as such was forbidden
to appear as a contractor with the government,[61] but it is more
than likely that he was a silent partner in the shares held by
Winslow and Griswold, for they kept him informed of the
negotiations with Washington and later of the progress of the
ironclad. A subcontract for the construction of the vessel was
given to Thomas F. Rowland, of the Continental Iron Works,
Green Point, Brooklyn, but the Albany Iron Works and the
Rensselaer Iron Works, together with Holdane and Company
of New York and Abbott and Son of Baltimore, furnished the
iron.[62]

In December, 1861, more than two months before the *Moni-*
tor was ready for duty, the Navy Department solicited bids for
twenty additional ironclads. According to Bushnell, the *Moni-*
tor contractors "by acting promptly & energetically" could get
an order for six or eight of the proposed vessels. Winslow's re-

[58] William F. Durand in *Dictionary of American Biography*, VI, 171–176.

[59] The letting of the contract and the building of the ship are dealt with at
length in James Phinney Baxter, 3rd, *The Introduction of the Ironclad Warship*
(Cambridge, Mass., 1933). Cf. Winslow to James M. Swank, Woodcliff, N.Y., Sept.,
1891, in Francis B. Wheeler, *John F. Winslow, LL.D. and the Monitor* (Poughkeepsie, N.Y., 1893), 52–54.

[60] Baxter, *Introduction of the Ironclad Warship*, 267.

[61] Winslow to Corning, Troy, Sept. 3, 1861, CP.

[62] Baxter, *Introduction of the Ironclad Warship*, 265–266.

action was that this would be desired only "if the pay is made reasonable safe & certain." [63] There is good evidence that through timely action on the part of Corning and other political friends of Winslow, Griswold, and their partners the awarding of contracts for the additional ironclads was delayed until after the successful action of the *Monitor* against the *Merrimac* on March 8, 1862.[64] Six days later, on March 14, 1862, Winslow reported to Corning: "We have closed for 6 Boats on the plan of the Monitor for $400,000 each—they are to be a trifle larger in size—*this will do.*" [65] The contract was indeed a favorable one. The price which had been paid by the government for the *Monitor* was only $275,000, of which nearly $80,000 was net profit. Even if allowance is made for the slightly larger size of the new ships and for mounting wartime inflation, the contractors stood to make a worth-while sum on the six new gunboats.[66]

The closing years of the Civil War saw the introduction of a method of steelmaking—the Bessemer process—which revolutionized the industry. In the winter of 1864–1865 one of the first Bessemer plants in America was built as an addition to the rail mill of the Rensselaer Iron Works at Troy. Corning, Winslow, and Griswold had become interested in the new steelmaking process through Alexander L. Holley, an engineer and one of the editors of the *American Railway Review,* who had inspected Sir Henry Bessemer's works in England in 1862. In 1863 Holley returned to England and this time obtained, in the name of Winslow, Griswold, and himself (a partnership formed for the purpose), the American rights to Bessemer's patents. Winslow, Griswold and Holley was not a manufacturing concern, nor did it become one. The Bessemer plant at Troy, built under Holley's direction, was owned and operated

[63] Winslow to Corning, Troy, Dec. 28, 1861, CP.

[64] Baxter, *Introduction of the Ironclad Warship,* 278, 279, 281.

[65] Winslow to Corning, March 14, 1862, CP.

[66] On at least three of the ironclads built by the contractors a royalty of $5,000 each was paid to T. R. Timby, who held a patent on a turret which Ericsson's design apparently infringed (Wheeler, *John F. Winslow . . . and the Monitor,* 57).

by the Rensselaer Iron Works, in which Corning, Winslow, and Griswold, but not Holley, had a financial interest. Here on February 15, 1865, was produced the first successful "Bessemer" steel in America.[67] It was not, however, the first steel manufactured in the United States by the process which has come to be associated with the name of Bessemer, and indeed, the Troy ironmasters were violating an American patent.

While Bessemer had been experimenting in England, William Kelly, a Pittsburgher who with his brother owned the Suwanee Iron Works near Eddyville, Kentucky, was carrying on similar experiments. As early as 1856, hearing that Bessemer had applied for a patent in Washington, Kelly filed a claim to priority. His claim was upheld and a patent granted to him. In the panic of 1857 Kelly went bankrupt, which doubtless accounts for his selling his patent rights in 1861. The purchasers were Z. S. Durfee and Eber B. Ward, both of Detroit. The following year, in 1862, Ward erected a plant at Wyandotte, Michigan, for the purpose of carrying out further experiments with the Kelly process. Not long after that, the Kelly Pneumatic Process Company, consisting of Ward, Durfee, and three other ironmasters, was organized. At the Kelly works in Wyandotte in September, 1864, five months before the successful manufacture of Bessemer steel by Winslow, Griswold, and Holley in Troy, steel was produced under the Kelly patent. In manufacturing the steel the Kelly Pneumatic Process Company violated the Bessemer rights, for although Bessemer had been refused an American patent on the main idea involved in his process (that is, the forcing of cold air through molten pig iron to burn out the carbon), he had been granted patents on his machinery. Some of the machinery used at the Wyandotte works infringed upon those patents.[68]

[67] Carl W. Mitman in *Dictionary of American Biography*, IX, 148–149; James M. Swank, *History of the Manufacture of Iron in All Ages* (Philadelphia, 1892), 411; Fritz Redlich, *History of American Business Leaders: A Series of Studies* (Ann Arbor, Mich., 1940–1951), I, 96.

[68] Allan Nevins, *Abram S. Hewitt, with Some Account of Peter Cooper* (New York, 1935), 126, 130–131; Redlich, *History of American Business Leaders*, I, 94–96; Swank, *History of . . . Iron in All Ages*, 409, 411.

Further to complicate the situation, it was soon found that Bessemer steel could be manufactured with consistent success only by making use of the patent of yet a third person. The experiments in Wyandotte and Troy, it was discovered, had terminated favorably (as had Bessemer's original experiments in England) only because of the quality of raw material which had been used. In each case, the pig iron which went into the converter happened to come from ore which contained little phosphorus and which in other respects was suitable. When inferior ores or ores of different chemical content were used, the product of the Bessemer process was not steel, but only wrought iron. It was Robert Mushet, an Englishman, who discovered a method of transforming the molten iron into steel by mixing with it fused carbonized iron containing manganese. In October, 1864, Z. S. Durfee obtained for the Kelly Pneumatic Process Company the American rights to Mushet's patent.[69]

After that time, then, the company in Michigan held the rights to both the Kelly and Mushet processes, but could not use Bessemer's machines, the American rights to which were held by Winslow, Griswold and Holley. On the other hand, whereas the group in Troy had undisputed right to the use of the Bessemer machinery, they could hardly continue to violate Kelly's patent on the method of manufacture. They were further handicapped by having no authority to employ Mushet's process. There was only one way out of the impasse —a pooling of the interests of the holders of the Bessemer rights and the owners of the Kelly and Mushet rights.

Early in 1866 an arrangement was made by which the Kelly patent, the American rights to the Bessemer machines, and those to the Mushet process were all invested in Winslow, Griswold, and a member of the Kelly firm, Daniel J. Morrell. The Troy interests managed very well for themselves, for Winslow and Griswold emerged as seven-tenths owners of the

[69] Victor S. Clark, *History of Manufactures in the United States* (New York, 1929), II, 70; Nevins, *Abram S. Hewitt*, 127–128, 130; Redlich, *History of American Business Leaders*, I, 94–95; Swank, *History of . . . Iron in All Ages*, 409.

consolidated rights, and Morrell held a three-tenths interest in trust for the Kelly Pneumatic Process Company.[70] No one has been able to explain satisfactorily why the undisputed holders of the rights to both the Kelly and Mushet processes should have retained only a three-tenths interest in the combined patents, whereas a seven-tenths interest went to Winslow and Griswold, who originally had held only the American rights to the Bessemer machines.

About 1867 the Bessemer works at Troy was enlarged to a capacity of five tons.[71] In the winter of 1869–1870 there was a further expansion, for Erastus Corning in January wrote to Nathaniel Thayer of Boston:

I am call'd upon for rather more money than I anticipated for our Iron Works—in particular for Mr Griswolds Bessemar [sic] Works, hence I can not take as much of the Kentucky Bonds as I should otherwise do.[72]

During the depression of 1873 the Troy Bessemer plant temporarily suspended operations, but by 1875 it was once again running at full capacity, sometimes turning out in excess of 270 tons of ingots in 24 hours. The following year it was claimed that the steel produced by this plant was one of the best grades to be found in the United States. On the eve of the panic of 1893 the capacity of the steelworks was 450 tons a day.[73]

As the Bessemer plant expanded, so did the rest of the Rensselaer Iron Works. In 1870 a new mill was erected on the

[70] Swank, *History of . . . Iron in All Ages*, 409, 410. "This arrangement continued until the formation of the Pneumatic Steel Association, a joint-stock company organized under the laws of New York, in which the ownership of the consolidated patents was vested. . . . The ownership of the patents was afterwards vested in the Bessemer Steel Company Limited, an association organized in 1877 under the laws of Pennsylvania. This association has been succeeded by the Steel Patents Company, organized in 1890. All the original English and American patents have expired [1896]" (*ibid.*, 410).

[71] Weise, *Troy's One Hundred Years*, 266.

[72] Letter dated at Albany, Jan. 14, 1870, CP.

[73] Clark, *History of Manufactures*, II, 231; Swank, *History of . . . Iron in All Ages*, 411; Weise, *Troy's One Hundred Years*, 266.

north side of Poesten Kill for the rolling of steel rails, and
sometime prior to 1872 the company acquired blast furnaces
at both Fort Edward and Hudson, New York. Nor did the
Albany Iron Works fail to expand. So successful was this concern in the post-Civil War period that a division of profits
made in April, 1866, amounted to $75,000 for each of the three
owners—Erastus Corning, John F. Winslow, and Erastus Corning, Jr. Whether this sum represented profits for one year or
for a longer period is not clear. In July, 1870, the spike factory
of the Albany Iron Works was reported to be turning out
150,000 pounds of hook-headed spikes a week. In 1872 the annual product of the whole works was said to be nearly 15,000
tons of cut nails, spikes, rivets, band, bar, rod, and scroll iron,
railroad car axles, wagon axles, crowbars, and wrought-iron
railroad chairs. The firm's New York agent reported sales
amounting to $330,786.03 for the year ending December 31,
1869. The following year sales through this agent rose to
$520,342.34.[74]

Despite the success of the Albany Iron Works in the late
sixties, John F. Winslow decided that he wanted to sell his
interest and go abroad for a time. To accomplish this he
promised to name a very low price and suggested to Corning
that he purchase the proffered share for Edwin, his younger
son. Corning, who had little respect for the business acumen
of either of his sons and who was himself old and sick, was
reluctant to take on new responsibilities. In the end, however,
he yielded and paid Winslow something in the vicinity of
$120,000 for his one-third interest in the real estate and ma-
chinery of the works. The amount to be paid for stock on hand
was to be determined by an inventory. After 1867, then, the
Cornings were the sole owners of the Albany Iron Works,
under the firm name of Erastus Corning & Co. Apparently
about this time also, Winslow disposed of his interest in the

[74] Winslow to Corning, Troy, April 2, 1866; Bainbridge to Corning, Troy,
July 12, 1870; George M. Davis to Corning, New York, Dec. 30, 1870; Corning,
Jr., to John A. Griswold, Albany, June 4, 1872: CP; *Contemporary Biography of
New York*, II, 353; Weise, *Troy's One Hundred Years*, 265.

Rensselaer Iron Works, either to the Cornings or to the Griswolds.[75]

Upon the death of Erastus Corning in 1872, Erastus Corning, Jr., his elder son and principal heir, took over the management of the Albany Iron Works. When, on March 1, 1875, the interests of Erastus Corning & Co. and John A. Griswold and Company were consolidated and incorporated under the name of the Albany and Rensselaer Iron and Steel Company, Corning (now no longer "Jr.") was named president. Ten years later, on September 1, 1885, the concern was reorganized as the Troy Iron and Steel Company, with a capital stock of $2,-500,000. The company built three blast furnaces in South Troy, enlarged the steelworks, and for a number of years was apparently in a flourishing condition. The panic of 1893, however, was more than it could weather. In that year the concern was sold by receivers [76]—a victim of financial crises, poor management,[77] and a reoriented industry.

[75] Winslow to Corning, Troy, Feb. 25, April 4, 1867; Corning, Jr., to Griswold, June 4, 1872: CP.

[76] George Baker Anderson, *Landmarks of Rensselaer County, New York* (Syracuse, N.Y., 1897), 309; Clark, *History of Manufactures*, II, 231.

[77] Contemporary evidence would seem to leave no doubt that Erastus Corning, Jr., was not the businessman that his father was and that his judgment in matters of business was usually not to be trusted. In 1876, only four years after his father's death, John Bigelow remarked of him: "Corning of Albany. . . . is a man of pleasure, who inherited a large fortune and a name associated with the triumphs of a political dynasty in this state in the last generation, of considerable influence. The heir, however, never had the ability to acquire these patrimonies, neither has he the ability to preserve them; and he has already squandered so much of them that he is only the shadow of a name" (Bigelow to William B. Beach, Albany, May 29, 1876, in John Bigelow, *Retrospections of an Active Life* [New York, 1913], V, 265).

· V ·

Man of the Rails, 1831-1853

NOT unrelated to Erastus Corning's mercantile and iron-manufacturing interests was his early interest in railroads. A connection between the railroads and the iron industry was noted by Henry Varnum Poor, editor of the *American Railroad Journal,* when he argued in 1852 that "the growth of a healthy American iron industry depended primarily on the healthy expansion of the American railroad network." [1] Two years later, in 1854, Abram Hewitt, the New Jersey ironmaster, stated that the way to sustain the domestic iron industry was not to raise the tariff, as was then being urged, but to build railroads. For every 5,000 miles of road built, Hewitt pointed out, 500,-000 tons of rails had to be supplied, and as much more metal for cars, engines, spikes, and so on. [2]

At least twenty years earlier Erastus Corning had grasped the interrelation of the iron and railroad industries. Although there was always an element of speculation in his railroad investments, beginning with the Mohawk and Hudson in the early 1830's and growing in importance as the years progressed, and although he was not indifferent to the advantages accruing to Albany, the headquarters of his many-faceted activities, by reason of its being a railway terminal, not a little of his early interest in railroads may be explained by his recognition of the new transportation medium as a first-rate market for iron.

[1] Alfred D. Chandler, Jr., *Henry Varnum Poor, Business Editor, Analyst, and Reformer* (Cambridge, Mass., 1956), 183.

[2] Abraham S. Hewitt to Charles Skelton, Feb. 18, 1854, cited in Allan Nevins, *Abram S. Hewitt, with Some Account of Peter Cooper* (New York, 1935), 156–157.

Corning has been so long regarded as a railroad leader that the fact that he was also an iron merchant and manufacturer is usually forgotten. When it is remembered, it goes far to explain his serving without salary as president of one railroad, the Utica and Schenectady, for twenty years and of another, the New York Central, for twelve.

It will be recalled from Chapter III that Corning's first railroad investment, made in October, 1831, was in the form of a one-third interest in 130 shares of Mohawk and Hudson stock. His partners in the stock-buying venture were two other citizens of Albany, Edwin Croswell and James Porter, and two New Yorkers, William G. Bucknor and Churchill C. Cambreling. The last name is especially significant since it was under the direct supervision of Cambreling that the Mohawk and Hudson was to be built, one of his specific duties being "to advertise for and enter into contracts for grading and forming the Road and for the materials for the same." [3]

Corning lost no time in identifying himself with the direction and administration of the Mohawk and Hudson, for in June, 1833, he was elected a director and vice-president of the company, a position which he filled for two years. [4] His service with the Mohawk and Hudson was, however, but a prologue to a much more important position, the presidency of the Utica and Schenectady.

The Utica and Schenectady Rail-Road Company was incorporated on April 29, 1833, with an authorized capital of $2,000,000, to consist of 20,000 shares having a par value of $100 each. The charter named twenty-one commissioners, among them Erastus Corning, to receive subscriptions to the stock of the company and, most importantly, to distribute the stock. [5] When the subscription books were opened in New

---

[3] Statement of purchase, Oct. 27, 1831, CP; Frank Walker Stevens, *The Beginnings of the New York Central Railroad* (New York, 1926), 22.

[4] Alvin F. Harlow, *The Road of the Century: The Story of the New York Central* (New York, 1947), 19; *Albany Argus*, June 24, 1834.

[5] *Laws of the State of New York, Fifty-sixth Session* (Albany, 1833), 462–468. Other provisions of the charter were concerned with compensation to the Mohawk Turnpike Company and with restrictions on the carrying of freight

York, Albany, Schenectady, and Utica (as provided in the charter), the stock was oversubscribed seven times. The commissioners therefore had a wide latitude of choice when it came to deciding who was to have stock and who was not. Ultimately, 5,500 shares were allotted to subscribers in the city of New York; 5,600 to subscribers in the counties of Albany, Rensselaer, Saratoga, Columbia, Ulster, and Dutchess; 2,500 to subscribers in Schenectady, Schoharie, and Montgomery counties; and 6,400 to subscribers in Oneida, Herkimer, and the other counties north and west of Albany.[6]

The *Albany Argus,* always loyal to Corning, commented that "the distribution was an extremely difficult, and in some respects an invidious task," and then went on to express confidence that "the interests of the company, and the interests of the public which are identical with them . . . have been secured." [7] But if this was true, it was only part of the story, for one criterion employed by the commissioners in determining individual allotments in the Albany area, at least, was the new stockholder's willingness to hand over his voting proxy to Corning.[8] One disappointed subscriber, Walker by name, sued the Utica and Schenectady, but received no sympathy from Chancellor Reuben H. Walworth, an old friend of Corning, who headed the courts of equity of New York State. In the case of Walker *vs.* the Utica and Schenectady, Walworth ruled that subscription gave a man no right to stock and then added the gratuitous comment that the commissioners were very modest in not taking more stock for themselves as a reward for their trouble and responsibility.[9]

In point of fact, Corning had no desire to hold a large block

---

in competition with the Erie Canal. This phase of the history of the road has been dealt with in other places. See David Maldwyn Ellis, "Rivalry between the New York Central and the Erie Canal," *New York History,* XXIX (July, 1948), 268–300; Harlow, *Road of the Century,* 26, 31.

[6] *Albany Argus,* June 25, July 16, 1833.   [7] *Ibid.,* July 16, 1833.

[8] J. McConihe to Erastus Corning, Albany, July 6, 1833, CP.

[9] James Porter to Corning, Saratoga Springs, N.Y., Aug. 20, 1833, CP. The commissioners had voluntarily limited themselves to 100 shares each (Stevens, *Beginnings of the New York Central,* 116).

of assessable stock. The Utica and Schenectady, a 78-mile line, had yet to be constructed, and dividends could hardly be expected for some time to come. It was more to Corning's purpose to control the road through others' proxies. Even before the stock distribution was made, one of his right-hand men, J. McConihe, was engaged in collecting promises of proxies in Troy and its vicinity. Subsequent to the distribution, but before the election of the first directors, James Hooker of Poughkeepsie collected Dutchess County proxies in the interest of Corning, and the Albany capitalist himself gathered in the proxies of his friends and personal acquaintances.[10]

The result of this foresightedness was that at the first Utica and Schenectady stockholders' meeting on August 17, 1833, Corning was elected to the board of directors. Others on the board were Alfred Munson, Henry Seymour, and Nicholas Devereaux of Utica; Nathaniel S. Benton of Little Falls; Tobias A. Stoutenburgh of Johnstown; Alonzo C. Paige of Schenectady; James Porter, John Townsend, and Lewis Benedict of Albany; James Hooker of Poughkeepsie; and C. C. Cambreling and John Mason of New York City. At the first directors' meeting, held on the same day, Corning was chosen as president of the road.[11]

Once in the president's chair, Corning took no chances of losing ground but kept his henchmen busy in his interests. Before each annual stockholders' meeting he conducted a drive for proxies and through the efforts of McConihe and others always managed to command enough votes to insure his controlling the election of directors. Just before the stockholders' meeting in 1840, and again in 1844, Corning sent Watts Sherman (cashier of the Albany City Bank, of which Corning was president) to New York City to obtain proxies there. On the second occasion Sherman visited the Boston stockholders also. At the same time Charles Livingston (of the Livingston and Wells Express Company) was, at Corning's behest, calling

[10] McConihe to Corning, Albany, July 6, 1833; same to same, Saratoga Springs, July 9, 1833; James Hooker to Corning, Poughkeepsie, N.Y., July 18, 1833; Power of Attorney, Silas Wright to Corning, July 27, 1833: CP.

[11] *Albany Argus*, Aug. 17, Aug. 19, 1833.

on shareholders in New Jersey and Philadelphia, soliciting their proxies for the road's president. As might be expected, the directors of the Utica and Schenectady who owed their positions to Corning also worked in his interest.[12]

Corning's control of the Utica and Schenectady by no means went unchallenged. According to Alfred Munson in May, 1835, more than a year before the line was in operation, a General Ostrom of Utica was applying to several stockholders at that place for their proxies, intimating that an effort would be made "to change the direction." [13] In the winter of 1840–1841, when Corning was in Europe trying to sell the New York state stock with which the Albany City Bank was rather heavily overloaded, it was reported to him by John V. L. Pruyn, his lawyer and nephew by marriage, that some "Troy people" were working against his interests.

[They] are jealous of the control Albany has over the Utica Road [Pruyn wrote], & we must take great care of that interest—Doct Craig of Sch[enecta]dy told me not long ago, he had heard some talk of an attempt at change in that direction—I do not conceive that there is any danger, but the Albanians have so little of that stock, that proxies must be obtained to a considerable amount to be safe— [14]

This was only the beginning of long-drawn-out difficulties with Troy, but a new issue soon temporarily obscured the intercity rivalry. The replacing of Gideon Hawley as secretary and treasurer of the Utica and Schenectady by the appointment of Pruyn to that position on July 1, 1843, gave all the disaffected elements a cause around which to rally. The result was that Corning found himself faced with perhaps the greatest challenge to his regime during his two decades as president of the road. As the time for the stockholders' meeting of 1844 approached, Hawley made himself rather troublesome, pre-

[12] McConihe to Corning, Troy, N.Y., May 30, 1834; Alfred Munson to Corning and James Porter, Utica, N.Y., May 26, 1835; Watts Sherman to Corning, New York, May 28, 1840, May 11, 1844; same to same, Boston, May 17, 1844; Charles Livingston to Corning, New York, May 18, 1844: CP.

[13] Munson to Corning and Porter, Utica, May 26, 1835, CP.

[14] John V. L. Pruyn to Corning, Albany, Jan. 10, 1841, CP.

senting his case to the New York City stockholders in the Utica and Schenectady and pointing out to them that since they owned such a large amount of stock in the road they should be represented on the board of directors by at least three or four members, instead of only two, as had always been the case.

This argument takes here [Watts Sherman reported to Corning from New York] & will to some degree have to be yielded to. But in selecting say *3* Directors here tis very important that the right kind of men should be taken. . . .

Great headway has undoubtedly been made by these people in obtaining proxies & the work has been going on so long that it will require a strong effort to retain power.[15]

Later Hawley circulated in New York what was described as *"his recently rec'd evidence against the present Board,"* [16] and Sherman subsequently reported from Boston that

the stories about the manner & object of Pruyns appointment and Mr Hawleys going out of office have been represented in the most base . . . light. It has even been asserted (as near as I can get at it) that *you* procured this arrangement for the purpose not only of having more unlimited controul over the affairs of the Co. but to cover up matters in relation to its financial or other affairs— [17]

So disturbed was Corning by Hawley's activities that in order to strengthen his position at the anticipated shareholders' meeting he bought additional stock in the Utica and Schenectady at $129 a share, but the meeting itself apparently passed off quietly enough, for there is no special notice of it in the press of the day. Perhaps Hawley came to a realization of where "his own true interest lay," as Charles Livingston had predicted he would.[18] It is more than likely, too, that most of the Utica and Schenectady's stockholders were pleased with Corning's management of the road.

[15] Sherman to Corning, New York, May 11, 1844, CP.
[16] Livingston to Corning, New York, June 1, 1844, CP.
[17] Sherman to Corning, Boston, May 17, 1844, CP.
[18] Livingston to Corning, New York, June 1, 1844; Sherman to Corning, New York, June 22, 1844: CP.

The history of the Utica and Schenectady sheds some light on the way in which America's earliest railroads were financed. It should not be supposed that those who so eagerly subscribed to stock were prepared to pay its par value at once—or, for that matter, ever. At most, the stockholders expected during construction of the road several small "calls" of perhaps five or ten dollars a share, and these at wide intervals. The rest of the authorized capital was to accumulate from the earnings of the road after the first section of it was in operation, dividends to serve in lieu of "calls." In January, 1835, with but $160,000 of the Utica and Schenectady's capital paid in (this was $8 on each share), the directors of the road, through Prime, Ward and King, New York City brokers, made arrangements to borrow $100,000 from John Jacob Astor. The money, which was to be used for the road's construction, was borrowed on the personal joint bond of Corning and two other directors from Albany, John Townsend and Lewis Benedict, Astor accepting as partial security some 1,500 shares of Utica and Schenectady stock at 10 per cent less than the amount that had been paid on it. The loan was to run for three years and was renewable for two years upon the option of the borrowers. Annual interest of 6 per cent, payable twice a year in New York, was charged by Astor, and the borrowers had to pay a commission of one-half of 1 per cent, amounting to $500, to Prime, Ward & King.[19] In all probability the Utica and Schenectady paid a commission to Corning, Townsend, and Benedict as well.

The first dividend of the company was declared on February 1, 1837, just six months after the road had begun operations. At this time the paid-in capital amounted to $1,500,000, which was half a million dollars less than the par value of the stock that had been issued. Further dividends, which with the first amounted to $20.85 on each $100 share, were declared on August 1, 1837, February 1, 1838, and August 1, 1838. Fifteen dollars of the dividend paid on each share offset calls on the

---

[19] *Documents of the Assembly of the State of New York, Sixty-fourth Session* (Albany, 1841), no. 147; Prime, Ward and King to Corning, New York, Jan. 28, Feb. 14, March 2, 1835, CP; Kenneth Wiggins Porter, *John Jacob Astor, Business Man* (Cambridge, Mass., 1931), II, 1003.

stock and so stayed in the treasury of the company. The paid-in capital had then reached $1,800,000. Dividends were continued at the rate of 10 per cent a year at least through 1840, but there was no further capital increase until May, 1842, when a special 10 per cent dividend was declared for the purpose of offsetting a final call on the stock.[20] Thus, any original stockholder who had retained his shares had paid for them only three-quarters of their par value. In addition, the paid-out dividends which he had received represented a handsome interest on his investment. By the early summer of 1844, the stock was selling for $129 a share.

But Corning was not so much concerned with large dividends as he was interested in protecting his position as favored contractor and in keeping the road free of legislative interference. Therefore, he wished the company neither to be financially weak nor to appear too prosperous. In line with this policy, it was probably at his instigation that the road's directors in the late 1840's decreed a cut in the rate of dividends.[21] When a New England stockholder complained and suggested that an extra dividend be declared in order to bring the earnings on the stock up to the usual amount, the Utica and Schenectady's president enlisted John V. L. Pruyn, no amateur in finesse, to make explanations.

We entered 1847 with about 4 to 5 pr ct surplus—having just made arrangements to relay the road with heavy Iron, the cost of which it was known would considerably exceed the amount [$500,000] the legislature had authorized us to borrow for the purpose—not knowing how heavy the calls might be during the year it would have been folly to have paid out this money at once, especially also as we wished to procure from the Legislature the right to increase our capital. . . . An extra dividend may in the opinion of some & perhaps will, lend strength to the project of reducing the fare on all the roads, which as the legislature is now in session it is de-

[20] *Documents of the Assembly of the State of New York, Sixty-fourth Session* (Albany, 1841), no. 147, pp. 2–3; copy of resolution adopted by the Directors of the Utica and Schenectady Rail-Road Company on May 10, signed by Gideon Hawley, dated at Albany, May 11, 1842, CP.

[21] David Watkinson to Corning, Hartford, Conn., Jan. 10, 1848, CP.

sirable to avoid. . . . Large dividends excite remark & invite legislation.[22]

Despite the caution of its president, however, by the time of the New York Central consolidation in 1853, the Utica and Schenectady was once again a "10 percent" road.[23]

In speaking of Corning's association with the Utica and Schenectady, a modern authority maintains that

throughout his two decades at the head of the U. & S., he . . . never accepted a cent of salary, asking only that he have the privilege of supplying all the rails, running gear, tools and other iron and steel articles used by the railroad, his profits on the same being his only recompense. No other dealer or manufacturer ever had a look-in with the U. & S. during those decades.[24]

The last statement is an exaggeration, for on another page the same writer tells of a contract for heavy rails let to Peter Cooper of the New Jersey Iron Company in December, 1846.[25] But although the quoted sentence is not the letter of Corning's relationship to the Utica and Schenectady, it is in the spirit of that relationship. No one who has worked with the Corning Papers can doubt the close tie-up between Corning the railroad president and Corning the iron manufacturer and dealer.

At the time of the building of the Utica and Schenectady in the 1830's, Corning was one of a committee of three appointed by the directors to purchase the materials for constructing the road. The other two members of the committee were his Albany associates, Lewis Benedict and John Townsend,[26] both of whom were also iron and hardware dealers. The initial contract for rails, entered into through the New York agent of an English house, was executed by Corning as president of the Utica and Schenectady, but was guaranteed by all three members of the committee,[27] Townsend and Benedict doubtless

[22] Copy of letter in Pruyn's hand, but probably sent over Corning's signature, to Watkinson, Albany, Jan. 4, 1848, CP.

[23] *American Railroad Journal,* IX (April 23, 1853), 267.

[24] Harlow, *Road of the Century,* 75.   [25] *Ibid.,* 30.

[26] A. and G. Ralston to Corning, Lewis Benedict, and John Townsend, Philadelphia, Jan. 26, 1835, CP.

[27] Benedict to Corning, New York (?), March 28, 1835, CP.

sharing in the commissions. It is probable, however, that the necessary spikes and other iron were furnished by Corning's Albany Iron Works, through Erastus Corning & Co. of Albany, and it is doubted that the commissions on these items were subject to division.

Corning's opportunities to supply the Utica and Schenectady with iron were not terminated with the completion of the first track. Between 1847 and 1850 the road's original strap rails [28] were replaced with heavier rails of new design, called in those days "H" rails. The first contract for the new rails was let at the end of 1846 to Peter Cooper of the New Jersey Iron Company—a contract for 4,000 tons of rails at $71.75 a ton, amounting to a total of $287,000. Nothing has been found to indicate that this particular order was funneled through Corning's Albany house or that the Utica and Schenectady's president profited by it in any other way. But in 1850 the directors of the Utica and Schenectady reported that the cost of laying the heavier rail had actually come to something over a million dollars,[29] and it seems unlikely that Corning failed to profit by this large expenditure.

At the end of 1846 John F. Winslow, Corning's partner in the Albany Iron Works, was writing him concerning a large order for hook-headed spikes which the firm was confident of obtaining from the Utica and Schenectady.[30] Apparently the order was received, the road purchasing through Erastus Corning & Co., for on June 30, 1848, Gilbert C. Davidson, one of Corning's partners in the Albany store, reported, "I received from Utica & Schenectady R R Co this morning dft. for $12,-569.73 balance due on a/c."[31] On such an order Corning reaped a double profit—the first his profit as manufacturer, the second his merchant's commission. In July, 1850, the Mount Savage Iron Company of Mount Savage, Maryland, in which

[28] Strap rails were flat iron bars fastened to the top of wooden rails that were called "stringers."

[29] Stevens, *Beginnings of the New York Central*, 295–296.

[30] John F. Winslow to Corning, Troy, Dec. 14, 1846, CP.

[31] Gilbert C. Davidson to Corning, Albany, June 30, 1848, CP.

Corning also had a large financial stake, was turning out a thousand tons of rails for the Utica and Schenectady.[32] Moreover, some of the road's heavy rails doubtless came from England, Corning in his role as merchant entering into contracts with the English houses, arranging credit, and claiming a commission, as he and his colleagues, Lewis Benedict and John Townsend, had done at the beginning of the Utica and Schenectady's history and as he was to do again in the case of the New York Central and other roads in the middle 1850's.

Thus Corning used his position as president of the Utica and Schenectady to advance his interests as an iron manufacturer and merchant, but he also used every means at his command to advance the interests of the railroad. As has been intimated, he preferred to act circumspectly and to keep the Utica and Schenectady from the unfavorable attention of the legislature, but he was not without political influence when it seemed desirable to exercise it. His association with the Albany Regency assured him of favors from his own party, and his friendship with Thurlow Weed, whom he had early taken pains to cultivate, gave him a strong ally among the opposition.[33] When Corning felt that the occasion warranted it, he hired lobbyists to present the Utica and Schenectady's point of view to the legislators, and at least one member of the Assembly itself, William H. Bogart of Cayuga County, was for some years in the pay of the Utica and Schenectady and later of the New York Central.[34]

In April, 1848, George C. Pomeroy presented a bill to Corning for "services at the Legislature eight months protecting R. R. from harm and sundry evil desposed [sic] persons." An attached note, addressed to Corning, reads:

With the above I pledge you that on no consideration will I again consent to go in the lobby of the legislature. We have succeeded

[32] Winslow to Corning, Mount Savage, Md., July 26, 1850, CP.
[33] Glyndon G. Van Deusen, *Thurlow Weed, Wizard of the Lobby* (Boston, 1947), 85.
[34] William H. Bogart to Corning, Aurora, N.Y., May 6, 1853, CP.

against fearful odds but how and by what sacrifice of personal respect you will know.[35]

In hiring lobbyists during the 1840's and early 1850's Corning acted with the presidents of the other railroads which by that time formed a line between Albany and Buffalo. Nor was this the only instance of co-operation among the component parts of what early became known as the Central Line. On January 31, 1843, less than a year after the last section of the line was completed, representatives of the several roads met in convention to decide upon a uniform policy regarding schedules, fares, and the handling of immigrant travel. Through the years such meetings were held regularly, the delegates in time coming to deal with such matters as the pooling of equipment, the handling of freight, uniform tariffs, and competition with the New York and Erie.[36]

In all co-operative arrangements the president of the Utica and Schenectady had a powerful, if not a deciding, voice. Doubtless his prestige accounted for this in great part, for Corning was by far the outstanding capitalist associated with the Central Line in the years before its consolidation into the New York Central (as, indeed, he was to be for a decade and more after the consolidation). Moreover, he held stock in at least some of the roads besides his own Utica and Schenectady.[37] When the actions of a given board of directors failed to suit him, he could send out his proxy gatherers and at the next

[35] Rail Road from Sch[enectad]y to Buffalo to Geo. C. Pomeroy, Dr., dated April, 1848, CP. See also Utica & Schenectada [*sic*] Rail Road Co. to George W. Bull, Dr., for seven weeks services in Albany, attending to interests of Company . . . at last session [of the] Legislature—78 miles road @ 93¢ per mile $72.56, dated March–April, 1843, CP.

[36] Charles Seymour to Corning, Canandaigua (?), N.Y., April 24, 1843; John Wilkinson and Thomas Y. How to Corning, Syracuse, N.Y., Oct. 5, 1846; Dean Richmond to Corning, Buffalo, N.Y., Dec. 14, 1852; printed copy of minutes of meeting of delegates from the several companies composing the Central Route between New York and Buffalo, at the Globe Hotel, in Syracuse, Nov. 5, 1851: CP. See also Stevens, *Beginnings of the New York Central*, 317–335.

[37] Call for installment of $500 on Lockport and Niagara Falls Railroad stock, Sept. 14, 1836, addressed to Corning; James Horner to Corning, New York, May 28, 1845; Nathaniel Thayer to Corning, Boston, May 20, 1846: CP.

stockholders' meeting whip the recalcitrants into line or replace them.[38] Another effective, though indirect, hold which he exercised was through his banking connections. Several directors of the roads on the western end of the line were associated with banks at Buffalo, Canandaigua, and Syracuse—banks in which Corning had an interest or which were dependent in some manner upon the Albany City Bank, of which he was president.[39] Finally, at least one of the roads, the Auburn and Syracuse, was at one time indebted to Erastus Corning & Co. for iron.[40] It may be readily supposed that some, if not all, of the others upon occasion found themselves in a similar position and perhaps were under the necessity from time to time of asking for an extension of credit.

It was partly Corning's interest in the Central Line of railroads which induced him in 1846, along with Bostonian John Murray Forbes and others, to "take hold" of the Michigan Central, a 145-mile, state-owned, decaying line between Detroit and Kalamazoo. The usefulness of the Michigan road (in conjunction with a line of steamboats on Lake Erie) as a "feeder" of the New York roads was obvious, but this was only one

[38] When, however, Corning attempted this maneuver in an effort to remove John Wilkinson from the board of the Syracuse and Utica in May, 1846, he was unsuccessful, apparently because the Boston and New York stockholders in the road were reached by Wilkinson before Corning requested their proxies. The Bostonians were especially strong in the roads west of Utica; however, Matthew Vassar of Poughkeepsie, friend and admirer of Corning, spoke of himself as owning "the largest amount of stock" in the Syracuse and Utica, and it is likely that Corning always had Vassar's vote. In addition, through Schuyler Livingston, the New York agent of Benjamin Ingham, a wealthy Englishman resident in the Two Sicilies, Corning always commanded the proxy of Ingham, who, according to John V. L. Pruyn, had large investments in this country, "especially in the Central line of Rail Roads between this [Albany] and Buffalo, in which he is said to be the largest owner." See Sherman to Corning, Boston, May 17, 1844; Thayer to Corning, Boston, May 20, 1846; Matthew Vassar to Corning, Poughkeepsie, March 28, 1853: CP; Pruyn Journal, July 27, 1852, Pruyn Papers, New York State Library, Albany, N.Y. On Benjamin Ingham, see Irene D. Neu, "An English Businessman in Sicily, 1806–1861," *Business History Review*, XXXI (Winter, 1957), 355–374.

[39] Henry B. Gibson to Corning, Canandaigua, May 12, 1843; Horner to Corning, New York, May 28, 1845; Jacob Gould to Corning, Rochester, N.Y., April 1, 1853: CP.

[40] How to Corning, Auburn, N.Y., Oct. 5, 1838, CP.

reason for Corning's becoming involved in the Michigan enterprise. Another was that he held a debt against the Michigan
road for iron which he had supplied,[41] a debt that he probably
had little hope of collecting unless it was applied to the purchase of the road. Lastly, he planned to sell the rejuvenated
road the additional iron necessary to carry it to its projected
termination on Lake Michigan. When negotiations over the
purchase of the road temporarily broke down in June, 1846, a
Detroit correspondent warned Corning that unless the sale
went through "some of the iron contracts will have to be post-
poned for sometime to come." [42] This was a powerful argument
with the Albany merchant.

The Michigan Central Railroad had evolved from the Detroit & St. Joseph, a line chartered in 1832 and taken over
by the state in 1837 as part of its program to bring all public
transportation under public ownership. Unfortunately for
Michigan's experiment, the panic of that year followed almost
immediately, and although the state's other railroad projects
were halted in order that the Michigan Central might be
pushed to completion, at the end of eight years the road had
reached only as far as Kalamazoo. What was perhaps as bad,
there was so little money for maintenance that "as the head
crawled forward, the tail was falling apart." [43]

Between July and September, 1845, several letters urging
the sale of the Michigan Central to private interests appeared
in a Detroit newspaper. Published under the nom de plume
"Taxpayer," the letters were the work of James F. Joy, a
Detroit attorney. Attracted perhaps by Joy's efforts, John W.
Brooks, the young superintendent of the Auburn and Rochester (one of the roads of the Central Line in New York), went
out to Michigan to look over the Michigan Central and to appraise its possibilities. That was toward the end of 1845. Brooks
carried with him letters from John E. and Nathaniel Thayer,
two of Boston's outstanding capitalists, and from Erastus Corning, who by this time had extensive mercantile, banking and

[41] John Murray Forbes to Corning, Boston, Sept. 8, 1846, CP.
[42] Henry N. Walker to Corning, Detroit, June 10, 1846, CP.
[43] Harlow, *Road of the Century*, 213–218.

land interests in Michigan and was not unaware, as already noted, of the financial condition of the Michigan Central.[44]

At this time the "Young Lochinvar . . . out of the East"— so Brooks has been described by one of our contemporary writers [45]—had not severed his connection with the Auburn and Rochester, in which J. E. Thayer and Brother were large stockholders, and he shortly resumed his duties with that road. But in mid-January, 1846, the Thayers wrote to Henry B. Gibson, president of the Auburn and Rochester, saying that they wanted Brooks to return to Michigan and make an attempt to purchase the Michigan Central. That same day they wrote to Brooks, sending him a draft of the charter which they hoped to obtain from Michigan's lawmakers.[46]

Brooks returned to Michigan, where, with important help from James F. Joy, he saw the necessary bill through the legislature. During the two months which this task consumed, he made frequent reports not only to his Boston backers but also to Corning. Nonetheless, Corning took the precaution of sending his partner, Gilbert C. Davidson, to Detroit to keep an eye on the matter. It was well that he did, for Davidson quickly discovered that "Brooks had managed to place the first Nine Names [that is, incorporators] in the bill from Boston." Upon the insistence of Davidson and of one of Corning's Detroit friends, the name of Thomas Perkins, Jr., was dropped and that of Erastus Corning substituted.[47] Other incorporators named in the bill included John E. Thayer and John Murray Forbes. The last mentioned had made a fortune in the China trade and while still in his thirties had "retired" to devote his attention to his investments.

The act passed by the Michigan legislature on March 28,

[44] M. C. McConkey, "James F. Joy" (manuscript biography in Michigan Historical Collections, University of Michigan, Ann Arbor), III, 233–238. Cf. Harlow, *Road of the Century*, 213–218; Richard C. Overton, *Burlington West: A Colonization History of the Burlington Railroad* (Cambridge, Mass., 1941), 25–26; Henry Greenleaf Pearson, *An American Railroad Builder, John Murray Forbes* (Boston, 1911), 24–25; William J. Peterson, "The Burlington Comes," *Palimpsest*, XIV (Nov., 1933), 382.

[45] Harlow, *Road of the Century*, 218.

[46] McConkey, "James F. Joy," III, 237–238, 242.

[47] Davidson to Corning, Detroit, Feb. 16, 1846, CP.

1846, provided for the sale of the railroad to the Michigan Central Railroad Company for $2,000,000. One-quarter of that sum had to be paid within six months. The remaining $1,500,000 was due at the end of eighteen months, that is, by the end of September, 1847. Payment might be in cash; in bonds of the "five-million loan" that had been entered into by Michigan in 1838; in "Butler bonds"; [48] in the stock of the Palmyra and Jacksonburgh, another state-projected railroad; or in certain other evidences of state indebtedness (for instance, "iron bonds" which had been issued by the state in lieu of payment for rails, spikes, and equipment). [49]

Years later Forbes was to say that the Michigan Central had been purchased from the state at "seventy cents on the dollar." [50] By this he meant that the purchasers acquired various bonds, coupons, and warrants at an average discount of 30 per cent and applied their par value to the purchase price of the road. Nevertheless it was something of a scramble to get together the first payment of $500,000. As late at September 8, 1846, twenty days before the payment was due, Forbes was skeptical of success. "We may have to resort to the N York Bondholders liberality," he wrote to Corning, "or let the whole thing go." [51] The principal bondholder that Forbes had in mind was the Farmers Loan and Trust Company of New York City, which held a large amount of the "five-million loan."

In the meantime, subscriptions for stock in the Michigan Central were being accepted, and if Boston failed to show the

[48] When Michigan had threatened to default on the "five-million loan" in 1843, Charles Butler, a young New York lawyer, was hired by London and New York interests to go to Detroit and attempt to stop repudiation. He was successful in his mission. On March 8, 1843, a law was approved which empowered the governor of Michigan to issue bonds (afterward known as "Butler bonds") in payment of the interest which had accrued on the original bonds. The law also provided for the eventual payment of both the original and the Butler bonds (G. L. Prentiss, *The Union Theological Seminary in the City of New York . . . with a Sketch of the Life and Public Services of Charles Butler, LL.D.* [Asbury Park, N.J., 1899], 434–451; *Laws of Michigan, 1843*, no. 73, pp. 150–153).

[49] *Laws of Michigan, 1846*, no. 40, pp. 38–39.

[50] Reminiscences of Forbes, quoted in Edith P. Cunningham, *C.E.P. and E.F.P.: Family Letters, 1861–1869* (Boston, 1949), 27–28.

[51] Forbes to Corning, Boston, Sept. 8, 1846, CP.

enthusiasm for the enterprise which had been anticipated, "the spirit" shown by western New York made up for "the dullness" of the Athens of America.[52] Had it been possible to collect an assessment on the stock in time, Forbes, who had assumed the task of raising the half-million initial payment, would have experienced less difficulty in doing so, but the subscription books had been opened too late for a call on the stock to meet the end-of-September deadline. Forbes, therefore, was resorting to other means. Corning, it will be remembered, held a debt against the old Michigan Central for iron that he had sold the road—a debt that was secured by so-called "iron bonds." These bonds were acceptable to the state as part of the purchase price of the road, and now in something like desperation Forbes appealed to Corning:

Can you give the Company *any* credit on [the Iron Bonds] . . . to give us time to collect our assessments? If you were disposed to take in pay for them or any part of them Bonds of the R Road with interest at 7% semi annually & the principal in five years it would help.[53]

Forbes's appeal was unavailing, for Corning was not inclined to exchange his claim on the state of Michigan for the bonds of a railroad company which had so far failed to acquire a railroad. Finally, however, he consented to take the notes of the Michigan Central at 60 to 120 days "on interest," thus assuring himself of repayment as soon as the first calls on the stock had been collected. The Farmers Loan and Trust Company was more generous, offering to accept for some of its Michigan state bonds the five-year, 7 per cent Michigan Central bonds proffered by Forbes.[54] D. D. Williamson, president of the Farmers Loan and Trust, was named a director of the Michigan Central.

Doubtless in recognition of the important service they had rendered, Williamson and Corning were appointed a com-

---

[52] *Ibid.* By Sept. 8, 1846, according to Forbes, 8,992 shares had been subscribed in New York, whereas only 4,060 shares had been taken in all of New England.

[53] Forbes to Corning, Sept. 8, 1846, CP.

[54] *Ibid.;* Forbes to Corning, Sept. 15, 1846: CP.

mittee to go to Detroit, make the first payment to the state treasurer, and take formal possession of the Michigan Central. This they did on September 23, 1846.[55] Forbes was chosen the road's first president. Together with Brooks, who was appointed superintendent, the Bostonian was to be largely responsible for the success of the enterprise, but at the time of the purchase Corning received much of the credit. "I find all along the Central Rail Road," a friend wrote to him from the West, "that you are spoken off [sic] as 'The Man' who has brot about so great a *good* for the State of Michigan." [56]

This was an understandable tribute, for Corning through his Detroit mercantile and banking connections was a familiar figure in Michigan, whereas Forbes and Brooks were comparatively unknown there. Besides Corning, Forbes, the Thayers, and the Farmers Loan and Trust Company, the chief backers of the Michigan Central were William Dwight of Boston and George Griswold and John C. Green of New York City.[57] The last two, like Forbes, had made fortunes in the China trade. Although it has always been assumed that the Michigan Central was principally a Boston concern, it was stated in 1848 by one of the directors that "New York and Michigan own a majority of the Road, and can take the power in their own hands if they please." [58]

Immediately after the purchase of the Michigan Central, Corning was in consultation with Forbes about "the buying of Iron," and even before the date on which the railroad passed into the hands of the new incorporators, the Albany Iron Works was bidding for an order of spikes.[59] In the course of the next few years Michigan Central purchases through Erastus Corning & Co. were to prove considerable in amount, and

[55] Forbes to Corning, Sept. 15, 1846, CP; Pearson, *An American Railroad Builder,* 30.
[56] Pomeroy to Corning, "off Cunninghams Island," Oct. 13, 1846, CP.
[57] Reminiscences of Forbes in Cunningham, *C.E.P. and E.F.P.,* 27–28.
[58] D. D. Williamson to John W. Brooks, Feb. 4, 1848, quoted in McConkey, "James F. Joy," III, 276. Cf. Overton, *Burlington West,* 26–27.
[59] Forbes to Corning, Boston, Oct. 1, 1846; Winslow to Corning, Albany, Sept. 14, 1846: CP.

Forbes, at least, suspected that commissions were sometimes too high. In December, 1854, he made a secret request of Tracy Howe, the Michigan Central's "local treasurer" at Detroit, for a copy "of items of Mess Corning & Co bill"—a request with which Howe immediately complied and news of which was sent posthaste to Gilbert C. Davidson by one of his Michigan friends.[60] Davidson certainly told Corning, but this, like Corning's openly expressed criticism of the Boston management of the Michigan Central, occasioned no unpleasant incident to mar the amicable relationship between him and Forbes.

On April 23, 1849, the Michigan Central reached Lake Michigan at New Buffalo, 218 miles from Detroit, whence a ferry carried passengers and freight across to Chicago, a city then in the throes of a phenomenal growth. That same spring a boat owned by the Michigan Central, the *Mayflower*, began to ply the lakes between Buffalo and Detroit. Thus through service was established. In December, 1851, the Michigan Central paid a 14 per cent dividend on its stock.[61] At that time Corning owned perhaps 710 shares, having a par value of $71,000.[62]

Throughout his life Corning was to maintain an active interest in the Michigan Central. For the first eight years after the purchase of the road he made annual trips to the West to inspect the line. He seems always to have taken liberally of the company's bonds and as late as 1869 was keeping a jealous eye on the road's iron orders. He served on the board of directors until his death in 1872.[63]

The fact that the Michigan Central was a bridge line between East and West made it imperative that it have good connec-

[60] George Davis to Davidson, Detroit (?), Dec. 30, 1854, CP.

[61] Harlow, *Road of the Century*, 220–221; circular of DeLauney, Iselin and Clarke, dated May 7, 1852, CP.

[62] In Dec., 1848, he held 510 shares, and in Oct., 1851 (perhaps in anticipation of the dividend), he purchased 200 shares (Stock list of the Michigan Central Railroad Company, dated Dec. 19, 1848; George B. Upton to Corning, Oct. 13, 1851: CP). In 1860, and perhaps at other times, Corning was speculating in Michigan Central stock (Sherman to Corning, New York, June 26, 1860, CP).

[63] Corning to Williamson, Albany, May 29, 1854; Corning to Isaac Livermore, Albany, Dec. 10, 1869: CP.

tions. This led its promoters to become involved in the affairs of the Great Western of Canada, a railroad which was to span the Ontario Peninsula from Niagara Falls to Windsor, opposite Detroit. The first segment of the line had been chartered in the 1830's, but so difficult was it to obtain capital in Canada at that time that construction was not begun until 1851. As early as 1847, however, John Murray Forbes, in writing to Corning, remarked of the Canadian road, "The more I think of that enterprise the more important it seems to me that it should go." [64]

In the spring of 1851, Forbes, Brooks, Corning, and others who were interested in the Michigan Central tried to obtain an amendment to the company's charter that would permit it to subscribe to stock in the Great Western. There is reason to believe that the Michigan legislature would have obliged the Central in the matter if the road's officers had come to terms with certain solons who were friendly to the Michigan Southern, the Central's rival. The Southern was at that time also suing for a change in its charter, for it wished to extend its line around the end of Lake Michigan into Chicago. "I doubt the expediency of letting the Southern Road out of the State for the sake of getting the Canada Bill," Forbes wrote; ". . . it would be paying high for the priveledge [sic] of subscribing to the Canada Road." [65] Corning shared Forbes's opinion and was

[64] Letter written from Brattleboro, Vt., Oct. 25, 1847, CP. For the early history of the Great Western see A. W. Currie, *The Grand Trunk Railway of Canada* (Toronto, 1957), chs. viii–ix; Tracy Ferris, "Railways of British North America," *Ontario Historical Society Papers and Records*, XXXVIII (Toronto, 1946), 31–42; W. M. Spriggs, "Great Western Railway of Canada," *Railway and Locomotive Historical Society Bulletin*, no. 51 (Feb., 1940).

[65] Forbes to Corning, Boston, March 25, 1851, CP. The Michigan Southern was a formidable rival, largely because of its superior eastern connections through Cleveland, Pittsburgh, and Philadelphia. In winter, when traffic on the lakes was halted, eastbound passengers over the Michigan Central route had to endure 256 miles of staging (through Canada to connect with the New York roads), 140 of which were "intolerably muddy in bad weather." Michigan Southern passengers, on the other hand, were subjected to only 88 miles of staging and that over roads which were "all Mcadamised" (Henry W. Walker to Corning, Detroit, Jan. 12, 1852, CP).

already at work on another means of pumping American capital into the Great Western. Balked he might be in Michigan, but the eastern end of the Canadian road was to connect with the Central Line in New York, and there his influence was practically unlimited.

An appeal to the New York legislature, backed by Corning,[66] resulted in a law that granted any railroad in the state permission to subscribe to stock in the Great Western up to the amount of 5 per cent of the capital of the subscribing road, provided the consent of two-thirds of the stockholders was obtained. This was all that Corning needed. He now began an active campaign to induce the shareholders in the roads between Albany and Buffalo to subscribe to Great Western stock. There was some resistance, especially among the investors in Corning's own Utica and Schenectady, whose dissatisfaction, it was reported, was fanned by "outside interests" opposed to the project.[67] The president of the Utica and Schenectady, however, was undaunted. "It was well they pitched upon his road," John W. Brooks observed, "for any other man might not have used so much exertion to get . . . [the plan] through." [68] In the end the Utica and Schenectady took $200,000 worth of Great Western stock, while other roads between Albany and Buffalo subscribed to a total of almost $300,000 worth. Thus, the subscriptions of the New York roads came to just under half a million dollars.[69] This represented about one-fifth of the original capital stock of the Canadian road.

A number of Michigan Central stockholders, forbidden to subscribe to Great Western stock as a group, subscribed as individuals. Their subscriptions, together with other subscriptions obtained in Detroit, came to $300,000. The American ob-

---

[66] Timothy C. Dwight to Corning, Albany, Dec. 18, 1851, CP.

[67] *New York Tribune*, Nov. 28, Dec. 27, 1851; Schuyler Livingston to Corning, New York, Jan. 29, 1852, CP; Brooks to James F. Joy, Detroit, Dec. 5, 1851, Joy Papers, Burton Historical Collection, Detroit Public Library, Detroit, Mich.

[68] Brooks to Joy, Detroit, Dec. 5, 1851, Joy Papers.

[69] New York Central Consolidation Agreement, 1853, in Stevens, *Beginnings of the New York Central*, 394.

ligation to the Canadian road, then, amounted to at least
$800,000. Another and larger block of stock was taken in Eng-
land.[70]

In June, 1851, Corning was elected a member of the Great
Western's board of directors, a position to which he was annually re-elected for the next three years. When, in 1852, fric-
tion developed between the New York stockholders and the
Canadian management over the proposed gauge of the road and
other matters, it was Corning who brought about at least temporary agreement. But the Canadians were not disposed long
to heed the wishes or advice of their neighbors across the border. Successfully appealing for support to the English stockholders, they managed to defeat the American investors at almost every turn. Finally, in the fall of 1854, Corning tendered
his resignation from the Great Western's board. Forbes and
Brooks, who at this time were also serving on the board, likewise resigned.[71]

Three months before Corning left the board of the Great
Western he had written to Henry B. Gibson: "I wish we [that
is, the New York Central] were clear of our stock in the Great
Western rail road.—It is now in London & I trust will be sold
before long." [72] One of Corning's complaints against the Canadian management was that the road was operated with no attention to economy. Another was that the directors tended to
overextend, proposing to build and buy branch lines and purchase docks at Niagara—ill-advised moves in the opinion of the
New Yorker. Despite his resignation from the board, Corning's
break with the Great Western was not complete. In July, 1855,

[70] Forbes to Corning, Boston, Nov. 26, 1851; Corning to Forbes, Albany, May
24, 1854: CP; Williamson to Corning, New York, Dec. 29, 1851, letterbook of
the Farmers Loan and Trust Company, Nov. 3, 1849—March 2, 1854, microfilm
copy, Collection of Regional History, Cornell University, Ithaca, N.Y. Currie
says that the American investment in the Great Western totaled $1,000,000
(*Grand Trunk Railway*, 162).

[71] J. S. Gilkinson to Corning, Hamilton, Canada West, June 3, 1851; Henry B.
Gibson to Corning, Canandaigua, March 24, June 14, 1852; Forbes to Corning,
Boston, Nov. 22, 1852; Corning to Forbes, Albany, June 15, Dec. 28, 1854; Corn-
ing to C. J. Brydges, Albany, Sept. 28, 1854: CP.

[72] Letter dated at Albany, June 7, 1854, CP.

he still held forty shares of the company's stock in his own name; in the winter of 1855–1856 the Canadian road was a customer of the Albany Iron Works; and, of course, the Great Western continued to exchange traffic with the New York roads and with the Michigan Central.[73]

As the Michigan Central's need of an eastern outlet had caused its directors to take an interest in the Great Western of Canada, so its search for a western connection was to involve its promoters in the affairs of the short Illinois roads which were soon to be forged into the Chicago, Burlington and Quincy. These roads were four in number—the Aurora Branch, the Central Military Tract, the Peoria and Oquawka, and the Northern Cross.[74]

One of the first indications of the presence of eastern capital in the Illinois roads is found in the election on February 22, 1852, of John W. Brooks and Gilbert C. Davidson (Corning's Albany partner) to the board of directors of the Aurora Branch, a 12-mile line between Aurora and Turner Junction.[75] By June of that year the Aurora Branch had acquired pretensions and had changed its name to the Chicago and Aurora. At the first meeting of the directors of the renamed road Brooks and Davidson were appointed a committee "to negotiate for and purchase the necessary Iron [for a proposed extension to Mendota] . . . of such form and pattern as they may determine, and also to purchase such other Iron as may be required for this road." It was further ordered that Erastus Corning of Albany was to be associated with them in discharging this duty.[76]

At that time Brooks seems to have been in a position to con-

---

[73] Corning to Forbes, Albany, May 17, May 24, 1854; Winslow to Corning, Albany, Jan. 16, 1856; circular of the Great Western Railroad, signed by the treasurer, dated July 10, 1855: CP.

[74] The story of the building of the Michigan Central around the end of Lake Michigan and into Chicago is told in Overton, *Burlington West*, 27–31. For the early history of the Illinois roads see *ibid.*, 20–23, 31–43.

[75] A. W. Newton, "The Chicago and Aurora Railroad," *Railway and Locomotive Historical Society Bulletin*, no. 76 (March, 1949), 7. From Turner Junction the trains of the Aurora Branch ran into Chicago over the tracks of the Chicago and Galena Union.

[76] Stephen F. Gale to Corning, Chicago, Feb. 14, 1853, CP.

trol the stock distribution of the Chicago and Aurora, while
by mid-summer, 1852, James F. Joy, the Detroit attorney who
had been instrumental in focusing the attention of eastern
capitalists on the Michigan Central and who had continued to
be associated with that enterprise, could boast that he had made
very good terms for the control of the Central Military Tract
Railroad, which was to stretch from Mendota to Galesburg.
Two of Joy's financial backers were Forbes and Corning. The
Albany capitalist subscribed to 166 shares of stock and took
$50,000 of the road's bonds. A third eastern investor in the
Central Military Tract was Erastus Fairbanks, the scale manufacturer of Saint Johnsbury, Vermont. All three capitalists
were likewise interested in the Chicago and Aurora. Within
the year this group was also in control of the Northern Cross,
the road from Galesburg to Quincy.[77]

Meanwhile, both Corning and Forbes were making a good
thing of the iron contracts. For the most part, rails for the Chicago and Aurora and the Central Military Tract were ordered
in England through the house of Erastus Corning & Co. or by
Forbes through the Boston agent of Thompson & Forman of
London. A smaller quantity of rails for the roads came from the
Mount Savage Iron Company in Maryland, in which both Corning and Forbes had a large interest.[78]

From the sources available, it has been impossible to estimate how much Erastus Corning & Co., the Mount Savage Iron
Company, or Forbes made on the contracts. It can be stated,
however, that the amounts involved were large. In August,
1853, the manager at Mount Savage was writing to Corning
concerning a bill for $120,000 held by the iron firm against

[77] Erastus Fairbanks to Corning, St. Johnsbury, Vt., Aug. 14, 1852; Forbes to
Corning, Boston, Aug. 18, 1852, Oct. 19, 1853; same to same, Nashua, Mass.,
July 26, 1853; J. E. Thayer and Brother to Corning, Boston, June 10, 1854: CP;
Corning to Joy, Albany, Aug. 23, 1852, Joy Papers. The Central Military Tract
Railroad subsequently purchased the Peoria and Oquawka (Overton, *Burlington
West*, 39–40).

[78] Davidson to Corning, Albany, Dec. 2, 1852; Gale to E. Corning & Co., Chicago, Feb. 14, 1853: CP; copy of contract between Central Military Tract Railroad Company by their agent John M. Forbes and Thompson & Forman of London by their agent William F. Weld & Co., Jan. 3, 1854: Joy Papers.

the Chicago and Aurora for the "first 2000 tons" of rails contracted for. In October of the following year Erastus Corning
& Co. was dunning James F. Joy, then president of the Central Military Tract, for $43,888.66 due the company, while the
amount involved in the transaction between Forbes and the
London house of Thompson & Forman was $139,500. This may
have been part of the £83,000 (a sum in excess of $400,000) owed
by Forbes in September, 1854, to Baring Brothers of London for
purchases of rails which that firm had underwritten. In November, 1854, Forbes ordered another 2,200 tons of English rails for
the Central Military Tract and the Chicago and Auroa, the contract being negotiated by Baring Brothers.[79] Corning and Forbes
also undertook purchases of rails for the Northern Cross, Corning contracting for half the order and the other half being
taken by the two men on joint account. The Northern Cross
bill came to a total well in excess of $140,000.[80]

In 1857, by which time the Chicago and Aurora had been
consolidated with the Central Military Tract, a group of five
easterners, including Corning and Forbes, were elected to the
board of directors of the new road, which was optimistically
calling itself the Chicago, Burlington and Quincy. Corning held
his position on the board for the rest of his life, a period of
fifteen years. He served for almost as long on the board of the
Burlington and Missouri River Railroad in Iowa. His investments in that road as well as in the Hannibal and St. Joseph,
the Burlington's Missouri connection, were large, but they be-
long to a period later than that which is covered in this chapter.

In the early period of his career, however, Corning held
stock in a number of railroads in addition to those which have
been discussed. Many were in the state of New York, but some
were outside the state. In 1835, for instance, he is mentioned
as a director of the Saratoga and Whitehall, the Saratoga and
Washington, and the Castleton and West-Stockbridge. At the

---

[79] Winslow to Corning, Albany, Aug. 6, 1853, CP; copy of contract between
Forbes and William F. Weld & Co., Jan. 3, 1854; E. Corning & Co. to Joy, Albany,
Oct. 30, 1854: Joy Papers; Ralph M. Hidy, *The House of Baring in American
Trade and Finance . . . 1763–1861* (Cambridge, Mass., 1949), 603.

[80] Forbes to Corning, Boston, Aug. 30, 1853 (?), Feb. 21, 1855, CP.

same time he held stock in at least two other roads—the Long Island and the Hartford and New Haven.[81]

In 1844 and 1845 Corning flirted briefly with the New York and Albany, but it does not appear that he was a stockholder in the road at that time, although he may later have taken some shares in the New York and Harlem, with which the New York and Albany was consolidated in 1846. From 1849 to 1854 he served on the board of the Hudson River Railroad, resigning in the latter year because of a clash between what he regarded as New York Central and Hudson River Railroad interests.[82]

When the Albany, Bennington and Rutland Rail Road Company was organized in 1850, Corning was named a director. The following year he is found among the directors of the Albany and Northern. When this road failed in the late 1850's, he and John V. L. Pruyn lost a considerable amount of money which they had invested in the road's bonds. As one of the trustees of the mortgage which had secured the bonds, Corning was sharply criticized by other investors who lost heavily.[83] There was some talk, evidently, of reviving the enterprise in 1859, and it was in connection with this that Corning showed a somewhat uncharacteristic flash of humor.

I have not any objection [he assured one of his correspondents] to be interested in the Albany & Northern road with other Gentlemen whose interests are similar to my own altho the New York papers say "that the public interests would be promoted if certain men should be hung"—if at any future day this threat should be carried out I should like to have good company.[84]

Corning was also interested in two other New York roads— the Watertown and Rome and the Lewiston, but his invest-

---

[81] *Albany Argus*, April 28, June 5, July 3, 1835; commissioners of the Long Island Rail-Road Company to Corning, New York, May 23, 1835; G. Allen to Corning, New York, Aug. 3, 1835: CP.

[82] J. Boorman to Corning, New York, June 11, 1849, CP; Edward Hungerford, *Men and Iron* (New York, 1938), 162.

[83] Joel Munsell, *The Annals of Albany*, 2d ed., II (Albany, 1870), 337; III (Albany, 1871), 257; Pruyn Journal, I, Jan. 22, 1858, Pruyn Papers; Corning to William M. Clarke, Albany, April 14, 1859, CP.

[84] Corning to A. Mann, Albany, Aug. 23, 1859, CP.

ment in the former, at least, was very small. Out-of-state roads (besides those already mentioned) in which he held stock in the 1850's were the Philadelphia and Reading (28 shares), the Mississippi and Atlantic (200 shares), the Toledo and Illinois (150 shares), and the Lake Erie, Wabash and St. Louis (450 shares).[85] This is only a partial list.

In addition to stock, Corning held the bonds of a number of the roads which have been mentioned and of others besides. Many of the railroad securities in his "portfolio" came into his possession through Erastus Corning & Co.'s having furnished the roads with iron, for it was the practice of iron manufacturers and merchants to accept part of their payment in the bonds of the roads which they supplied, always, of course, at a large discount.[86]

Erastus Corning's railroad interests were thus diverse. In terms of money invested, he was by 1853 probably as deeply interested in the Michigan Central and in the Illinois roads as he was in the Utica and Schenectady. The increasing competition offered the Central Line by the New York and Erie, the Pennsylvania Central, and the Baltimore and Ohio, however, was to result that year in the formal consolidation of the New York roads. When Corning was elected president of the consolidated company, the New York Central, he entered upon the phase of his railroad career for which he has been chiefly remembered. That will be the theme of a later chapter.

[85] John Parker to Corning, New York, Jan. 23, 1852; Winslow, Lanier and Company to Corning, New York, Nov. 13, 1852; Daniel Lee to Corning, Watertown, N.Y., Feb. 24, 1853; J. B. Plumb to Corning, n.p., Oct. 12, 1853; Edward Whitehouse to Corning, n.p., June 20, 1854: CP.

[86] Corning to A. B. Smith, Albany, Feb. 6, 1855, CP; Chandler, *Henry Varnum Poor*, 74.

· VI ·

Erastus Corning, Banker

IN the latter part of the 1830's and for the rest of his active career, Erastus Corning's progress from his home on State Street to the store on South Broadway was often interrupted by a stop at the Albany City Bank. There, in the back room, he settled himself briefly at the president's desk.

The charter of the Albany City Bank dated from April, 1834. At that time New York's general banking law was still four years in the future, but individual charters, including that of the Albany City, followed an established pattern, incorporating each bank with the usual power of a commercial bank to lend, discount, and invest and to accept deposits and issue notes. The Albany City Bank was authorized to have a capital of $500,000, and Erastus Corning was one of thirteen commissioners appointed "to receive subscriptions for and distribute the said capital stock." [1]

The subscription books were opened on June 9; by the time they were closed in midafternoon on June 11 the stock of the bank had been oversubscribed by $642,900. "Another illustration," sarcastically observed the pro-Corning, pro-Jackson *Albany Argus,* "of the reality of 'distress' statistics and predictions." [2] As a matter of fact, oversubscription of bank stock,

[1] *Laws of the State of New York, Fifty-seventh Session* (Albany, 1834), 385–391; Bray Hammond, *Banks and Politics in America from the Revolution to the Civil War* (Princeton, N.J., 1957), 593. See this work, pp. 149–164, 556–563, 593–598, and scattered pages, for the most recent interpretive history of banking in New York State.

[2] *Albany Argus,* May 30, June 13, 1834.

as of railroad stock, was common, perhaps because a subscriber expected to receive only a percentage of the number of shares that he indicated he would like to have. In 1833, a year before the shares of the Albany City Bank were offered for subscription, the stock of the Chemung Canal Bank in Elmira, New York, had been oversubscribed by $1,234,000.[3]

On July 24, 1834, Corning was elected a director of the Albany City Bank. The following day he was chosen president—an honor that could hardly have come as a surprise to him, for he had been the promoter of the bank and from the beginning it had been his intention to head it. On October 1 the Albany City opened its doors in a building on the south side of State Street, halfway between the Corning home and the place of business of Erastus Corning & Co. on South Broadway.[4]

The date of the Albany City's founding was significant. In 1834 the country was in the midst of the war against the Second Bank of the United States, a war that, according to a modern authority, had had its real beginning with the Albany Regency, the Democratic political machine of New York.[5] Such was the prosperity of New York by the late 1820's and such was its ability to take care of its own needs that any move on the part of the federal government to encroach upon states' rights was resisted, not only by the new generation of businessmen who dominated the Regency, but by all who feared the draining away of New York's capital to less favored areas. More specifically, the businessmen of New York resented the control exercised over their financial affairs by a federal bank with headquarters in Philadelphia.[6]

For years New York businessmen had paid large sums into the customs office of the port of New York with the knowledge that the revenues of the port were deposited in the Wall Street branch of the Bank of the United States, to pass into the control of directors who were, for the most part, Philadelphians.

[3] Ausburn Towner, *Our County and Its People: A History of the Valley and County of Chemung* (Syracuse, N.Y., 1892), 147.
[4] *Albany Argus*, July 29, Aug. 8, Oct. 3, 1834.
[5] Hammond, *Banks and Politics*, 351–355.　　　　　[6] *Ibid.*, 353.

"New York's jealousy in this matter was no empty question of first place in an honorific sense but a lively question of whose pockets the profits were going into." For years, too, New York bankers had been compelled to submit to the regulatory action of the federal bank in lending what they considered to be their own money, and New York's businessmen had resented the concomitant restrictions upon their freedom to borrow. The purpose of the Regency's attack on the Bank of the United States was, then, the destruction of an institution which was not only the outstanding current example of federal encroachment on states' rights, but was also "a material block in the way of New York's interests." [7]

As a Democrat, a businessman, and a supporter of Martin Van Buren, who, as governor of the state had been largely responsible for the passage of New York's Safety Fund Law, Erastus Corning had taken an active part in the Regency's program. The Safety Fund Law, enacted in 1829, required all banks in New York to contribute to a fund administered by the state for the payment of the obligations of those banks that might become insolvent.[8] It was the climax of a series of laws, beginning with the first restraining act of 1804, designed to establish a sound banking system in a state with great commercial interests. But the system so established accomplished more than that: its success cast doubt on the wisdom of maintaining a federal bank.[9]

Shortly after the passage of the Safety Fund Law, Van Buren moved from the state capital to Washington, where he took up his post in the President's cabinet and added his voice to those that were directing Jackson's ingrained suspicion of all banks toward a specific antagonism to the Bank of the United States. The result of their efforts was the veto in 1832 of a bill that

[7] *Ibid.*

[8] *Laws of the State of New York, Fifty-second Session* (Albany, 1829), 167–173. This was the first law passed by an American legislature that "recognized an obligation on the part of the public authorities to protect the creditors of banks" (Fritz Redlich, *History of American Business Leaders: A Series of Studies* [Ann Arbor, Mich., 1940–1951], II, pt. 1, 88).

[9] Hammond, *Banks and Politics,* 352.

would have renewed the charter of the federal bank, a veto that was gratifying not only to state bankers and seekers of easy credit, but to all who advocated abstention by the federal government from fields of enterprise regarded as rightfully belonging to the states.

By 1834 the federal funds were being transferred from the Bank of the United States to state banks—"pet" banks, they came to be called—and the wave of state-bank incorporations which attended the attack on the Bank of the United States was perhaps at its peak. It was from this background that the Albany City Bank emerged, its promoter, Erastus Corning, enjoying the favor of the Regency-dominated New York legislature.

At this period of his career Corning had much to gain through control of a bank. Because of the expansion of his activities in several areas he was in need of working capital, and the laws of the times did nothing to discourage a bank's extending loans to its officers.[10] He had been a director of the New-York State Bank of Albany since at least as early as 1826 and as such enjoyed a favorable position as borrower; but borrowing from his own bank perhaps amplified the amounts upon which he could draw and surely was more convenient. Further, as president of a bank he was not only privy to what was happening in the business circles of the city (since all applications to his bank for loans were reviewed by him), but he was also in a position to extend or withhold practically any accommodation that was requested. To a man who intended to be a power in Albany and in the state, this was important.

No record of Corning's financial stake in the early Albany City Bank has been found, but a list of shareholders and their investments in the rechartered Albany City Bank of 1864 (the old charter expired on December 31, 1863) is extant.[11] Since the number and value of the shares in the second bank corresponded precisely to those in the first (5,000 shares of $100 each),

[10] *Ibid.*, 468.
[11] Copy of certificate of organization, dated Dec. 28, 1863, Banking Department, State of New York, State Office Building, Albany, N.Y.

it is probable that some valid inferences concerning the ownership of the stock in the earlier bank may be drawn from what
is known of the shareholdings in the rechartered bank.

The list referred to shows Erastus Corning as possessing 573
shares. Erastus Corning, Jr., his son, held 121 shares, and John
V. L. Pruyn, the elder Corning's lawyer and his associate in the
New York Central Railroad, was listed as holding 472 shares.
The cashier of the bank held 272 shares in his own name and
1,233 shares as "attorney." There is a possibility that some, if
not all, the shares held by the cashier in this way really belonged
to the bank's president, who may have preferred to keep the
actual size of his holdings secret. In any event, in addition to
his own shares, Corning controlled those of his son and of
Pruyn and all that were held in the name of the cashier, who, it
should be remembered, held his position only during Corning's pleasure. Thus Corning had the voting power of at least
2,671 shares out of 5,000—a clear majority.

Although ownership of the stock of the original Albany City
Bank doubtless changed over the thirty years between 1834
and 1863, it is nonetheless safe to infer that Corning always
held a sizable block of stock in the first bank and that he controlled a number of votes in addition to his own.[12]

From the beginning the Albany City Bank was on a sound
basis. According to the *Albany Argus*, its entire capital of half
a million dollars was paid in before its doors were opened.[13]
The mercantile community of which it was a part afforded
ample business demand for loans and discounts, provided a
market for investment securities, and preferred deposit credit
to circulating notes for the bulk of its payments.[14] The fact

[12] Some of the bank stock had been judiciously distributed to persons who
promised Corning their proxies. A letter to Corning from J. McConihe, who for
many years served the Albany capitalist as a kind of political pay-off man, reads
as follows: "The bearer . . . is desirous of getting a few shares of stock in your
bank which he wishes to hold— He is a true friend of the admstn—& a worthy
man & you can have his proxy & it would be gratifying to have him get some."
The letter is dated at Troy, June 11, 1834, CP.

[13] *Albany Argus*, May 30, Aug. 19, Oct. 3, 1834.

[14] With a legal top limit of $750,000, the Albany City Bank's circulation at the
end of 1834 did not exceed $78,000 (*Albany Argus*, Feb. 10, 1835); in January,

that the bank weathered the major panics of 1837 and 1857 attests to the quality and conservatism of its leadership.

One of the factors in the success of the Albany City Bank in its early history was the character of its cashier, Watts Sherman, a "live wire" and an indefatigable worker. Born in Utica, New York, in 1809, Sherman received his earliest training in the Ontario County Bank of Canandaigua, New York, of which his cousin, Henry B. Gibson, was cashier. By 1830, at twenty-one years of age, Sherman was himself cashier of the Herkimer County Bank at Little Falls, New York.[15] It was in this capacity that he first came to the attention of Erastus Corning.

In selecting Sherman as cashier of his bank Corning once again demonstrated his ability to choose able lieutenants and bind them to him and his interests. As Gilbert C. Davidson was a loyal partner in the hardware house and John F. Winslow a co-operative manager of the Troy ironworks, as John V. L. Pruyn identified his interests with those of Corning in the Utica and Schenectady Railroad (and later in the New York Central), so Watts Sherman, cashier of the Albany City Bank from 1834 to 1851, served the bank's president with unquestioning loyalty.

In July, 1833, as cashier of the Herkimer County Bank, Sherman had visited Albany for the purpose of selecting a city correspondent.

Mr. Watts Sherman Cashier of the Herkimer County Bank at Little Falls has been at the Bank this morning [Richard Yates, cashier of the New-York State Bank, wrote to Corning, who was a director of that bank], & from his conversation I should think he was anxious to open their account with us. . . .

I should like to have you see him and get his good will.[16]

This was more than a year before the Albany City Bank came into being, but Corning seems to have kept an eye on Sherman, who, indeed, gave the Albany capitalist little chance to forget

---

1841, when it was remarked that "the circulation of the Bank is getting up some," the figure quoted was only $125,000 (John V. L. Pruyn to Erastus Corning, Albany, Jan. 29, 1841, CP).

[15] Redlich, *History of American Business Leaders*, II, pt. II, 352.

[16] Richard Yates to Corning, Albany, July 5, 1833, CP.

him. Thereafter, the Little Falls cashier sent Corning weekly statements of the affairs of the Herkimer County Bank [17] and during the stringency of 1834 solicited his help with a stubborn board which refused to accept the cashier's estimate of the state of the money market.[18] Perhaps Corning, who always had a high regard for Sherman's ability, would have chosen him for cashier of the Albany City Bank without urging, but Sherman, who was ambitious, took no risks.

I can *safely* promise [he wrote to Corning on July 24, 1834] . . . that I can obtain the account of the Bank of Monroe for the Alby. City Bank—moreover I will *pledge* myself in case of my appointment to the Cashiership of the latter Institution, to bring with me the accounts of *this* Bank & the *Ontario Bank*. I think also that Mr. Johnson will give me the a/c of the *Ontario Branch* beyond a doubt. Besides these I am very confident that I can obtain the a/cs of two or three other of the Western Institutions.[19]

The following day, July 25, 1834, Sherman was appointed to the position he sought. After the spring of 1835 he was not only Corning's business associate, but by reason of his marriage to Sarah Turner, Harriet Corning's niece, he had also become a member of the Corning family.[20]

Although it is clear that Corning placed great trust in Sherman's judgment, there is no doubt that the president of the Albany City Bank had the final word in the affairs of the in-

[17] See, for instance, Watts Sherman to Corning, Little Falls, Oct. 15, Oct. 29, 1833, CP.

[18] "I will be obliged to you if you will write to some member of our Board of your acquaintance and arouse him to a sense of the times as they really exist. I am at present avoiding any discount that it is possible for me to get rid of, but I cannot make our Board realize the true state of the Money Market—or the actual madness that it is for ourselves or any other Country Bank to go on extending themselves in view of the prospect we have before us. We must stop discounting let the disappointment fall where it may" (Sherman to Corning, Little Falls, Feb. 19, 1834, CP).

[19] Sherman to Corning, Little Falls, July 24, 1834, CP.

[20] *Albany Argus,* March 3, 1835. Sarah Turner Sherman died in 1838, and Watts Sherman later married his cousin, Sarah Gibson, daughter of Henry B. Gibson, cashier of the Ontario County Bank and president of the Auburn and Rochester Railroad. Sherman's close association with the Corning family continued after his second marriage, his wife being taken into the circle.

stitution, just as his dictum was decisive in matters concerning the hardware house and the ironworks. When, in the early summer of 1838, a faction in the bank's board of directors challenged his control, he was equal to the situation.

Anthony Blanchard, one of the board members, was an attorney. Quite naturally he had expected to take care of some, if not all, of the bank's legal matters. But Corning had put such affairs into the hands of his own lawyer and friend, John V. L. Pruyn, and Pruyn's law partner, Henry L. Martin. Neither Pruyn nor Martin was at the time a member of the board, but Corning and Sherman were maneuvering for Pruyn's election. In June, 1838, Corning went to Detroit on business, and during his absence Blanchard forced matters to a head. Although commanding sufficient strength to keep Pruyn off the board, Blanchard failed in the attempt to remove him from his position as the bank's attorney. Doubtless Corning's hasty return to Albany had much to do with the maintaining of the *status quo*. In any case, by 1840 Pruyn was referring to "our bank" with a proprietary air, and by 1850 he was the bank's vice-president.[21]

The manner in which Corning imposed his will on the board of directors might be resented, but no one could deny that the position and prestige of the president were distinct assets to the bank. To cite only one instance, Corning's long-standing friendship with Silas Wright, United States Senator from New York, was to result, during the Van Buren administration, in the Albany City Bank's being named a bank of deposit for public funds.

The attempt to gain government patronage for the Albany City Bank began very early in the bank's history. A letter of December, 1835, from Watts Sherman to Silas Wright outlined why, in the opinion of the cashier, the Albany City deserved the favors of the government. Sherman's first argument was frankly political. The officers of his bank were all Democrats, he pointed out, as were most of the stockholders. Further, the Albany City had a larger capital than any other Albany bank

[21] Sherman to Corning, Albany, June 14, June 22, 1838; Pruyn to Corning, Albany, July 17, 1840: CP; Amasa J. Parker, *Landmarks of Albany County, New York* (Syracuse, N.Y., 1897), pt. 1, 369.

"yet was compelled & pained to witness the favors of the government falling almost exclusively into the hands of the Mechanics & Farmers Bank," which, like all the other banks in Albany, with the exception of the Albany City, was of a "political character" that was "hostile to the administration." [22]

Sherman's second argument concerned a specific hardship under which the Albany City Bank operated because it did not handle the government's business. The two banks in Detroit, Michigan, that were government depositories made their eastern remittances to the Albany City Bank. The funds which the Detroit banks accumulated with Sherman's bank consisted chiefly of the collections of the public land offices in Michigan and were in the form of bank notes from country banks in New York and the New England states. In order to convert these bills into funds current in Albany and New York City, the Albany City Bank was obliged to send them to the banks which had issued them "which costs us from ⅜ to ½ pr cent." Seldom, Sherman asserted, were the deposits of the Detroit banks with the Albany City long enough to compensate that bank for the risk, expense, and trouble of converting the funds which were sent to it. He gave a specific instance:

We were drawn upon on Saturday for $100,000 payl on the 15th Inst.—which was for a government draft on the Bank of Michigan in favour of the Mechs & Fars Bank of this City (& we anticipate similar ones hereafter). Now you will perceive the hardship of our being compelled to pay over to our Neighbors this $100,000 in funds current in the City of N. York receiving as we have for it various kinds of Country funds.[23]

Although Sherman stated his case well, his appeal failed, at least for the time being. Corning, however, did not propose to let the matter rest, but kept after Wright, with the result that sometime between March, 1837, and the end of 1839, the Albany City Bank was named a bank of federal deposit.[24]

The difficulty experienced by Sherman in redeeming country

[22] Sherman to Silas Wright, Albany, Dec. 6, 1835, CP.   [23] *Ibid.*
[24] William Seymour to Corning, Washington, March 1, 1837, CP; Wright to Corning, Washington, Feb. 7, 1840, Silas Wright Papers, Manuscript Division, State Library, Albany, N.Y.

bank notes was the common lot of the officers of all city banks. A New York law of 1840 sought to mitigate the inconvenience. The law provided that all the banks of the state must henceforth redeem their notes in New York City or Albany, as well as in the place of issue. Each bank was to name a redemption agent in one of the designated cities and was, presumably, to provide funds current in those cities for the redemption of its bills.[25] In this new order the Albany City Bank played a leading role.

By July, 1840, four of the commercial banks then carrying on business in Albany—the New-York State Bank, the Mechanics and Farmers Bank, the Canal Bank, and the Albany City Bank—had entered into an agreement for transacting the business in connection with the new law. The Albany City Bank, seemingly the leader of the alliance, was appointed "corresponding agent." The system worked in this way: At the close of business on alternate Saturdays, each Albany bank "sealed up" the notes of each country bank that had come into its possession during the preceding two weeks. Through the Albany City Bank the country banks were then informed of the amount of their notes being held for redemption.[26] In the opinion of a present-day scholar, "it is possible that the sealed packages were exchanged among the four [Albany] banks each of which under the law must have been the redemption agent of some of the country banks concerned." According to the same authority, this early alliance of the Albany banks may well have represented "the beginning of what was known in the 1850s as the Albany assorting house"—one of the early regional agencies for the redemption of bank notes.[27]

Another area in which the Albany City Bank was active was

[25] *Laws of the State of New York, Sixty-third Session* (Albany, 1840), 154–156.
[26] Pruyn to Corning, Albany, July 17, 1840, CP. I am indebted to Dr. Fritz Redlich for interpreting the meaning of Pruyn's letter.
[27] Redlich, *History of American Business Leaders*, II, pt. II, 270. The Albany assorting house was organized in 1858 under the joint management of the Bank of the Interior (which had been chartered in 1851) and the Merchants' Bank (the charter of which dated from 1853). This agency redeemed not only the notes of the New York country banks, but those of the New England, Pennsylvania, and New Jersey banks as well (*ibid.*, II, pt. I, 79; Parker, *Landmarks of Albany County*, pt. I, 371, 372).

in the purchase of state securities. Here Corning's experience as a director of the New-York State Bank was of value to him. As early as 1830 that bank had been a successful bidder for at least part of the Chemung Canal Loan, which had been floated by the state of New York to obtain funds for the building of that canal. Four years later, in 1834, the State Bank, this time acting jointly with the Mechanics and Farmers Bank of Albany, had entered a successful bid for the Chenango Canal Loan. On both occasions the bank was acting a role which was later filled by brokers and investment houses—that is, the bank purchased a large block of securities, then marketed them in smaller lots at whatever profit could be made.[28]

In April, 1834, Richard Yates, cashier of the State Bank, was in New York City for the purpose of disposing of the Chenango Canal securities. Of his endeavors he wrote to Corning in some detail:

I have made an offer to sell $300,000 of our Chenango Canal Stock at a premium of 8 per cent—$50,000 to be paid down & the balance in installments of about $50,000 per week—The stock to be transferred as the payments are made & five per cent Interest to be allowed by purchaser; so that the Interest acct will be squared—

Prime Ward King & Co will probably be the purchasers & I shall have to pay a Brokerage of ¼ per cent.

. . . This will be a far better operation for us than to be pedling [*sic*] out the Stock even though we should make a little more.[29]

A second Chenango Canal Loan in 1836 was successfully bid for by the Albany City Bank. Corning's offer on behalf of the bank was for $100,000 at $101.40 and a like amount at $101.55. Thomas W. Olcott, president of the Mechanics and Farmers Bank, bidding for that bank and the New-York State Bank together, offered only par. A few years later, in 1839 or 1840, several of the Albany banks appear to have taken on joint account a very large amount of New York state securities. The share of the Albany City Bank was $300,000.[30]

---

[28] Redlich, *History of American Business Leaders,* II, pt. II, 330.

[29] Yates to Corning, New York, April 17, 1834, CP.

[30] G. Hawley to Corning, Albany, July 9, 1836; Sherman to Corning, New York, Nov. 12, 1840: CP.

In November, 1840, Corning, accompanied by his wife, set sail for Europe. Intending to combine business with the grand tour, he hoped to dispose of perhaps $150,000 worth of the Albany City's state securities, as well as to visit his correspondents in the iron trade at Birmingham and Liverpool.[31] The winter of 1840–1841 was not a propitious time to carry American securities to the European market. In the crises of 1837 and 1839 foreigners had lost heavily on their American banking, canal, and mercantile investments. The repudiation of state debts had not yet begun, but the London market was flooded with large quantities of state securities.[32] Nonetheless, in the British capital Corning arranged to leave $35,000 worth of New York state stock with Baring Brothers and Company, to be sold to the best advantage, and in all managed to dispose of $65,000 worth of the stock in England. "I am glad . . ." wrote Watts Sherman to Corning in February, "but would have been still better pleased if you had got rid of a much larger amt." The stock was not selling well in America, and $250,000 worth which had been sent to Europe by the Albany banks on joint account was also failing to move.

The prospect of the State soon bringing a further amt. into market serves to depress the present value [Sherman wrote]. This added to recent explosions of the Phila Banks will I apprehend very much affect the English Market & almost render American securities non saleable.[33]

Sherman's apprehensions were justified. New York state securities continued to sell in the London market through 1841, but at depreciated prices.[34] In May, 1842, John V. L. Pruyn was suggesting that the Albany City Bank take some of the cur-

[31] Sherman to Corning, New York, Nov. 12, 1840; same to same, Albany, Nov. 30, 1840; Pruyn to Corning, Albany, Jan. 29, 1841: CP.

[32] Ralph W. Hidy, *The House of Baring in American Trade and Finance . . . 1763–1861* (Cambridge, Mass., 1949), 279, 289–290; Leland H. Jenks, *The Migration of British Capital to 1875* (New York, 1927), 103–104.

[33] Sherman to Corning, Albany, Feb. 26, 1841, CP. The Bank of the United States in Philadelphia (operating under a Pennsylvania charter since 1836) had finally collapsed earlier in the month in which Sherman was writing.

[34] Hidy, *House of Baring*, 291.

rent state loan, which he thought would soon command a premium and "might do something towards making up for losses on the former stock operation." [35] So far as the European market was concerned, Pruyn's was a vain hope for the immediate future, since in the course of 1841 and 1842 nine states (though not New York) stopped payment of interest on their indebtedness, a minority repudiating their obligations outright. By the winter of 1842–1843 the resentment of British investors had reached such a pitch that Americans in London felt distinctly uncomfortable and Anglo-American business relations were definitely strained. The market for American public securities disappeared almost entirely. By 1846 the domestic demand for American stocks had begun to revive, and large blocks of earlier issues of state stocks that had been held in London were returned to the United States for sale.[36]

Corning's success in obtaining government patronage for the Albany City Bank has been mentioned. He was no less successful in attracting the accounts of country banks. Here he not only used his influence as a merchant and capitalist well known in the West, but also, in the case of a number of such banks, his influence as an investor. As early as April, 1833, he was said to own $32,875 worth of stock in these New York institutions: [37]

Madison County Bank (Cazenovia)	$5,000
Oswego Bank	3,000
Broome County Bank (Binghamton)	3,675
Whitehall Bank	5,250
Buffalo Bank	6,250
Genesee Bank (Batavia)	9,700

This was probably only a partial list, for in August, 1830, Corning was the possessor of twenty shares in the Onondaga County Bank at Syracuse,[38] and in December, 1831, Judge

[35] Pruyn to Corning, New York, May 7, 1842, CP.

[36] Hidy, *House of Baring*, 368; Jenks, *Migration of British Capital*, 103–108.

[37] *Albany Argus*, April 2, 1833.

[38] John Wilkinson to Corning, Syracuse, Aug. 28, 1830, CP; Franklin H. Chase, *Syracuse and Its Environs: A History* (New York, 1924), II, 784.

Elial T. Foote, president of the Chautauqua County Bank at Jamestown, was promising the Albany investor "$2,000 more of our stock." [39]

At a later date Corning appears as a stockholder in the Hudson River Bank at Hudson, New York, the Westchester County Bank at Peekskill, the Bank of Monroe at Rochester, and the Genesee Valley Bank at Geneseo. [40] Doubtless there were others in which he had small amounts invested, and by 1844 there was at least one in which his investment was very large. This was Oliver Lee and Company's Bank at Buffalo.

Oliver Lee was a native New Englander who in 1814 moved to Genesee County, New York, and in 1828 settled at Silver Creek in Chautauqua County. During the 1820's he became associated with Corning in a land-development and harbor-promotion project centering in Irving, New York, on the shores of Lake Erie. The acquaintanceship of the two men seems to date from that period. In 1836, and perhaps earlier, Lee was a director of the Commercial Bank of Buffalo, but it was not until 1841 that he took up residence in that city. At that time he entered into private banking there, probably with the support of Corning and Watts Sherman. [41] By the middle of 1843 both Corning and Sherman were deeply engaged financially in the Lee venture.

Lee's office continues to do a very heavy business [Sherman observed to Corning in July of that year]—We can make a *great affair* of that by taking care of it & paying in as you say an amt sufficient to make our cash capital at least $50,000. [42]

[39] Elial T. Foote to Corning, Jamestown, Dec. 5, 1831, CP; John P. Downs and Fenwick Y. Hedley, eds., *History of Chautauqua County, New York, and Its People* (Boston, 1921), I, 45.

[40] Isaac Seymour to Corning, Peekskill, Oct. 7, 1833; Ralph Lester to Corning, Rochester, Jan. 1, 1848; C. Murdock to Corning, Hudson, Dec. 1, 1848; William H. Whiting to Corning, Geneseo, May 1, 1852: CP.

[41] *Memorial and Family History of Erie County, New York* (New York, 1906–1908), II, 358. The prohibition against private banking in New York State had been removed in 1838 by the repeal of the "restraining law" of 1818 (*Laws of the State of New York, Sixty-first Session* [Albany, 1838], 245–253).

[42] Sherman to Corning, Albany, July 19, 1843, CP.

In a short time their investment was to be more than that, for the following year, 1844, when Lee's bank was converted to an incorporated institution, the capital was set at $170,000, and Corning and Sherman held the controlling interest. Lee held 400 shares, and Israel T. Hatch, former president of the Commercial Bank of Buffalo, was also a shareholder.[43] At the end of the bank's first year as a chartered institution Lee reported: "I can pay 25 per cent I think this year over and above Expenses." [44] The dividend actually paid, however, was 12 per cent. This dividend was repeated in 1845.[45]

In midsummer of 1846 Oliver Lee died, and Sherman hastened to Buffalo to make an inventory of the bank's affairs. It was then that he discovered that, good as the return on his and Corning's Buffalo investment had been, it might have been somewhat better had the president of Oliver Lee and Company's Bank been honest.

It now appears by the Books of the Bank [Sherman reported to Corning] that Lee never really paid in but about $25,000 towards the capital of the Bank instead of $40,000 as represented by him— But he has nevertheless been drawing and paying to himself annually 12 prct dividends on $40,000 instead of on $25,000 his real amt of stock— [46]

After this Corning and Sherman were counseled to give up the practice of banking at a distance, but it was far from their thoughts to lose the "great interest" they had been obtaining on their money in Buffalo. Typically disregarding their would-be advisers, they bent their efforts to the finding of a capable man to place in charge of Oliver Lee and Company's Bank. F. H.

---

[43] W. W. Vanzandt to Sherman, Albany, Feb. 1, 1844; Sherman to Corning, undated, but probably written at Buffalo in July, 1846: CP; Henry Wayland Hill, ed., *Municipality of Buffalo, New York: A History, 1720–1923* (New York, 1923), I, 427; *The Merchant's and Banker's Almanac for 1856* (New York, 1856), 35; "Notes on the Service of Israel T. Hatch in Behalf of New York's Canals," *Buffalo Historical Society Publications*, XIV (1910), 389.

[44] Oliver Lee to Corning, Buffalo, Dec. 17, 1844, CP.

[45] Sherman to Corning, undated, but probably written at Buffalo in July, 1846.

[46] *Ibid.*

Tows, their first choice, was a poor one, but Henry L. Lansing, who had worked in the Albany City Bank and who was appointed president of Oliver Lee and Company's Bank in late 1851 or early 1852, served them well.[47]

For a period of five or six years subsequent to Lansing's appointment the affairs of the Buffalo bank went smoothly. The institution enjoyed state patronage in the form of canal-toll deposits, and after 1853 it received the Buffalo deposits of the New York Central Railroad. In October of that year the railroad's account stood at approximately $130,000. Eastern remittances were made to the Albany City Bank, and that bank was depended upon for help in emergencies.[48] The system worked well until the panic of 1857.

A debt in excess of $264,000 against several insolvent or failing companies, including the Buffalo Car Company, had embarrassed the resources of Oliver Lee and Company's Bank even before the financial crisis of the late summer of 1857 hit with full force. The failure of the Reciprocity Bank of Buffalo on August 29, followed almost immediately by that of the Hollister Bank, caused a further strain on Oliver Lee and Company's Bank. Added to this came a call on the bank from the city comptroller for the $45,000 in city funds on deposit there,[49]

all of which taken together and coming together [the *Buffalo Courier* observed], formed a combination of circumstances so untoward and paralyzing, that to avert suspension seemed scarcely possible. But the officers of the bank were still hopeful that the proprietors would take some action to relieve it from peril.[50]

Unfortunately "the proprietors" were so busy saving the institutions in which their financial stake was larger that they had little time or thought, and no resources, to bestow upon Oliver Lee and Company's Bank. In early September the bank was

[47] Erastus Corning, Jr., to Corning, Geneva, Switz., Sept. 27, 1846; Pruyn to Corning, Paris, Oct. 14, 1846; Sherman to Corning, New York, Dec. 6, 1851: CP.

[48] Henry L. Lansing to Corning, Buffalo, Nov. 15, 1851, Oct. 5, 1853; Sherman to Corning, New York, July 16, 1852: CP.

[49] *Buffalo Courier*, Sept. 4, 1857, quoted in *Bankers' Magazine and Statistical Register*, XII (Oct., 1857), 324.

[50] *Ibid.*

forced to suspend payment. It never opened for business again. In due course a receiver was appointed to wind up its affairs.[51]

At the time of the failure of Oliver Lee and Company's Bank the principal stockholders were Corning, Sherman, and Henry B. Gibson of Canandaigua. Corning's investment in the bank was $60,000, and in the course of the settlement by the receiver he was assessed an additional $60,000.[52] This was in conformity with the New York State Constitution of 1846, which provided that stockholders in a bank were liable to twice the amount of their investment. Thus, Corning's losses were large. Yet in view of the sizable dividends which the bank paid (in 1852, for instance, a "nett profit" of 22 per cent was anticipated)[53] it seems likely that his aggregate earnings went far to offset the loss of his investment and the final assessment. Moreover, in the summer of 1860 he regained a little more than a quarter of the money he had originally invested, for at that time the receiver paid a 27 per cent dividend to the stockholders—the 27 per cent representing the division of assets after all liabilities were satisfied.[54] This brought to a close the affairs of Oliver Lee and Company's Bank.

Corning had a happier experience in Detroit. It will be remembered that when Watts Sherman in 1835 was exhorting Senator Silas Wright to use his influence in Washington in behalf of the Albany City Bank he mentioned "two Banks in the City of Detroit that . . . make their Eastern remittances to this Institution [that is, the Albany City Bank]." One of the Detroit banks to which he referred was the State Bank of Michigan; the other was doubtless the Farmers and Mechanics Bank of Detroit. In July, 1835, in reply to an inquiry from a correspondent in that city, Sherman had written:

We should be most happy to keep the Acct. of the Fars & Mechs Bk. of Detroit in which you are interested on the same terms we extend to other Banking Institutions.

[51] *Ibid.;* Corning to John Ganson, Albany, Sept. 15, 1857, CP.
[52] Ganson to Corning, Buffalo, May 16, 1860, CP.
[53] Lansing to Corning, Buffalo, Dec. 25, 1852, CP.
[54] Ganson to Corning, Buffalo, June 29, 1860, CP.

. . . . We keep no running acct. on which we allow interest, our interest accts. are called *special*, to the credit of which we place *current* funds when directed by our correspondents to do so. All uncurrent items must go to the credit of a running acct. and remain with us long enough to be converted into current before they are drawn for—

On the *Special Acct* we will allow interest at the rate of 5 prct pr ann. We will also agree to your proposition in relation to the Redemption of Fars & Mechs Bk notes and stipulate as you desire in relation to over-drafts.[55]

By June, 1837, if not earlier, Erastus Corning had a financial interest in the Farmers and Mechanics Bank. On July 1, 1837, the president of the Albany City Bank collected $500 (probably a semiannual dividend) on his stock in the Detroit bank. Eleven years later he was using his influence with Michael Shoemaker, a member of the Michigan Senate, in a successful effort to procure a renewal of the Farmers and Mechanics charter. In the rechartered bank Corning held 200 shares of the capital stock, having a par value of $10,000.[56]

Meanwhile, Corning and John V. L. Pruyn had become interested in the Michigan Insurance Company, another Detroit bank. This institution had been incorporated as an insurance company in 1834; in 1843 an amendment to its charter gave it specific banking powers.[57] A letter to Corning, dated November 18, 1851, from Henry B. Gibson of the Ontario County Bank in Canandaigua, New York, not only indicates the esteem in which Corning was held by the country bankers but also gives a clue to the high degree of control which he exercised in the Michigan Insurance Company:

[55] Sherman to William B. Welles, Albany, July 30, 1835, CP.

[56] J. Wills to Corning, Detroit, June 30, 1837; Corning to Michael Shoemaker, Albany, Jan. 29, 1848; E. C. Litchfield to Corning, Detroit, Sept. 20, 1849: CP. There was a considerable amount of New York capital in the Farmers & Mechanics Bank of Detroit. A number of persons in the vicinity of Rome, as well as Charles Seymour of Canandaigua and Henry H. Martin and John V. L. Pruyn of Albany, had an interest in it (Pruyn to Corning, Detroit, Oct. 21, 1849; H. W. Walker to Corning, Detroit, March 26, 1851: CP).

[57] Pruyn to Corning, Detroit, Oct. 21, 1849, CP; *Laws of Michigan, 1834,* pp. 81–88; *1843,* no. 94, pp. 207–211.

If *you* are satisfied with the affairs, and management of the Michigan Insurance Bank I am content, for I consider that Institution under *your* immediate supervision, *and control,* and as long as that is so, my investment in the Stock of that Bank is safe, and will be *productive.*[58]

On October 1, 1850, Corning received a dividend of $1,000 on his Michigan Insurance stock. Two years later the bank's cashier was promising him "as a New Years memento" a dividend of 8 per cent. When reorganization of the bank was discussed in 1858, it was stated that the stock was fully worth par and that the surplus after all debts were paid would be about $20,000—this in addition to the bank building, which was worth between $35,000 and $40,000.[59]

Aside from the dividends which Corning received on his investments in the Michigan banks, he enjoyed at least two less direct but no less important returns from his interests in those institutions. It has already been mentioned that the Albany City Bank served as the eastern correspondent of the Detroit banks. In turn, the Michigan Insurance Company, if not the Farmers and Mechanics Bank, served as a distributing agent of the Albany City's circulating notes. As was the custom at the time, the Detroit bank was careful to send the notes to remote parts of Michigan, thus insuring the delay of their return to Albany for redemption.[60]

Another by-product of Corning's investments in the Detroit banks was of more personal benefit. In 1849, by reason of political connections, Henry W. Walker, the Michigan Insurance Company's cashier, made an arrangement "by which our Bank will receive the deposites from the State Treasury, or so much

[58] Henry B. Gibson to Corning, Canandaigua, Nov. 18, 1851, CP.

[59] Walker to Corning, Detroit, Oct. 1, 1850, Dec. 8, 1852, CP; Journal of John V. L. Pruyn, vol. I, entry for Aug. 3, 1858, New York State Library, Albany, N.Y.

[60] "Mr. Sherman in his letter complains that the notes sent here for circulation find their way back rapidly. This is to be expected when such large amounts are paid out, as in the last two months. . . . The last package of last month $5000 did not arrive here until after all payments were made save in this city, and we gave them other N.Y. money, and sent yours to the remote parts of the State" (Walker to Corning, Detroit, Oct. 28, 1848, CP).

thereof as will assume at all the nature of permancy [*sic*]." [61]
The funds so obtained were to be placed in the hands of Corning for investment rather than deposited with the Albany City Bank, for as Watts Sherman pointed out, he and Corning could use the money more advantageously to themselves if it were placed with Corning personally. This seemed an entirely equitable arrangement to Walker, since Corning had provided the necessary security (in the form of Michigan Central Railroad stock) for the obtaining of the state deposit in the first place.[62]

Perhaps the best illustration of the dovetailing of Corning's Michigan interests was to be found in the relationship between the Michigan Insurance Company and the Michigan Central Railroad. Through his large investment in the Michigan Central, Corning was able to procure the banking business of the road for the Michigan Insurance Company, and the bank in turn was sometimes in a position to bring pressure to bear on the officers and friends of the Michigan Southern Railroad, the Michigan Central's competitor. This reciprocity, which dated from the 1840's, endured for more than two decades, chiefly because Corning used his influence with the Boston stockholders in the Michigan Central to keep the road's account for the bank. In 1863, and again in 1869, when rival interests threatened the withdrawal of the railroad's deposits from the Michigan Insurance Company, Corning appealed to Nathaniel Thayer, a Boston capitalist and a Michigan Central director, to intervene on behalf of the Insurance Bank.[63] It may be readily imagined that Thayer, through whom Corning each year was buying many thousands of dollars' worth of state and railroad bonds, was disposed to do all that he could to keep his Albany client happy.

The Michigan Insurance Bank became a national bank in 1865. In 1869 it merged with the First National Bank of Detroit, the consolidated institution continuing to bear the latter name. Corning retained his interest in the consolidated bank until the

[61] Walker to Corning, Detroit, Oct. 18, 1849, CP.   [62] *Ibid.*
[63] Walker to Corning, Detroit, Oct. 28, 1848, March 26, 1851; Corning to Nathaniel Thayer, Albany, Oct. 13, 1863, Feb. 22, 1869: CP.

end of his life. A short time after his death, in the spring of 1872, his estate was collecting dividends on $25,000 invested in the institution.[64]

In the meantime, the Albany City Bank was flourishing. After 1838 Corning seems to have had little difficulty with his board, and he managed the bank's affairs to his own satisfaction. Once, in 1847, a report was widely circulated that he, Sherman, and other directors were speculating heavily in flour, to the prejudice of the bank's interests. That Corning and Sherman were speculating in flour was probably true, for they had been doing so since 1843.[65] But that they were speculating with large amounts of the bank's funds was probably not the case. Sherman, whose later career shows him to have been rather too inclined to take chances, may have been willing to trifle with the safety and reputation of the Albany City, but not so Corning, who was a sound and careful banker and was jealous of the Albany City's good name.

Until 1851 Corning continued to have the competent services of Sherman in handling the affairs of the Albany City Bank. In that year, however, Sherman moved to New York, where he became a partner in the private banking house of Duncan, Sherman and Company. His business and social ties with Corning remained firm. At times the two men were in almost daily correspondence. Their friendship continued until Sherman's death during a holiday in Madeira in 1865.[66] Henry H. Martin succeeded Sherman as cashier of the Albany City. Martin was honest and amenable, but he lacked Sherman's competence and boldness, and unlike most of Corning's "lieutenants," he seems not to have been personally devoted to his chief.[67]

[64] J. Owen to Corning, Detroit, June 13, 1865; Corning to Thayer, Albany, Feb. 22, 1869; Emory Wendell to Corning, Jr., Detroit, July 2, 1872: CP.

[65] Sherman to Corning, Albany, Jan. 19, 1843; Chicago, July 8, 1847: CP.

[66] Corning Papers. For information about Duncan, Sherman and Company see Muriel Hidy, "George Peabody, Merchant and Financier, 1829–1854" (unpublished Ph.D. dissertation, Radcliffe College, 1939), 302–304, 313, 322, and Redlich, *History of American Business Leaders*, II, pt. II, 352.

[67] George H. Thacher to Corning, Albany, Aug. 8, 1869, CP.

The charter of the Albany City Bank expired on December 31, 1863. During the thirty years of its existence the bank had paid a regular dividend of 8 per cent—by no means the largest return which could be had on an American investment in those years, but a steadier return than most such investments yielded. At the end the stockholders were "paid eighty per cent. in addition to their regular dividends, and the sum of $90,000 of the undivided profits of the old bank was carried as a surplus fund of the new one." The bank, reorganized under its new charter, continued under the same name, with the same officers, and with the same amount of capital—that is, $500,-000.[68]

In 1865 the Albany City became a national bank. Two years earlier, in 1863, Congress had passed "an Act to provide a national Currency, secured by a Pledge of United States Stocks, and to provide for the Circulation and Redemption thereof." [69] In effect, this act was a free-banking measure, for in addition to the currency clauses, it provided that any group of persons, under certain conditions, might form a banking association under the national authority. At least one-third of the capital of the banks had to be invested in United States securities, upon which the Comptroller of the Currency would issue circulating notes to 90 per cent of the value. The act was amended and amplified in 1864,[70] but the basic provisions of the law of 1863 were retained. State banks were permitted to enter the national system, but such banks showed marked reluctance to do so. The Internal Revenue Act of 1865 introduced an element of coercion by imposing a 10 per cent tax on state bank notes.[71] This had the desired effect so far as many state banks were concerned,[72] but circulation was generally unimportant to well-established city banks and many of these gave up note issue rather than their state charters.

According to Hugh McCulloch, president of the Bank of

[68] Parker, *Landmarks of Albany County*, pt. 1, 369.
[69] *U.S. Statutes-at-Large*, 37 Cong., 3 Sess., ch. 58, 1863, 665–682.
[70] *U.S. Statutes-at-Large*, 38 Cong., 1 Sess., ch. 106, 1864, 99–118.
[71] *U.S. Statutes-at-Large*, 38 Cong., 2 Sess., ch. 78, 1865, 484.
[72] Hammond, *Banks and Politics*, 733.

Indiana and afterward Comptroller of the Currency, one of the objections of many state bankers to the new national banking system was that they believed it would encourage banks of circulation only. By the time of the Civil War careful bankers looked askance at note issue, "except as it was subordinate to a commercial banking business with deposit liabilities." To them the national banking act was a "wild cat" law. Another important objection to converting to national charters was that the state bankers feared the caprices of Congress and the Treasury Department.[73] At any time the terms of the law might be changed. They preferred their charters from a legislature closer to home.

The directors of the Albany City Bank shared the reluctance of city bankers generally to convert to a national charter. Nonetheless in 1865 the step was taken. The reason for this move on the part of the officers is significant. On May 11 John V. L. Pruyn, vice-president of the bank, noted in his journal:

Conversed today with Mr. Martin & Mr. Corning as I had done several times before, about changing the organization of the Albany City Bank, and bringing it under the National System—Both Mr. C. & I are very reluctant to give up our State organization—but it seems to be almost unavoidable—The turning point is that National Banks (and most banks are becoming such) must keep their reserve fund on deposit with a National Bank—If therefore we do not change, we shall lose our Country Bank accounts— [74]

And so the change was made. The Albany City National Bank continued in operation until 1902 when it was merged with the National Commercial Bank and Trust Company, which is still doing business in Albany.

Erastus Corning remained president of the bank until his death in 1872. As he grew older and his physical infirmities confined him more and more to Albany, he gave increased attention to his banking activities there. After he withdrew from the hardware business in 1867, the old gentleman could

[73] *Ibid.*, 728–731. On the attitude of the state bankers, see also Redlich, *History of American Business Leaders*, II, pt. II, 105–113.

[74] Pruyn Journal, vol. III.

be found almost any morning in a back room of the Albany
City National Bank at 47 State Street (the move from the south
side of State had been made in 1840), keeping an eye on
things.[75] He was something of a trial to the cashier and clerks,
and their relief was great when the president went off to Newport for the summer. Until the very end, however, Corning remained an asset to the bank, for his mind was clear, his experience was valuable, and his name commanded respect.

[75] There is a description of Corning at this period in a letter from Peter Winne,
an Albany coach and carriage manufacturer, to John McBain Davidson, dated
at Albany, June 29, 1869, CP.

· VII ·

The Land Speculator: New York

AS an eastern merchant whose customers were drawn largely from the West, Erastus Corning early understood the potentialities of the western country. Frequent trips on the Erie Canal after 1825 and on the roads of the Central Line beginning in the 1830's gave him opportunity to observe the growth of upstate cities, and his acquaintances in western New York drew his attention to sites on rivers and lakes which might well be the cities of the future. When his business took him to Michigan, as it often did after 1840, he became intimately acquainted with the Great Lakes country and the possibilities for its exploitation. The small parcels of land which, like other merchants of his day, he sometimes took in settlement of a debt whetted his desire for more. Scarcely had the decade of the thirties reached the halfway mark when his investments in western lands were absorbing an important part of his capital.

Corning's principal land speculations may be conveniently divided into two groups. The first included three localities in New York State: the townsites of Corning and Irving and a town-lot promotion and real-estate development in Auburn. The second group consisted of out-of-state speculations: shares, first, in the American Land Company and in the Half-Breed Tract in Iowa and, second, in the Sault Canal lands in Michigan and the lands of the Fox and Wisconsin Improvement Company in Wisconsin.

Of the New York projects, the first was Corning, dating from the late summer of 1835. This townsite was in the western part of the state, on the south bank of the Chemung River, in the town of Painted Post (now Corning), Steuben County. Two years before Corning was projected the Chemung Canal had been completed from Elmira to Lake Seneca, with a feeder from a point near the future townsite.[1] Corning was therefore at the head of navigable waters. The purpose of the Chemung Canal was to join New York's southern tier of counties to Albany and the eastern seaboard, for the traveler or freight, once having reached Lake Seneca, found easy conveyance to the east by way of the lake, the Erie Canal, and the Hudson River. A water route to eastern New York, so promoters of the canal urged, would increase the profits of the lumbermen of the southern tier by giving them access to another market. Hitherto they had been dependent on Philadelphia, Baltimore, and Wilmington, where, it was charged, prices were held down by the buyers, who knew that the New Yorkers had no choice but to come to them. A second reason given for building the canal was that it would provide easy access to the coal deposits in Tioga County, Pennsylvania.[2]

Erastus Corning was familiar with both these arguments and was likewise appreciative of the resources of the Chemung-Steuben-Tioga region, as the cause of the canal was championed by Edwin Croswell, editor of the *Albany Argus*,[3] a newspaper which Corning seldom failed to read. The impetus for the townsite speculation, however, came from Hiram W. Bostwick, a resident of Otsego County, whose acquaintance with Corning probably dated from the six-year period, 1818–1824, when Bostwick had lived and worked in Albany.[4]

At some time prior to August, 1835, Bostwick visited Albany and tried to interest Corning, Thomas W. Olcott (president of the Mechanics and Farmers Bank), and Watts Sherman (cashier

---

[1] Charles H. Erwin, *History of the Town and Village of Painted Post and of the Town of Erwin* (Painted Post, N.Y., 1874), 46; Harlo Hakes, *Landmarks of Steuben County, New York* (Syracuse, N.Y., 1896), 260.

[2] Erwin, *History of Painted Post*, 45–46; Hakes, *Landmarks of Steuben County*, 259–260.

[3] See *Albany Argus* for Feb., March, and April, 1829.

[4] See W. W. Clayton, *History of Steuben County, New York* (Philadelphia, 1879), 254.

of the Albany City Bank) in the purchase of "a track [*sic*] of land in Steuben Co." When Bostwick returned to the capital city in the late summer, Sherman, at least, was willing to enter into the Steuben County venture provided his mentor, Erastus Corning, had confidence in Bostwick's judgment and honesty and provided, too, that the land could be bought "*very low*."[5] It is probable that the Corning Company was formed about this time.

The original members of the company were nine in number: Corning, Olcott, Sherman, Bostwick, Ansel Bascom of Seneca Falls, New York; Joseph Fellows and Bowen Whiting of Geneva, New York; William A. Bradley of Washington, D.C.; and Levin I. Gillis of Montgomery County, Maryland.[6] Between November, 1835, and April, 1837, these associates purchased 1,144 acres in the town of Painted Post for a total of $42,200.[7] In April, 1839, the group paid $9,000 for an additional 250 acres in the same town.[8] Five years later, in July, 1844, another purchase of 420 acres was negotiated.[9] This last parcel brought the company's holdings to a total of 1,814 acres. For this $53,198, or an average of $30.10 an acre, had been paid.[10] The land was on both sides of the Chemung, but the townsite, to which the name Corning was given, was platted south of the river. At that time Erastus Corning's stake in the

[5] Watts Sherman to Erastus Corning, Albany, Aug. 11, 1835, CP.

[6] *Register of Deeds, Steuben County*, book 36, p. 342, Office of the Clerk of Steuben County, Bath, N.Y. Subsequently two of the original members (Bascom and Sherman?) withdrew from the venture, so that by mid-March, 1848, there were but seven proprietors (Hiram W. Bostwick to Corning, Corning, N.Y., March 15, 1848, CP).

[7] *Register of Deeds, Steuben County*, book 24, pp. 562–564; book 25, pp. 435–436, 437–438; book 26, p. 13; book 36, pp. 342 ff. Cf. Bostwick to Corning, Thomas W. Olcott, and Sherman, Seneca Falls, N.Y., March 13, 1836, CP.

[8] *Register of Deeds, Steuben County*, book 37, p. 37.

[9] Bought for $1,998, this last-mentioned acreage was located in the northeast corner of the town of Painted Post and was not contiguous to the other land owned by the company north of the river (*ibid.*, book 41, pp. 179–180).

[10] Orginally Ansel Bascom was the Corning Company's agent, and it was in his name that all purchases prior to April 10, 1837, were made. Subsequently Hiram W. Bostwick and Bowen Whiting acted together with Bascom as "trustees." After Nov. 23, 1840, Corning and Joseph Fellows were the company's trustees, with Bostwick as its agent in Corning (*ibid.*, book 36, pp. 344, 348; book 37, p. 38).

Steuben County venture was apparently no larger than that
of any of his partners, but evidently it was felt that his name
carried the greatest prestige.[11]

So far as Corning himself was concerned, the venture in
Steuben County was more than a simple land speculation. As
early as May, 1838, he described himself as being associated
with "eight gentlemen" who were "engaged in the building"
of the New York section of a railroad which would join the
new townsite with the coal fields in Tioga County, Pennsylvania.[12] The Pennsylvania segment of the road was backed by
Philadelphians, including James R. Wilson, Coffin Calket,
J. W. Ryerss, and others who were described as having an interest in the resources of Tioga County.[13] Corning's Albany
Iron Works furnished spikes for both the Pennsylvania and
New York roads. Early in 1840, the year in which the line was
opened to Blossburg, its Pennsylvania terminus, the New York
company owed Corning almost $4,000. For this debt he ac-
cepted twenty-year bonds, "drawing six per ct int semi annually." [14]

[11] At the same time promoters of a speculation in Chautauqua County, N.Y.,
in which Corning was interested, wished to name their townsite for him and
were deterred from doing so only because the Steuben County promotion was
called Corning (Lewis Eaton to Corning, Buffalo, N.Y., April 7, May 2, 1836,
CP). Later a town on the Burlington Railroad in Iowa was also named for
Corning.

[12] Corning to John Dunn, Albany (?), May 20, 1838, CP. This road was built
by the Tioga Coal, Iron Mining, and Manufacturing Company, which was incorporated in 1828 and authorized to improve the navigation of the Tioga
River. The company's charter was amended in 1833 to permit the construction
of a railroad. The venture was not a success, for despite the voting of a $70,000
state loan in 1840 the property (renamed in 1851 the Corning and Blossburg
Railroad) was sold by the sheriff in 1852. In June, 1854, the line came into the
possession of the Blossburg and Corning Rail Road Company. After several other
corporate changes it was taken over by the New York Central in 1914 (*Laws of
New York, 1828*, ch. 191, pp. 232–233; *1833*, ch. 81, p. 104; *1840*, ch. 296, p. 241;
Interstate Commerce Commission, *Valuation Reports*, XXVII [1930], 12,
217).

[13] *Laws of New York, 1833*, ch. 81, p. 104; Clayton, *History of Steuben County*,
255; John L. Sexton, "Coal Mines and Mining," *Papers and Proceedings of the
Tioga County Historical Society*, I (1906), 171.

[14] James R. Wilson to Corning, Philadelphia, May 13, 1840; Bostwick to Corning,
Corning, Jan. 31, 1840: CP.

By 1840, if not earlier, the Albany capitalist was also interested in property in Tioga County, Pennsylvania. In that year he came into possession of 450 shares of stock in the Arbon Coal Company and 100 shares in the Arbon Land Company, both in Tioga County. The companies had been formed by a group of Pennsylvanians, some of whom were members of the company that had built the Pennsylvania section of the Corning-Blossburg railroad. One incorporator, Bowen Whiting, was also a member of the Corning Company, and by the end of 1841 Hiram W. Bostwick was a director of the Coal Company.[15]

Not only did Corning own shares in the Arbon Coal Company, but he also advanced money to the company. This he did on his private account, as a member of the firm of Erastus Corning & Co., as president of the Albany City Bank, and as an interested party in the store operated by his nephew, Thomas Turner, Jr., at Blossburg. By mid-December, 1841, the Coal Company owed Corning personally a sum in excess of $6,000, and it owed the Albany City Bank in excess of $12,000. Undetermined, but large, amounts were also owed to the Corning firm in Albany and to Turner's store in Blossburg. For all these debts, totaling about $45,000, Corning agreed to take some 20,000 tons of coal, delivered at the river bank in Corning, to be credited toward the debts at the rate of $2.25 a ton. At this time the Coal Company was advertising its product at $3.50, delivered in any quantity at Corning, and coal was selling in Albany, in small lots, at about $7 a ton.[16]

The transaction between Corning and the Arbon Coal Company points up the difficulty that the company had in finding a market for its coal (a problem not yet resolved as late as

[15] Bostwick to Corning, Corning, Jan. 31, 1840; receipt dated Dec. 10, 1841, signed by James R. Wilson, Treasurer, and H. W. Bostwick and James H. Gulick, Directors, Arbon Coal Company: CP; Sexton, "Coal Mines and Mining," 173; *History of Tioga County, Pennsylvania* (Harrisburg, 1897), I, 104–105, 124–125.

[16] Receipt for $18,000 from Albany City Bank, signed by James R. Wilson, Dec. 10, 1841; receipt for 2,700 tons of coal from Arbon Coal Company, signed by Corning, Dec. 11, 1841; copy of minutes of directors' meeting, Arbon Coal Company, Dec. 10, 1841; copy of agreement between Arbon Coal Company and Corning, Dec. 24, 1841: CP; *Albany Argus*, Dec. 11, 1841.

1846).[17] Corning, however, had no such problem, for, by reason of his diversified interests, he had access to a ready-made market. As fast as the coal for which he had contracted was delivered, he disposed of it to the Utica and Schenectady Railroad and to the Albany Iron Works.[18] To the ironworks, of which he was the principal owner, he seems to have sold the fuel at only a small advance in price,[19] but it can at least be questioned if this was the case with the railroad, in which his investment in proportion to the total investment was never very great.

By the time that the Corning-Blossburg railroad went into operation, that is, by 1840, the village of Corning had acquired a post office and the Corning Company had erected a hotel, a block of four stores, and another block of ten offices.[20] But the financial affairs of the company had not been going so well. In July, 1839, Bostwick, the company's agent at the townsite, in reply to a demand from Erastus Corning that he account for some sales of timber, had explained that the lumber had been sold to meet current expenses. Six weeks later he was complaining that he had "no Co. funds in hand," and by the end of the year he stated flatly, "I am dunned and perplexed beyond endurance." [21]

In June, 1840, the indebtedness of the company in the form of demands against it stood at $20,000. In addition, parts of the property were mortgaged. At the end of that year another mortgage was placed on the company's holdings. The year 1840 seems to have marked the nadir, however, for by November, 1841, Bostwick could report substantial sales of village lots.[22] The change in the company's fortunes was to be at-

[17] Bostwick to Corning, New York, June 5, 1846, CP.

[18] John F. Winslow to Corning, Blossburg, Pa., July 20, 1842; same to same, Troy, N.Y. (?), May 15, 1843; J. Jones Smith to Corning, Corning, Sept. 22, 1842: CP.

[19] Winslow to Corning, Troy, June 11, 1845, CP.

[20] Clayton, *History of Steuben County*, 255; Bostwick to Corning, Washington, Dec. 11, 1839, CP; letter of "W" to the editor, *Corning Journal*, July 2, 1857.

[21] Bostwick to Corning, Corning, July 17, Aug. 30, Dec. 28, 1839, CP.

[22] Bostwick to Corning, Corning, Jan. 31, 1840, Nov. 17, 1841; William A. Bradley to Corning, Washington, June 5, 1840: CP; *Register of Deeds, Steuben County*, book 37, p. 38.

tributed in large measure to the opening of the Corning-Blossburg railroad. By midsummer, 1844, Watts Sherman was rejoicing that "our Compy debts are now all liquidated but the 2 mortgages."[23]

In 1849 the Erie Railroad, which had been projected through the village of Corning almost a decade earlier, finally reached that place. "The village is improving very much," Joseph Fellows reported in the fall of that year, "and extensive sales [of lots] have been made."[24] About this time Erastus Corning was so impressed with the prospects of the place that he agreed to advance $8,000 for the building of another block of stores.[25]

As early as 1842 a division of the Corning Company's assets among the individual members was contemplated, and in 1853 railroad stocks held by the company were actually apportioned to the members. That same year further attempts were made to reach agreement on the final terms of partition, but it was not until March, 1854, that a division of assets was effected. A second and final division followed, in October, 1855.[26]

In the scheme for division, Erastus Corning was probably one of the principal movers, as he was to be in the case of the Sault Canal lands at a somewhat later date, because he always preferred having his interests under his personal direction and was impatient when operating through a company in which he could not exercise nearly complete control. But perhaps the most important factor in the decision to dissolve the Corning company was the belief on the part of some of the members that Hiram W. Bostwick was no longer to be trusted with the management of its affairs. Joseph Fellows and William A. Bradley both expressed dissatisfaction with him.[27] Yet Bostwick, of all the proprietors, gave most of himself to the venture.

[23] Sherman to Corning, Albany, Aug. 10, 1841, CP.

[24] Joseph Fellows to Bradley, Geneva, N.Y., Sept. 3, 1849, CP.

[25] Bostwick and A. B. Dickinson to Corning, Corning, Aug. 24, 1850, CP.

[26] Bostwick to Corning, Corning, Nov. 1, 1842, Oct. 10, 1853; Fellows to Corning, Bath, N.Y., Aug. 2, 1853; Corning to Sherman, Albany, April 11, 1854: CP; *Register of Deeds, Steuben County*, book 74, pp. 84 ff., book 78, pp. 6 ff.

[27] Fellows to Corning, Geneva, Sept. 3, 1849; Fellows to Bradley, Bath, Aug. 2, 1853; Bradley to Corning, Washington, Sept. 11, 1853: CP.

In 1857 an early settler of Corning recalled "in grateful remembrance" Bostwick's many services in the promotion of the village.[28]

In the division of 1854 Erastus Corning received as his share 168 lots having an estimated value of $41,575. In addition, contracts amounting to $10,000 for lands already sold were assigned to him. In the division of the following year he came into possession of 68 additional parcels of land, having an estimated value of $32,450.[29] Subsequent to the division the Albany financier acquired other lots in and near Corning. On September 17, 1855, he bought 48 lots in the village, plus two "river lots" (these also on the south side of the Chemung) and two lots of "the Knox farm" north of the river, all from Hiram W. Bostwick for $14,742. Later purchases from James H. Gulick, W. M. Mallory, C. C. B. Walker, and Horace Turner added eleven more village lots to Erastus Corning's holdings.[30]

A modern writer has said that "Corning was a speculative enterprise that succeeded." [31] The man for whom the place was named, at least, had no grounds for complaint, even though he always maintained that he realized on the venture less than he had anticipated. Between 1855 and 1872 he seems to have received only some $32,000 for land which he disposed of in the town,[32] but at the time of his death in the latter year it was estimated that his remaining property in the village was worth $200,000.[33]

Although the village of Corning in 1849 stood third on the list of inland shipping points in the state of New York [34] and the *Corning Journal* could report in June, 1854, that "there has never been a time since the settlement of this village, when

[28] *Corning Journal,* June 18, 1857.

[29] *Register of Deeds, Steuben County,* book 74, pp. 84, 93–94; book 78, p. 6.

[30] *Ibid.,* book 76, p. 401; book 78, p. 262; book 82, pp. 76, 117.

[31] Alexander C. Flick, *History of the State of New York* (New York, 1933–1937), VIII, 63.

[32] See *Register of Deeds, Steuben County,* books 76–141.

[33] *Daily Knickerbocker,* Albany, April 13, 1872.

[34] Millard F. Roberts, *Historical Gazetteer of Steuben County, New York* (Syracuse, N.Y., 1891), 256.

its prospects were as fair for growth and importance, as at present," [35] Corning missed being the metropolis its promoters had envisioned. The very railroads which brought it temporary prosperity in the course of time condemned it to being just another small, inland city, since its only advantage over its neighbors—that it lay at the head of navigable waters—was rendered unimportant by the increased efficiency of the iron horse. Today it is known chiefly as the home of the Corning Glass Works, an industry lured there from Brooklyn in 1868 by a subsidy of $50,000 subscribed by the citizens of Corning.[36]

Later in the same year that Erastus Corning had become interested in promoting the townsite of Corning, that is, in 1835, he had joined another group of men in a townsite speculation in Chautauqua County, westernmost county of New York State. The land purchased there was on Lake Erie, at the mouth of Cattaraugus Creek. This was within the Holland Land Company Purchase and, in fact, included part of a townsite called Cattaraugus which had been laid out by that company at an earlier date.[37] But by the time that Corning and his partners made their investment the land had passed from the possession of the Holland Company to individual owners.[38] It was from these owners that Corning and his associates bought lots one to twenty-four of the old townsite of Cattaraugus, as well as a number of adjoining lots. Part of the purchase was effected in 1835, when one Rufus Reed conveyed six lots in the village of Cattaraugus to Alexander C. Stevens, one of the

[35] *Corning Journal*, June 23, 1854.

[36] Corning Junior Chamber of Commerce, *Focus on Corning* (Corning ? 1948 ?), 41.

[37] *The Centennial History of Chautauqua County* (Jamestown, N.Y., 1904), 610. The post office at this place was called "Acasto" (*ibid.*, 616). For a history of the Holland Land Company see Paul Demund Evans, *The Holland Land Company* (Buffalo Historical Society *Publications*, XXVIII [1924]).

[38] According to the tax-assessment reports submitted by David E. Evans, Holland Land Company agent at Batavia, N.Y., the last of the company's lands in the town of Hanover, in which the village of Cattaraugus was located, were sold in 1827 or 1828. See Evans' reports for 1827 and 1828 in Buffalo Historical Society *Publications*, XXXIII (1941), 446, 458.

associates of Erastus Corning. It was not until August 17, 1836, however, that the Irving Company was formed, "Irving" being the name finally given to the new townsite.[39]

Among the members of the Irving Company, in addition to Corning and Stevens, were at least three other citizens of Albany: Thomas W. Olcott (who will be recognized as a member of the Corning Company), John V. L. Pruyn, and Thurlow Weed. Oliver Lee and Lewis Eaton of Buffalo were also members.[40] The company had great plans for its townsite, and not without reason, for the venture got off to a promising start. In April, 1836, Eaton wrote to Corning:

Our place at Cattaraugus has allready attracted the attention of monied men here as well as abroad. We can sell in parcels of 20 to 30 lots for 200 to 300$ all the desirable lots at once. We have sold as high as $500 the single lot.[41]

A month later Eaton was even more sanguine, reporting that he had no doubt he could "sell the whole out" in Buffalo in a week and at a fair profit.

If we derive all the advantages that nature has designed for our place, To wit, the termination of the Erie Rail Road, the Extension of the erie Canal or the Cenewengo [Conewengo], it will be an im-

---

[39] Oliver Lee to Corning, Buffalo, Oct. 26, 1845, CP; *Centennial History of Chautauqua County*, 616. It was decided to call the Chautauqua County development Irving only after several other names, including Acasto, Iroquois, and Corning, had been discussed and rejected—the last-mentioned because that name had already been given to the Steuben County townsite (Eaton to Corning, Buffalo, April 7, May 2, 1836, CP).

[40] Other members of the Irving Company were William Kent, Dr. Henry P. Wilcox, William Samuel Johnson, Hamlet Scranton, Pierre A. Barker, Hiram Pratt, Thomas B. Stoddard, and Samuel B. Ruggles (Lee to Corning, Silver Creek, N.Y., April 24, 1842, CP; John V. L. Pruyn to Samuel B. Ruggles, Albany, April 5, 1845, Miscellaneous Papers no. 58, Collection of Regional History, Cornell University, Ithaca, N.Y.; *Centennial History of Chautauqua County*, 616). One source adds the names of William L. Marcy (afterward governor of New York), Addison Gardner, Heman J. Redfield, John Cotes, and Ezekiel B. Gurnsey (Andrew W. Young, *History of Chautauqua County, New York* [Buffalo, 1875], 415). The name of Thurlow Weed among the associates is especially interesting, as the venture was early labeled a "Regency" (that is, Democratic) concern (Eaton to Corning, Buffalo, April 7, 1836, CP).

[41] Eaton to Corning, Buffalo, April 7, 1836, CP.

portant concern and we should not part with too much to speculators. . . . If the senate should not pass the Genesee Valley Canal, another year would satisfy the Legislature that the Cenewengo is much the cheapest and most important avenue to be opened.[42]

In the same letter Eaton refers to a reported "appropriation," doubtless for the harbor which the United States government had commenced building at Cattaraugus soon after 1830. By 1836 a considerable amount had been spent on piers and a lighthouse and on keeping the channel open, and the harbor was providing an outlet for lumber, an article in which the area was rich.[43]

For a time Irving prospered. The townsite was on the main road along the lake shore, and it has been reported that on some days as many as 300 wagons passed through on their way to Ohio's Western Reserve. Many stopped for the night in or near the village. A shipyard was built close to the mouth of Cattaraugus Creek, and several large boardinghouses were erected to shelter the workers. Meanwhile, efforts were made by the Irving promoters, Lewis Eaton in particular, to attract business away from the neighboring villages of La Grange and Silver Creek.[44]

But the continued prosperity of the new townsite was dependent upon its attracting the Erie Railroad and upon the federal government's continuing its interest in Cattaraugus harbor. This meant that all possible influence had to be used in three different quarters: in the United States Congress, in the state legislature, and with the officers of the Erie. In these endeavors Erastus Corning was active,[45] but he and his associates failed of success. The reasons for their failure are not clear, but by 1840 Dunkirk had won the battle for the Erie terminus, and the government's loss of interest in Cattaraugus

[42] Eaton to Corning, Buffalo, May 2, 1836, CP.

[43] *Centennial History of Chautauqua County*, 616; William J. Doty, ed., *The Historic Annals of Southwestern New York* (New York, 1940), II, 568.

[44] Doty, *Southwestern New York*, I, 285, 286; *Centennial History of Chautauqua County*, 617; Eaton to Corning, Buffalo, Feb. 1, 1838, CP.

[45] Olcott to Corning, Albany, May 29, 1836; Eaton to Corning, Lockport, N.Y., Aug. 2, 1836; William Seymour to Corning, Washington, March 1, 1837: CP.

harbor followed inevitably. When, in 1851, the Erie was actually completed and the following year the Buffalo and State Line (later the Lake Shore Railroad), from Buffalo west, also bypassed Irving, the village's fate was determined.

In the meantime the holdings of the Irving Company had been divided among the individual members. This was a course which had been urged by Oliver Lee as early as 1842, but the division was not effected until August 19, 1845, when a public sale was held. On that occasion the shareholders bid for such lots as they wished, and it was anticipated that those members of the company who did not choose to take a share of the land would be paid in cash, presumably from the proceeds of sales to outside parties. Erastus Corning at this time came into possession of a large block of lots.[46]

Information concerning the extent of investments in Irving by the Irving Company or investments of individuals in the company is meager. In April, 1845, John V. L. Pruyn offered a sum in the vicinity of $3,000 for William Kent's share,[47] but this was after it was decided to carry the Erie to Dunkirk, and the Irving property had consequently fallen in value. In September, 1845, Corning was advised to take an offer of $15 a lot for four of his lots in Irving. (Gone were the days when those same lots would have commanded $200 a piece.) A month later he had an offer of $6 a lot for village lots and $4 an acre for "wild lands." [48]

If Corning, New York, was "a speculative enterprise that succeeded," Irving was one that did not. Even before the Lake Shore Railroad bypassed the village, the post office had been moved to La Grange, which gradually took on the name "Irving." Although Erastus Corning as late as 1860 was hopeful of realizing something from his property in old Irving, he was

[46] Lee to Corning, Silver Creek, April 24, 1842; same to same, Buffalo, Aug. 18, 1842, Oct. 26, 1845; Pruyn to Corning, Albany, Aug. 14, Aug. 16, 1845; Haven Powers to Corning, Irving, Sept. 4, 1845: CP.

[47] Pruyn to Ruggles, Albany, April 5, 1845, Miscellaneous Papers no. 58, Collection of Regional History, Cornell University.

[48] Powers to Corning, Irving, Sept. 4, 1845; Lee to Corning, Buffalo, Oct. 26, 1845: CP.

to be disappointed. Today that place is completely deserted, and only a few timbers remain to mark where the old lighthouse once stood in the harbor.[49]

Corning's real-estate venture in Auburn, in Cayuga County, New York, began in much the same manner as his speculations at Irving and Corning and at about the same time. But Auburn in the mid-1830's was already a forty-year-old settlement which had been an incorporated village for two decades. Its population was above the 5,300 mark, it was the county seat, and it was the site of the state prison, while the outlet from Owasco Lake, on which it was situated, provided water power for a fairly-well-diversified industry, including carding and fulling mills, sawmills and gristmills, and distilleries. All of this went far to insure the prosperity of the place.[50]

Corning had an interest in Auburn as early as 1833, when he made a bid for some of the stock of the newly organized Cayuga County Bank at that place. The bid was made through Nathaniel Garrow, one of the bank's commissioners, who was subsequently to be its president.[51] Then, prior to October, 1835, the Albany capitalist became associated with Garrow, Henry Martin, John Seymour, Martin Van Buren (the vice-president of the United States), and some 60 other persons in the purchase of about 400 acres of land in and around Auburn.[52] Stone quarries—one of which by 1843 was described as "extensively worked" [53]—were located on a portion of the property, but the venture was essentially a town-lot speculation.

Within two years of the purchase the proprietors were in financial trouble. The property had been mortgaged to the extent of $45,000 to the Farmers Fire Insurance and Loan Com-

[49] Corning to Charles H. Lee, Silver Creek, Aug. 27, 1860, CP; *Centennial History of Chautauqua County*, 611; Doty *Southwestern New York*, II, 568.

[50] *History of Cayuga County, New York* (Auburn, N.Y., 1908), 18, 19, 27, 32.

[51] Nathaniel Garrow to Corning, Auburn, April 8, 1833, CP. See also *History of Cayuga County*, 34.

[52] *Register of Mortgages, Cayuga County*, book V, pp. 139, 155, 186; *Register of Deeds, Cayuga County*, book 67, pp. 406 ff.: Office of the Clerk of Cayuga County, Auburn, N.Y.

[53] *Register of Deeds, Cayuga County*, book 67, p. 408.

pany of New York City,[54] and the hard times following the
panic of 1837 made it impossible for the mortgagors to meet
their obligations to the New York concern. Accordingly, in
August, 1843, the mortgagee, now known as the Farmers Loan
and Trust Company, foreclosed on the property.[55]

The foreclosure was not unexpected, for on July 23, 1842,
a full year before, Corning had submitted to the Farmers Loan
and Trust a "proposition," the terms of which are unknown,
but which was concerned with the buying in of the Auburn
property by Corning in his personal capacity. Six days later
the board of the Farmers Loan and Trust approved the offer,
and from that time the company regarded the Auburn real
estate as belonging to Corning.[56] In February, 1843, Corning
entered into an "agreement of settlement" with the other members of the group having a financial interest in the property,[57]
thus paving the way for an uncontested bid at the sale which
was scheduled for August. At the August sale the Albany
capitalist bought the Auburn land (slightly in excess of 405
acres) for $17,350,[58] an average of $42.82 an acre. This com-
pared with $30.10 an acre paid for the land at Corning eight
years before, but the Auburn land was more valuable from the
outset since it was located in a village which was already well
established.

Prior to the August, 1843, purchase Corning had an interest
in at least one other parcel of land in Auburn, a lot comprising
about two-fifths of an acre, which he had taken in payment of
a debt owed by one Isaac S. Miller, hardware dealer, to Erastus
Corning & Co. of Albany.[59] Subsequent to the purchase from
the Farmers Loan and Trust, Corning from time to time added
to his holdings in Auburn, but these transactions all involved

[54] *Register of Mortgages, Cayuga County*, book V, pp. 139, 155, 186.
[55] *Register of Deeds, Cayuga County*, book 67, p. 406.
[56] R. R. Delafield to Corning, New York, July 29, Nov. 2, 1842, microfilm copy
of Farmers Loan and Trust Company Letter Book (July 2, 1841—Aug. 2, 1845),
Collection of Regional History, Cornell University.
[57] G. B. Throop to Corning, Auburn, April 6, 1843; Thomas Y. How to Corning, Auburn, Sept. 15, 1845: CP.
[58] *Register of Deeds, Cayuga County*, book 67, p. 406.
[59] *Ibid.*, book 64, p. 1.

parcels which were small in comparison with the purchase of 1843.[60]

For some of the lots which he bought at the foreclosure sale, Corning found a market almost immediately. By the end of 1846 he had already realized on the land a sum in excess of $20,000 (more than he had paid for the whole purchase). By the end of 1848 he could chalk up an additional $13,000. When 1850 drew to a close, the total sales approximated three times the purchase price, and as yet only a fraction of the land had been sold.[61]

Through the years Corning built houses, stores, and offices on some of his lots. A letter of January 28, 1867, from Isaac S. Allen, his Auburn agent, refers to the "Corning Block," which evidently included a meeting hall or auditorium and for which the agent had refused an offer of $24,000 cash, deeming the property worth from $28,000 to $30,000. The same letter includes a reference to the "State St. Block." [62] Three years later the Corning Block was actually sold for the $28,000 which the agent thought it was worth. Shortly before Corning's death Allen was still forwarding Auburn collections quite steadily.[63]

[60] *Ibid.,* book 72 and following books.

[61] See *ibid.,* books 67, 69–81. A glance through the index of grantors to the Register of Cayuga County deeds for the years subsequent to 1843 reveals the name of Erastus Corning many times over.

[62] Issac S. Allen to Corning, Auburn, Jan. 28, 1867, CP.

[63] Allen to Corning, Auburn, Sept. 20, Oct. 1, Dec. 2, 1870, CP.

· VIII ·

Western Land Speculations

ABOUT the time that Erastus Corning became involved in the speculations at Corning, Irving, and Auburn, New York, he also became a stockholder in the American Land Company, organized in 1835 by certain capitalists of Boston, New York, and Albany for the purpose of buying lands in the West.[1] Corning was one of the original shareholders in the company and along with Charles Butler and Edward A. Nicoll of New York and John B. Jones and John W. Sullivan of Boston was from the outset a member of its board of trustees.[2] Butler, who was chosen president of the company, had formerly been a law partner of Bowen Whiting,[3] with whom Corning was associated in promoting the townsite of Corning.

The American Land Company's speculations were on a very large scale. In January, 1836, Butler reported that he was that month paying out $88,000 on account of lands purchased.[4] By the time of the first annual report, in June, 1836, more than 130,000 acres in nine states had been contracted for by the company, at a price in excess of $318,000. The reported purchases amounted to 81,178 acres in Arkansas, 6,874 acres in

[1] *First Annual Report of the Trustees of the American Land Company* (New York, 1836), 5.

[2] *Ibid.*, 26.

[3] G. L. Prentiss, *The Union Theological Seminary in the City of New York . . . with a Sketch of the Life and Public Services of Charles Butler, LL.D.* (Asbury Park, N.J., 1899), 429.

[4] Watts Sherman to Erastus Corning, Albany, July 27, 1835, CP; Charles Butler to Bowen Whiting, New York, Jan. 22, 1836, Butler Papers, Library of Congress, Washington, D.C.

Mississippi, 1,500 acres in Florida, more than 10,000 acres in Ohio, something in excess of 25,000 acres in Michigan, and smaller acreages in New York, Pennsylvania, Illinois, and Wisconsin. Further large purchases in Arkansas, Mississippi, and Tennessee were anticipated. It was expected, for instance, that in the last-mentioned state $300,000 would be invested in land at $1.25 an acre, and no less a person than the governor had been appointed the company's agent to examine and approve the deeds. According to this first report the capital stock of the company had been set at $1,000,000, one-half of which had already been paid in by the stockholders. Oak timber which had been sold off the Florida land had brought $4,000 into the company's treasury, and the sale of some of the company's property in Toledo and Chicago had netted $42,837.[5]

Immediately upon its organization the American Land Company came under public censure, the newspapers charging that certain Democrats in Washington, including Vice-President Van Buren, Attorney General Benjamin F. Butler, Senator Silas Wright, and Amos Kendall, a prominent member of the Kitchen Cabinet, were speculating in government land through the agency of the company. The circumstance that Charles Butler was a brother of the Attorney General was not overlooked. Further, the papers labeled the company a monopoly, the worst, perhaps, of all epithets in Andrew Jackson's day. In a letter of August 17, 1836, to a Chicago editor, Charles Butler flatly denied that Martin Van Buren had any interest in the company which Butler headed,[6] but no such denial seems to have been made in the case of Amos Kendall, Benjamin F. Butler, or Silas Wright.

In the fall of 1839 the name of Martin Van Buren, who was by that time President of the United States, was again linked with that of the American Land Company, the *Cincinnati Gazette* charging that Kendall, then the Postmaster General, was to receive the profits on $40,000 worth of stock for procuring Van Buren's approval of the company's purchase of

---

[5] *First Annual Report of the American Land Company,* 5, 11–18.
[6] Butler to T. O. Davis, New York, Butler Papers.

Indian lands in Mississippi. According to the *Gazette* the actual projector of the American Land Company had been Attorney General Butler, at whose insistence his brother had been chosen to head it. Charles Butler, it was claimed, in addition to an ample salary, received 5 per cent of all subscriptions to the company's stock. The article ended on a satirical note, observing that, after a year of operation during which the Indians had been steadily cheated, the company had voted $1,000 for Bibles to be distributed among the aborigines of Mississippi and Alabama.[7]

Vigorous as were the expressions of the *Gazette*'s editor, they were matched by those of Thurlow Weed, editor of the *Albany Evening Journal*. The American Land Company, Weed stated, was such a combination of wealth and power as had never before existed in the Republic; the highest officers in the national and state governments were stockholders in the gigantic monopoly; the articles of association had been drawn up by the Attorney General himself; the company's agents were sent through new states and territories to engross valuable lands; government land officers were subsidized by the company; surplus revenue in the "pet" banks was at the service of the speculators, and millions of dollars had already been invested in Michigan, Illinois, Wisconsin, and Mississippi.[8]

Then, coming closer to home and getting down to cases, Weed claimed that at the head of the Albany stockholders in the American Land Company were Edwin Croswell and Thomas M. Burt, editors and owners of the *Albany Argus*, the state paper (and, incidentally, the *Journal*'s competitor). He also named John Van Buren, son of the President, and Senator Silas Wright as persons interested in the company. It was through the influence of Wright, he asserted, that the public deposits were placed within reach of the monopolizing speculators.[9]

[7] *Cincinnati Gazette*, copied in *Havana* (N.Y.) *Republican*, Nov. 27, 1839. I am indebted to Professor Paul Wallace Gates for this and the next item, as well as for the items cited in footnotes 23 and 25 of this chapter.

[8] *Albany Ev. Journal*, copied in *Chicago American*, Aug. 12, 1839.

[9] *Ibid.*

It is noteworthy that Weed, in speaking of the Albany stockholders, failed to include the name of Corning, whose 200
shares in the American Land Company represented over one-
quarter of the total Albany investment in the enterprise, his
holdings being twice as large as those of Burt and four times
as large as those of Croswell.[10] Although Weed may have been
unaware of Corning's interest in the company, it is more likely
that he knew of the interest but chose to ignore it, preferring
to concentrate his attack upon his more vulnerable, and less
useful, newspaper competitors.

While the motives and aims of the American Land Company
were being examined and criticized by the press, trouble was
brewing within the organization itself. In the fall of 1838 an
attempt had been made, presumably by some of the Boston
shareholders, to oust Corning and E. A. Nicoll of New York
City from the board. Shortly after, there was a rumored plot
to remove Charles Butler from the presidency of the company
and replace him with Franklin Dexter, a trustee from Boston.[11]
The course of ensuing events is unclear, but it seems that
Corning and Nicoll first joined forces to save Butler's position
and, having done so, presented their own resignations from
the board. By that time, however, the Bostonians apparently
had had a change of heart.

Our Land Co meeting was held on the 28th ult . . . [Butler wrote
to Corning on July 9, 1839]. The strongest expressions of kindness
& confidence were manifested towards you & Mr. Nicoll, & Mr.
Dexter would not listen for a moment to your resignation nor that

[10] Butler (per David Morice) to Erastus Corning & Co., New York, June 21,
1837, CP. Holdings in Albany at this time amounted to 725 shares, distributed
as follows: John F. Bacon, 20; Thomas M. Burt, 100; Erastus Corning, 200;
Edwin Croswell, 50; Sherman Croswell, 25; Edward C. Delavan, 100; Albert
Gallup, 25; Theodore Olcott, 55; James Porter, 50; Watts Sherman, 50; James
Vanderpoel, 50 (*ibid.*). In 1845 there were 1,159 shares of American Land Company stock held in Albany; in 1847, 1,029 shares; from 1850 through 1861, 628
shares (Butler to Corning, New York, July 25, 1845, Feb. 13, 1847, Jan. 14, 1860,
July 24, 1861; S. W. Fleetwood to Corning, New York, July 10, 1850, July 12,
1855: CP).

[11] E. A. Nicoll to Corning, New York, Feb. 14, 1839; Butler to Corning, New
York, July 8, 1839: CP.

of Mr Nicoll's— He expressed himself deeply mortified at the action of the shareholders last fall to harrass [*sic*] you & spoke of it as extremely improper.[12]

For a time after this the affairs of the company seem to have run more smoothly. In August, 1839, William B. Ogden, brother-in-law of Butler and Chicago agent of the American Land Company, observed to a correspondent that the agitation which had existed within the organization had mainly ceased.[13] The Bostonians, however, had not given up their struggle for control. Shortly the number of board members from New York City was reduced from two to one. By 1845 there were apparently but four trustees: one (Corning) from Albany, one (Charles Butler) from New York, and two (Franklin Dexter and John B. Jones) from Boston.[14] Thus it would seem that the power of the Boston faction at this time was equal to that of New York and Albany combined.

Events following the panic of 1837 did much to dim the first bright hopes of the investors in the American Land Company. But in the late summer of 1839 Ogden, writing from Chicago, referred to the continuing westward migration and expressed the opinion that as soon as financial affairs were normal the company would begin to realize "a portion" of their early anticipations.[15] Corning, at least, shared this faith in the future of the venture, for in February, 1842, he was buying additional stock in the company. That such optimism was not widespread may be deduced from his being able to purchase ten shares for $300, 30 per cent of their par value, while he was allowed an option on ten additional shares at the same figure.[16]

In June, 1842, shareholders were given an opportunity to exchange their stock for company lands in New York, Michigan,

[12] Butler to Corning, New York, July 9, 1839, CP.
[13] William B. Ogden to John B. Jones, Chicago, Aug. 9, 1839, Ogden Manuscripts (Letter Book, II), Chicago Historical Society, Chicago. Ill.
[14] Deed from trustees of American Land Company to John Stewart, dated Jan. 1, 1845, Miscellaneous Autographs no. 120, Collection of Regional History, Cornell University, Ithaca, N.Y.
[15] Ogden to Jones, Chicago, Aug. 9, 1839, Ogden Manuscripts.
[16] William E. Jones to Corning, New York, Feb. 12, 1842, CP.

Ohio, Indiana, Illinois, Wisconsin, Georgia, and Pennsylvania. Stock which came into the possession of the company through the exchange was "to be cancelled, thus reducing the number of shares holding the remaining properties." [17] A decade later, in 1852, reference is found to "lands in Ottawa County, Ohio, formerly belonging to the Land Co. and now to Mr Butler & some other parties." [18] By 1854, if not earlier, Corning had acquired from the company a considerable acreage in Michigan, but whether he paid for it in cash or in stock is not certain. In 1860 in a single Michigan county he held 860 acres which had formerly belonged to the company.[19]

In 1844 and again in 1847 the American Land Company published catalogues of certain of its holdings. The catalogue of the earlier year described "96,046 acres . . . situate and lying in" St. Francis, Phillips, Crittenden, Monroe, Arkansas, Chicot, and Jefferson counties, Arkansas. The publication also included a supplement listing 1,588 acres in Manitowoc and Rock counties, Wisconsin, and town lots in Adrian, Monroe, Tecumseh, and Berrien, Michigan; Erie, Pennsylvania; Toledo, Ohio; Evansville, Indiana; [20] and "in Bushnell's addition to Chicago." [21] The catalogue of 1847 concentrated on the "northwestern" states of Ohio, Michigan, and Illinois, listing 23,169 acres in the first, 24,890 acres in the second, and 5,432 acres in the third.[22]

A circular of February 15, 1850, signed by Butler and Dexter, claimed for the company 84,000 acres in Mississippi. The signers intimated that an offer not to exceed 60 cents an acre

[17] Copy of resolution of shareholders of the American Land Company adopted at the annual meeting, June 30, 1842, CP.

[18] Fleetwood to Corning, New York, March, 27, 1852, CP.

[19] The land was in Allegan County (Corning to John Ball, Albany, Dec. 2, 1854; Corning to Charles Seymour, Albany, July 3. 1860: CP).

[20] In a letter of Feb. 13, 1847, Butler reported to Corning: "The Indiana business has been successfully closed" (CP).

[21] *Catalogue of 96,046 Acres of Land Belonging to the American Land Company* (New York, 1844).

[22] *Catalogue of Lands in the North-western States Belonging to the American Land Company* (New York, 1847).

for the whole parcel was expected, but it was firmly stated that such a low figure would not be accepted.[23]

About that time the internal affairs of the company were once again in a state of agitation. In 1848 Butler had joyfully reported to Corning "the largest & best business meeting that we have ever had," at which "everything went off harmoniously."[24] But by 1850, although Butler remained in the presidency, the company's offices had been moved to Boston,[25] and from that time onward Franklin Dexter, and, presumably, the rest of "the Boston faction," came to exercise more and more influence in the affairs of the company. In 1854 Corning, writing in a testy mood, assured a correspondent: "—all I know is what I get from the [company's] reports."[26]

From the mid-1840's until the time of the Civil War, at least, the holding of stock in the American Land Company seems to have been a paying proposition. In July, 1850, a dividend of six dollars a share, referred to as "Dividend No. 9," was paid. Two of the preceding dividends had been paid in July, 1845, and in February, 1847, respectively. The former had amounted to two dollars a share, the latter to three dollars. During the decade of the 1850's no less than twenty-seven dividends were declared. One of these—that of July, 1855—amounted to three dollars a share. Between January 14 and May 21, 1860, a period of eighteen weeks, dividends thirty-seven to forty, inclusive, were paid. In the aggregate, these came to 5 per cent.[27]

At the outbreak of the Civil War the company unfortunately found itself with all its remaining lands concentrated in Mississippi and Alabama,[28] and as a result dividends ended abruptly. In 1866 an Albany shareholder solicited Charles

[23] The circular is in the Baring Papers, Public Archives, Ottawa, Ontario.
[24] Butler to Corning, New York, July 25, 1848, CP.
[25] Circular of the American Land Company, dated Feb. 15, 1850, Baring Papers.
[26] Corning to George Stull (?), Albany, Dec. 7, 1854, CP.
[27] Butler to Corning, New York, July 25, 1845, Feb. 13, 1847, Jan. 14, Feb. 9, April 11, May 21, 1860, July 24, 1861; Fleetwood to Corning, New York, July 10, 1850, July 12, 1855: CP.
[28] Butler to Edwin C. Delavan, New York (?), April 2, 1866, CP.

Butler's opinion concerning the value of the company's stock and was told that the shares would not bring ten cents on the dollar.[29] But if Butler's correspondent sold out for anything like that figure, his action was premature, for something was yet to be realized on the property in the South. In July, 1869, Corning, who still owned 181 shares in the American Land Company, received a check from Butler for $362—"a distribution in liquidation of Two Dollars to each share of the stock of this Company."[30] In 1871 a "further distribution, in liquidation" of one dollar on each share was made "out of collections received from Mr. Goodman," the company's southern agent.[31] Perhaps other payments followed.

Another large speculation in which Erastus Corning had a stake was in the Half-Breed Tract in Iowa. A casual glance at a map of that state will reveal in the southeastern corner a sizable wedge of land lying between the Mississippi and Des Moines Rivers. This 119,000-acre area was set aside by the United States government for the offspring of Indian women and white men, principally traders and trappers who had penetrated the red man's country in advance of the frontier.[32] The tract was originally given in common to the half-breeds, and Congress retained reversionary rights in it. In 1834, however, those rights were renounced. At the same time the half-breeds were authorized to divide and sell their land if they wished.[33]

In anticipation of congressional permission to divide and sell the tract, speculators had persuaded many of the original claimants to sign away their interest in the undivided holding. The first such transaction of record dates from the autumn of 1829.[34] By 1841, when the tract was actually divided, very few persons to whom the land had originally been given retained a right to it, and at that time the New York Land Company, of

[29] *Ibid.*

[30] Form letter signed by Charles Butler, Trustee, July 20, 1869, CP.

[31] Butler to Corning, New York, July 20, 1871, CP.

[32] *U.S. Statutes-at-Large*, VII, 229–230.   [33] *Ibid.*, IV, 740.

[34] *Iowa Advocate and Half-Breed Journal*, Montrose, Sept. 22, 1847, reprinted in *Annals of Iowa*, 3d ser., X (July, 1912), 461.

which Erastus Corning was a member, claimed more than half the 119,000 acres. This company dated from October 22, 1836, on which day Corning and eight others had entered into an agreement to buy land in the Half-Breed Tract. Even before that date, agents for the company had already "purchased lands" (that is, had bought individual rights to the undivided tract) to the sum of $20,000. Further purchases to the amount of $55,000 were authorized in the articles of association.[35]

At the time that the government released the tract to the half-breeds, no one had any clear idea of the number of persons who had rights in it. In addition, no provision was made for the mechanics of partition. It was this situation which the legislature of Wisconsin Territory (of which Iowa was then a part) hoped to remedy by the appointment early in 1838 of a commission to hear claims, survey the tract, and divide it.[36] That same year, however, Iowa Territory was cut off from Wisconsin, and one of the first acts of the new teritorial legislature was to recall the commission which had been appointed to settle the Half-Breed matter.[37]

In April, 1840, a group of St. Louisans, claiming about 24 shares in the tract, requested a decree of partition from the District Court of Lee County, Iowa, in which the tract was located. Subsequently the New York Land Company presented

[35] "Articles of Association of the New York Land Company," in *Annals of Iowa*, 3d ser., XIV (Oct., 1924), 437–438. The original members of the company, in addition to Corning, were Joshua Aiken and Isaac Galland, both of Illinois; Samuel Marsh, Benjamin F. and William E. Lee, George P. Shipman, and Henry Seymour, all of New York City; and Edward C. Delavan of Albany. Although Corning's share in the company at the time of its formation was only a twenty-fourth interest, he was to pay one-twelfth of the expenditures connected with the venture. The same ratio of two to one obtained in the cases of Delavan, Marsh, and Seymour, but the Lees committed themselves to the paying of expenses in the ratio of only four to three, Galland agreed to an outlay in exact proportion to his interest, and Aiken and Shipman, who together were listed as owners of nineteen forty-eighths of the assets, were to be held responsible for only one-twelfth of the expenditures (*ibid.*, 438–439). There is no explanation of this in the articles of association, but in all likelihood adjustments were made to compensate for services rendered. At the outset, at least, Aiken and Galland acted as agents for the company. (See *ibid.*, pp. 437–439.)

[36] *Laws of the Territory of Wisconsin, 1838*, no. 54, pp. 244–252.

[37] The recall was dated Jan. 25, 1839 (*Laws of the Territory of Iowa, 1839*, 225).

to the same court a claim for some 60 portions of the tract. The
requested decree was handed down on May 8, 1841, the pre-
siding judge, Charles Mason, having decided that there originally had been 101 valid claimants to the Half-Breed Tract
and that, of the 101 portions, approximately 22½ were at the
date of decision vested in the St. Louis claimants and 41 in
the New York Land Company.[38] Thus the company was entitled to approximately 48,000 acres.

The decision of Judge Mason was not generally well received. Isaac Galland, a member of the New York Land Company whose large private claims in the tract had been ignored
in the settlement, later charged that "the compromise mid-
night decree of partition" was rendered "under circumstances
of secrecy and most palpable collusion." [39] He further maintained that the court had given itself a "sweet morsel," [40] and
although Galland stopped short of saying that direct bribery
played a part in the settlement, such an implication is to be
found in his remarks. In this connection, it is worthy of note
that a large amount of money was paid out by the New York
Land Company in the early part of 1841, perhaps to quiet
those whose claims were subsequently disallowed. Just two
months before Mason's decree was issued, Watts Sherman,
cashier of the Albany City Bank, wrote to Corning, who was
then in Paris, that he had authorized Edward C. Delavan to
"draw on us for $7000 on his own a/c & $2000 on yours for the

[38] *Decree in Partition of the Half Breed Tract in Lee County, Iowa,* rendered
by Charles Mason, Chief Justice of the Territorial Supreme Court of Iowa, in
Annals of Iowa, 3d ser., XIV (Oct., 1924), 424, 436–437, 443, 444, 450.

[39] *Iowa Advocate and Half-Breed Journal,* Sept. 1, 1847, in *Annals of Iowa,*
3d ser., X (July, 1912), 456. As a matter of record, the compromise was reached
and "that whole business was arranged and closed" at ten o'clock on a Saturday
night (Charles Mason to Sophia Farrar, Burlington, Iowa, May 10, 1841, in
Charles Mason Remey, ed., "Life and Letters of Judge Charles Mason of Iowa,
Middle Western Pioneer, 1804–1882" [typescript, Cornell University Library],
I, ch. vi [volumes unpaged]).

[40] This was an allusion to Judge Mason's confirmation of a sister-in-law's right
to two shares in the tract. By his own admission Mason had been retained by the
sister-in-law to act for her, and therefore in this case he was both counsel and
judge. See Mason Diary, Aug. 5, 1860, in Remey, "Life and Letters of Charles
Mason," III, ch. xii.

settlement of the half Breed matter which he thinks he has now arranged just as it should be." [41]

Another complication, described by Galland as a device "to swindle the rightful owners out of all their land," arose from the Iowa law of 1839 which had recalled the commissioners who had been appointed by the Wisconsin territorial legislature to partition the Half-Breed Tract. The law of the Iowa legislature, in addition to recalling the commissioners, provided that they might sue the owners of the tract for the compensation to which they were entitled by reason of the services they had rendered before their recall.[42] Accordingly, suits were entered. When judgments in favor of the former commissioners were handed down, and those who claimed ownership in the tract refused to obey the court, the entire tract of 119,000 acres was sold by the sheriff for $2,884.66, the amount of the judgments.[43]

The sheriff's sale took place on January 1, 1842, the purchaser being one Hugh T. Reid, an attorney. After that date there were at least two "legal" titles to every acre of the tract— the title based on Mason's decree of May 8, 1841, and the title acquired by Reid eight months later. According to Galland, the same interests were behind both the Mason partition and the sale to Reid,[44] their theory perhaps being that two titles are safer than one when both are questionable. In any event, there were many claimants who were represented neither in Mason's partition nor by Reid, and, in addition, there were numbers of squatters—those who were living on the land without title to it. Little wonder that a group of Dutch immigrants, seeking a place to settle in the late 1840's, shied away from the Half-Breed Tract.

It became clear to us [one of their number wrote] that a purchase in this region was very dangerous because lawsuits were constantly brought to quiet title; while so many people lived there without

[41] Sherman to Corning, Albany, Feb. 28, 1841, CP.
[42] *Laws of the Territory of Iowa, 1839,* 225
[43] Webster *v.* Reid, 11 Howard, 457.
[44] *Iowa Advocate and Half-Breed Journal,* Sept. 1, 1847, in *Annals of Iowa,* 3d ser., X (July, 1912), 456.

being owners of the land that it was far from our thoughts to buy them out.[45]

It was not until 1850 that a decision of the United States Supreme Court invalidated Reid's title to the Half-Breed Tract and thus upheld the partition of 1841.[46]

Efforts by the New York Land Company to sell their holdings in the tract were begun as early as June, 1837, and were carried on thereafter through a series of western agents. The first of these were Joseph Aiken and Robert E. Little. At the same time Isaac Galland was also acting for the company, and he, at least, continued to do so until the partition of 1841. Galland was succeeded by David W. Kilbourne of Fort Madison and Keokuk, who by 1852 was in the bad graces of the company.[47] The company also had an eastern agent, Hiram Barney, a New York City lawyer,[48] who acted as liaison between the stockholders and their western agents. It was Barney who, early in 1852, was largely responsible for replacing the out-of-favor Kilbourne with Charles Mason, the judge who had rendered the decree of partition in 1841.[49]

Mason was not an agent in the usual sense, in that he simply sold land on commission. Rather, he entered into an agreement to purchase all the New York Land Company's property for $225,000, the company to hold a mortgage of $160,000. This was to be paid by Mason's releasing to the company all income from the sale of lands over and above expenses until his indebtedness had been discharged.[50]

[45] Henry Peter Scholte, *"Eene Stem uit Pella"* (Amsterdam, c. 1848), translated by Jacob Van Der Zee as "The Coming of the Hollanders to Iowa," in *Iowa Journal of History and Politics*, IX (Oct., 1911), 539.

[46] Webster *v.* Reid, 11 Howard, 437.

[47] Montrose *Western Adventurer*, Aug. 19, 1837, in *Annals of Iowa*, 3d ser., VII (Jan., 1907), 637; B. L. Wick, "The Struggle for the Half-Breed Tract," *Annals of Iowa*, 3d ser., VII (April, 1905), 21; David W. Kilbourne to Delavan, Fort Madison, Iowa, May 4, 1852 (copy), CP.

[48] Barney, at one time a law partner of Benjamin F. Butler, was collector of the Port of New York in the early years of the Lincoln administration (*Lamb's Biographical Dictionary of the United States* [Boston, 1900–1903], I, 199).

[49] Hiram Barney to Corning, New York (?), Feb., 1852 (?), CP.

[50] *Ibid.*; Barney to Corning, New York, June 21, 1852, CP; Mason Diary, March

In the seven years between 1852 and 1859 circumstances combined to prove Mason's undoing. Not only was he harassed by the squatters on the company lands, who resented having to pay for their farms, but he had to deal with at least three additional difficulties. Most serious of these was an oversight in the contract that he had signed by which it was not made mandatory upon the New York Land Company that it release its mortgage on parcels of land sold by him. When the company refused such releases, it was impossible to give a purchaser a clear title, and consequently Mason was unable to effect many sales. Secondly, in 1853 Mason went to Washington as Commissioner of Patents, leaving his affairs in connection with the Half-Breed Tract in the hands of an agent who proved something less than honest.[51] Finally, there came the panic of 1857.

In the late summer or fall of 1857 Mason offered to release his interest in the Iowa land to the New York Land Company for $80,000. The offer was rejected, but two years later Barney and Mason entered into a compromise. By the terms of this Mason gave up his right to most of the land for which he had contracted in 1852, and the company released its mortgage on the smaller acreage that Mason retained.[52] Mason felt that he had been cheated of $50,000 in the settlement, but Barney maintained that the New York company had given the former judge $150,000 in property rather than have any further connection with him.[53]

As the years went by, Erastus Corning's investment in the New York Land Company grew. His original share had been one twenty-fourth of the whole, but by 1842 he owned a little

---

16, 1859, in Remey, "Life and Letters of Charles Mason," III, ch. xii; cf. *ibid.*, I, ch. vi.

[51] Mason Diary, Sept. 19, 1857, July 18, July 22, 1859, in Remey, "Life and Letters of Charles Mason," III, ch. xii.

[52] Mason Diary, July 18, 1859, *ibid.*

[53] Barney to Corning, Washington, April 17, 1860, CP. Mason was not to forget the ill-treatment which he felt that he had suffered at the hands of Barney and the members of the New York Land Company. When in April, 1860, Barney and Corning were suggested as two incorporators of the Pacific Railroad, Mason, who had a part in preparing the railroad bill for Congress, objected, and both names were dropped (*ibid.*).

in excess of one-eighth of the company's stock, and by 1863 he was in possession of approximately one-quarter of it. Of the original members of the company, five had withdrawn by 1842, although their loss was offset in part by the appearance of two new stockholders—"Wiggin & Co." and "Goodwin & Fisher." By 1850 John T. Norton, Corning's former Albany partner, was also a member of the company. Fifteen years later the company consisted of Corning, Edward C. Delavan, Samuel Marsh, a man named Cambreling (perhaps the same Churchill C. Cambreling with whom Corning had been associated in the early days of the Mohawk and Hudson), and Horatio and John Seymour, the last two having inherited the original interest of their father, Henry Seymour.[54]

Opinions as to the value of the Half-Breed lands varied from time to time. In December, 1840, Hiram Barney estimated the worth of the whole 119,000-acre tract at $1,200,000. Six months later Charles Mason was telling his sister-in-law that the 2,350 acres she claimed were worth at least $10,000. This was about $4.25 an acre, and at that rate the whole tract would have brought approximately half a million. A decade later, in September, 1850, some members of the New York Land Company seem to have considered the sale of the company's holdings to David W. Kilbourne for two-thirds or three-quarters of the $150,000 that had been invested by the stockholders.[55] The price under consideration then, for what constituted perhaps 40 per cent of the Half-Breed Tract, was not more than $115,-000. At that rate all the lands in the tract would have brought perhaps $300,000. But in 1852 the New York Land Company actually entered into the agreement with Mason by the terms of which the company was to exchange its holdings for a promised $225,000—a sum that was probably not very far removed from Mason's estimate of the land's worth twelve years before. When in 1856 Mason was so far behind in his pay-

[54] Barney to Corning, New York, Sept. 8, 1842, Dec. 7, 1865; John T. Norton to Corning, Albany, Sept. 11, 1850; Corning to Barney, Albany, Oct. 29, 1863: CP.

[55] Delavan to Corning, Albany, Dec. 9, 1840; Norton to Corning, Albany, Sept. 11, 1850: CP; Mason to Sophia Farrar, Burlington, Iowa, May 10, 1841, in Remey, "Life and Letters of Charles Mason," I, ch. vi.

ments that he had to enter into new arrangements with Barney, he contracted to pay $375,000 to the company, but he still felt that he was getting a bargain, for by that time he believed himself "the possessor of property worth half a million or more." [56]

From the information that is available, it is impossible to tell whether or not, in the long run, the New York Land Company and its individual investors realized a profit, since no inclusive statistics or expressions of opinion have come to light. In the case of Corning, however, a few figures have been found. According to the articles of association that were drawn up in 1836, Corning committed himself to an expenditure of $6,250, but by 1850 his investment in the Half-Breed venture amounted to more than $18,000.[57] By the middle of the 1860's, when he was the owner of a one-quarter interest in the company, his investment had increased accordingly.

At the time that Mason entered into his contract with the New Yorkers in 1852, Corning probably received about $8,000. When that contract was renegotiated in 1856 and Mason promised to pay the company $375,000, the sum earmarked for Corning was $38,123.35, and by August of that year he had been paid $1,334.32 of that amount.[58] It is unlikely, however, that the company received much, if anything, from Mason after that. On the other hand, it is doubted that it lost anything on the transaction with the Iowan, for while the lands were in his care he was responsible for all expenses, including taxes, and the bulk of the property—once described by Barney as "the garden of the world" [59]—was reclaimed by the company in 1859.

Corning continued to believe in the ultimate worth of the venture, for he continued to buy the shares of his more faint-

---

[56] Delavan to Corning, Ballston Centre, N.Y., Sept. 17, 1853; Barney to Corning, New York, July 9, 1856: CP; Mason Diary, Nov. 2, 1856, in Remey, "Life and Letters of Charles Mason," III, ch. xii.

[57] "Articles of Association of the New York Land Company," 438–439; Norton to Corning, Albany, Sept. 11, 1850, CP.

[58] Norton to Corning, Albany, Sept. 11, 1850; Barney to Corning, New York, July 9, Aug. 11, 1856: CP.

[59] Delavan to Corning, Albany, Dec. 9, 1840, CP.

hearted partners who withdrew from the company. During the 1860's he was rewarded for his trust by the receipt from Barney of small, irregular, but frequent sums "collected in Iowa on half-Breed interests." [60]

The holdings of the New York Land Company, unlike those of similar companies in which Corning was an investor, were never divided, at least during Corning's lifetime. In the beginning there had been the matter of the disputed title to militate against division. Later, the "sale" to Mason lulled the stockholders, including Corning, into believing that they had disposed of their property. After the company's repossession of its holdings in 1859 Corning's interest in his Michigan and Wisconsin lands far outstripped his concern with matters in Iowa.

[60] See, for instance, Corning to Barney, Oct. 29, 1863, Aug. 19, Sept. 22, 1864, CP.

· IX ·

Later Speculations in the West

ALL the land speculations that have been discussed in Chapters VII and VIII dated from the 1830's. Two of the largest in which Corning became interested, however, were of a later vintage. In these—one in Michigan, the other in Wisconsin— he invested much money, and to them he gave a great deal of attention. Both differed from his earlier land ventures in that he and his fellow promoters were to be the recipients of large acreages in return for financing the construction of public works.

The speculation in Wisconsin grew out of a grant by Congress in 1846 of some 260,000 acres of public land to Wisconsin Territory to finance the building of a canal through the portage between the Fox and Wisconsin Rivers and to aid in the carrying out of other improvements in the old route between Lake Superior and the Mississippi. The territory (and, after 1848, the state) moved slowly with the project. In 1851 the legislature let a contract for that section of the work which was on the lower Fox to Morgan L. Martin of Green Bay. When in 1853 it was decided to turn over the entire project to a private contractor, Martin, who by then had invested heavily in the venture, brought about the organization of the Fox and Wisconsin Improvement Company. The new company undertook the completion of the improved waterway in exchange for the bulk of the land grant of 1846 and the income from the improvement itself for a period of twenty years.[1]

[1] Joseph Schafer, *The Winnebago-Horicon Basin* (Madison, Wis., 1937), 97,

Shortly after the organization of the company the Wisconsin investors, in the words of Martin, "were compelled to seek outside capital to swing the growing enterprise." Accordingly, they appealed to a group of New Yorkers. Martin's original contact was with William J. Averill and Isaac Seymour of New York City, but soon Erastus Corning, Hiram Barney, and Horatio Seymour were also drawn into the venture. Isaac Seymour was cashier of the Bank of North America and a business associate of Martin's brother.[2] He and Corning were old acquaintances, for in the 1830's Seymour had been cashier of the Westchester County Bank at Peekskill, New York, and had made weekly reports to Corning, who had an interest in the bank.[3] Perhaps it was Seymour who first drew Corning's attention to the Fox and Wisconsin Improvement Company or, more likely, drew the company's attention to Corning. In any event, on June 1, 1855, Hiram Barney wrote to the Albany capitalist:

Time is short in which to make the arrangement with the Fox and Wisconsin Co. They have very good propositions for all the money they want and I have had some difficulty in preventing acceptance. They will give better terms to you and Gov[ernor Horatio] S[eymour] than to anybody else because they want the benefit of your cooperation, which they consider of great importance. . . .

They require less money than I supposed—not more, they say, than $100,000.[4]

By mid-August, Corning, Horatio Seymour, and Barney had entered into what Barney called "a pact of purchase of said Co."

104, 106, 112, 116. Chapters vi and vii of this book are devoted to a detailed account of the Fox-Wisconsin improvement, including the financial and political aspects.

[2] *Ibid.*, 106–107, 119; "Narrative of Morgan L. Martin," *Collections of the State Historical Society of Wisconsin*, XI (1888), 413; *Merchant's and Banker's Almanac for 1854* (New York, 1854), xxv. Horatio Seymour, who was apparently unrelated to Isaac, was governor of New York in 1853–1855 and 1863–1865. Horatio and John F. Seymour, who was later president of the Fox and Wisconsin Improvement Company, were brothers.

[3] See, for instance, Isaac Seymour to Erastus Corning, Peekskill, N.Y., Oct. 7, Nov. 25, 1833, CP.

[4] Hiram Barney to Erastus Corning, New York, June 1, 1855, CP

At the annual stockholders' meeting Corning was elected president, succeeding Otto Tank of Green Bay.[5] The New Yorker's term was short. Preparing to go to Europe at the end of 1855 and planning to be away for some months, he resigned as president of the company, as it was "absolutely necessary for that officer to execute papers."[6] Morgan L. Martin was elected in his place. In 1858 John F. Seymour of Utica, New York, was president. By that time Samuel Marsh of Boston and perhaps Nathaniel Thayer of the same city had also become stockholders in the company. Subsequent to 1859 Edward C. Delavan of Albany was likewise a stockholder.[7]

In the meantime, by dint of successful lobbying in Washington, the Improvement Company had twice persuaded Congress to reinterpret and amend the terms of the original land grant and in this manner succeeded in increasing its claims by approximately 425,000 acres.[8] This still left it somewhat short of the 884,000 acres which were at one time claimed as rightfully belonging to the company,[9] but the total acreage finally granted was perhaps three times that which was promised in the company's original contract.

It should thus occasion no surprise that the New Yorkers were convinced that they had a good thing. A letter from Barney to Corning, dated December 27, 1855, reflected the general optimism. In November, Barney reported, the first boat had passed through the waterway from Green Bay, its eastern terminus, to Lake Winnebago, and already produce was beginning to pile up awaiting spring transportation. Indeed, Barney doubted if sufficient boats would be available to handle the anticipated freight. For a ten-year lease of the tolls the company had been offered 10.5 per cent per annum on the

---

[5] Barney to Corning, New York, Aug. 16, 1855, CP; Schafer, *Winnebago-Horicon Basin*, 123.

[6] Barney to Corning, New York, Dec. 27, 1855, CP.

[7] Barney to Corning, New York, Dec. 27, 1855, July 12, 1856; Corning to Drexel and Company, Albany, June 21, 1858: CP; Corning to John F. Seymour, Albany July 18, 1859, Seymour Papers, Wisconsin Historical Society, Madison, Wis.

[8] Schafer, *Winnebago-Horicon Basin*, 112–113, 118–123.

[9] Barney to Corning, New York, June 1, 1855, CP.

capital stock. Land sales, too, were going well, the company's
agent having sold between October 1 and November 25 some
10,000 acres of what Barney described as the poorest lands at
an average price of $3.60 an acre, one-half cash, one-quarter
in two years, and the final quarter in three years, with 8 per
cent annual interest on the delayed payments.[10]

Approximately four years later, in August, 1859, with the
improvement still uncompleted, Corning wrote to John F.
Seymour: "I think if the share holders pay sufficient calls to put
the Co out of debt and finish the work the owners may look
forward with confidence for remuneration—and they will hold
a good property." [11]

Corning as president of the New York Central could promise
Seymour that "a line of Propellors" would be put on from
Buffalo to Green Bay "and run regular." [12] Apparently prospective shippers, irked by the irregularity of vessels on the waterway and the lakes (and by the tendency of the owners to charge
high rates), had in the past often turned to other transportation routes, for in February and March, 1860, John F. Seymour
was in Wisconsin "adjusting rates of tolls and getting river
boats to run on time and on agreed prices for freight." Toward
the end of March he wrote to Corning, expressing the hope that
"the regularity of the New York Central propellors & the river
boats will increase business." [13] Perhaps traffic on the waterway
was increased by these and other measures, but nonetheless, by
the end of 1860, the Fox and Wisconsin Improvement Company was unmistakably insolvent.

The reasons for the failure of the company were clear. In
the first place, the panic of 1857 and its aftermath had reduced
anticipated land sales, while much land which had been sold
on credit reverted to the company. Secondly, although the
waterway was opened for navigation all the way from Green

[10] Barney to Corning, New York, Dec. 27, 1855, CP.
[11] Corning to J. F. Seymour, Albany, Aug. 11, 1859, Seymour Papers.
[12] *Ibid.*
[13] J. F. Seymour to Corning, Chicago, March 26, 1860; see also Barney to Corning, New York, Dec. 27, 1855: CP.

Bay to the Wisconsin in the spring of 1860,[14] there was much work yet to be done on it, and despite the earlier confidence of the promoters, income from tolls was negligible.

In December, 1859, Morgan L. Martin had charged that there was a deliberate policy on the part of the eastern directors to allow the Improvement Company to fail in order that they might profit by the failure.[15] Subsequent events would seem to give some credence to Martin's contention, but the persons whom Martin was accusing were at the time making valiant efforts to save the concern.

The eastern directors raised some money on their personal notes, taking twice the amount in bonds to use as collateral. Martin got a bill through the legislature permitting an increase of $1,500,000 in the company's stock, which the directors issued, but without noticeably affecting the market for their securities. They tried to sell lands in England and in Germany. They made the bondholders fund their coupons for three years. But all to little purpose. The company was going on the rocks.[16]

Early in 1861 the Wisconsin legislature, at the request of John F. Seymour, enacted a bill that permitted the sale of the Improvement Company, including its lands and works in perpetuity, for a sum sufficient to pay its indebetdness and complete the waterway.[17] In June, 1865, the property of the company was offered for sale under this law, the minimum price being set at $3,325,028.59. Although the sale was kept open for three months, no purchaser appeared. An appeal was then made to the court for permission to sell for whatever the property would bring. Permission having been granted, the tangible assets of the company were placed on the block a second time. The sale was held at Appleton, Wisconsin, between February 1 and 5, 1866. The amount which the property actually brought

[14] Circular, dated at Appleton, Wis., March 26, 1860, CP.

[15] Martin to Horatio Seymour, Green Bay, Wis., Dec. 5, 1859, Seymour Family Papers, Collection of Regional History, Cornell University, Ithaca, N.Y.

[16] Schafer, *Winnebago-Horicon Basin*, 126.

[17] *Ibid.; Laws of the State of Wisconsin, 1861*, ch. 289, pp. 306–309.

was approximately $300,000, only about one-tenth of the sum
set as a minimum eight months earlier. The purchasers were
the eastern shareholders in the Fox and Wisconsin Improvement Company, Erastus Corning among them.[18]

The easterners bought as a group, not as individuals. Corning seems to have subscribed $50,000 of the total purchase price,
and Samuel Marsh a like amount. A few months after the Appleton sale, in June, 1866, the purchasers formed themselves
into the Green Bay and Mississippi Canal Company, which was
projected as a $3,000,000 concern.[19] Second thought, how-
ever, dictated a lower capitalization, for, as Barney said,

the capital will probably be taxed and . . . it will be otherwise
injurious to the reputation and interests of the Company to state
it too high. We here [in New York City] concur in the opinion that
one million is large enough.[20]

The Green Bay and Mississippi Canal Company, of which
Corning was a director, took over the lands as well as the works,
leases, contracts, and franchises of the defunct Fox and Wisconsin Improvement Company,[21] but it held only brief title to the
lands, which were soon divided among the individual stock-

[18] Circular signed by Charles Butler, Alexander Spaulding, and M. M. Davis,
dated at New York, April, 1865; Barney to Corning, Lake Huron, June 21,
1865; same to same, New York, Dec. 7, 1865; Samuel Marsh to Corning, New
York, May 4, 1866: CP.

[19] Barney to Corning, New York, Dec. 27, 1865, May 16, 1866; Marsh to Corning, New York, May 4, 1866: CP.

[20] Barney to Corning, New York, May 17, 1866, CP.

[21] The Green Bay and Mississippi Canal Company ultimately completed the
planned work on the Fox River and on the canal which connected that river
with the Wisconsin, thus fulfilling its contract. No land had been appropriated
for the improvement of the Wisconsin, the early engineers having assumed that
it was navigable in its natural state. For much of its length, however, sand bars
prohibited the passage of all but the smallest boats. In 1872 the federal government determined to work on the Wisconsin and, as a preliminary, bought out
the navigation rights of the Green Bay and Mississippi Canal Company in the
entire Fox-Wisconsin waterway. Ultimately hundreds of thousands of dollars
were spend on the Wisconsin, but because of the propensity of the river to "fill
up," it remained unnavigable for larger vessels (Schafer, *Winnebago-Horicon
Basin*, 127–129, 131).

holders.[22] As early as July, 1866, Barney reported to Corning that "work for partition is progressing and we shall be ready to divide the lands . . . next month." [23]

At the time of the Appleton sale the lands of the Improvement Company had amounted to approximately 375,000 acres in the counties of Dunn, Eau Claire, Clark, Wood, Portage, Waupaca, Marquette, Shawano, Brown, and Door and "other of the best portions of the state." [24] Since the entire purchase price of the assets of the company amounted to but $300,000, it follows that the lands came to the easterners at a very low figure. On the assumption that Corning's interest in the purchase was $50,000, or one-sixth of the whole, the Albany capitalist came into possession of some 62,000 acres, much of it land which was covered with valuable stands of pine.

One writer has stated that the easterners bought themselves riches at the Appleton sale.[25] Perhaps they did. As another writer has shown in the case of a similar, though larger, speculation—that of Ezra Cornell on behalf of Cornell University —Wisconsin pinelands, if properly managed and held until a good price could be obtained, yielded large returns.[26]

From his speculation in Michigan in the 1850's Erastus Corning emerged the owner of perhaps 100,000 acres. This venture, like that in Wisconsin, was based on a federal land grant, one that Congress had bestowed upon the state of Michigan in the early 1850's. The grant consisted of three-quarters of a million acres to aid in the construction of a canal around the falls in the

[22] According to Schafer, the Green Bay and Mississippi Canal Company never held title to the lands, and the easterners bought at the sale as individuals (*Winnebago-Horicon Basin*, 127), but Barney in a letter to Corning, May 16, 1866, wrote: "The property purchased will be conveyed by the Trustees to the Company. The lands will then be divided rateably among the purchasers & conveyed by the Company to them" (CP).

[23] Barney to Corning, New York, July 10, 1866, CP.

[24] Circular signed by Charles Butler, Alexander Spaulding, and M. M. Davis, dated at New York, April, 1865, CP.

[25] Schafer, *Winnebago-Horicon Basin*, 127.

[26] Paul Wallace Gates, *The Wisconsin Pine Lands of Cornell University* (Ithaca, N.Y., 1943), 242–243. It has been estimated that the Cornell lands brought a net profit of about $10 an acre (*ibid.*).

Saint Marys River, which joins Lakes Huron and Superior. On April 5, 1853, the legislature of Michigan let the contract for building the canal to a group of eastern capitalists, one of whom was Corning. These men, in turn, assigned the contract to the Saint Mary's Falls Ship Canal Company, of which they themselves were directors and Corning was president. In the course of the next three years the company succeeded in building the canal at a cost of about $1,000,000. When it was turned over to the state of Michigan in the spring of 1855, the Ship Canal Company received as compensation the entire 750,000 acres of land which had been set aside for the purpose.[27]

According to the terms of the grant from Congress the 750,-000 acres were to be chosen from any legally unclaimed public land in Michigan. Therefore, while the canal was under construction, an agent of the Canal Company had selected and laid claim to some 563,000 acres of timberland "favorably situated on good streams" and some 187,000 acres of "mineral" (principally iron ore) land.[28] Most of the mineral land was located in the upper peninsula, 39,000 acres of it in Marquette County.[29] The pinelands, a small proportion of which were so lightly timbered as to be more correctly labeled farm lands, were spread through 38 counties—all but 48,000 of the approximate 563,000 acres in the state's Lower Peninsula.[30]

About the beginning of 1860 the bulk of the Canal Com-

---

[27] See Irene D. Neu, "The Building of the Sault Canal: 1852–1855," *Mississippi Valley Historical Review*, XL (June, 1953), 25–46.

[28] H. W. Walker to Corning, Detroit, April 9, 1853, CP. The selections were designated "St. Mary's Canal Lands" on the land-office books and were held in trust by the state for the Saint Mary's Falls Ship Canal Company (*Laws of Michigan, 1853*, 51).

[29] *Geological Survey of Michigan*, vol. I: *Upper Peninsula, 1869–1873* (New York, 1873), 24.

[30] The largest acreage was in Alcona County, where almost one-seventh of the county's area (about 54,000 acres) was absorbed by the Canal Company. Acreages which the company owned in some other counties were: Montcalm, 45,500; Isabella, 32,000; Mason, 31,000; Mecosta, 30,000; Schoolcraft, 25,000; Oceana, 20,000. Smaller acreages were located in each of the remaining 28 counties in which the company had lands. (Statistics have been compiled from *Catalogue of 525,000 Acres of Pine Timber Lands Belonging to the Saint Mary's Falls Ship Canal Company* [Detroit, 1863].)

pany's mineral land was sold to a newly chartered corporation, the Saint Mary's Canal Mineral Land Company. The price at which the land changed hands was $1.37 an acre, which was just about what it had cost the Canal Company. But no actual money figured in the sale, for the bill was paid in stock of the new company, 5,000 shares (one-quarter of the total number, with a par value of $250,000) being turned over to the Ship Canal Company in exchange for 182,592 acres of land.[31] Most of the remaining stock of the Mineral Land Company was taken by the directors of the Canal Company and their friends in Albany, Boston, and New York. Erastus Corning came to hold 1,825 shares.[32]

In the spring of 1860 the Mineral Land Company transferred 1,650 acres of its recently acquired holdings to another newly organized corporation, the Albany and Boston Mining Company, and received in exchange 5,000 shares of Mining Company stock. (This stock was subsequently distributed among the shareholders of the Mineral Land Company in proportions of one share to four Mineral Land shares.) The remaining shares in the Mining Company fell to the same group who controlled the Mineral Land Company and the Ship Canal Company. Corning, with more than 1,000 shares in the Ship Canal Company and 1,800 in the Mineral Land Company, took 640 shares in the Mining Company.[33]

Toward the end of the Civil War the Saint Mary's Canal Mineral Land Company sold most of its iron lands in Marquette County (about 38,000 acres) to the Iron Cliffs Company, the incorporators of which were William B. Ogden and John W. Foster of Chicago and Samuel J. Tilden of New York. The reported sale price was $500,000, which was approximately $13 an acre. Cor-

[31] *Laws of New York, 1858*, ch. 228, pp. 368–371; Corning to Erastus Fairbanks, Albany, Feb. 8, 1860, CP; Report of Cyrus Woodman [to the directors of the Saint Mary's Canal Mineral Land Company?], Sept. 1, 1863, Woodman Papers, Wisconsin Historical Society, Madison, Wis.

[32] John N. Denison to Corning, Boston, Aug. 3, Aug. 5, 1865, CP. Denison was treasurer of the Mineral Land Company.

[33] Cyrus Woodman to John V. L. Pruyn, Boston, June 11, 1863; Fred Beck to Corning, Boston, March 11, 1864; circular of Saint Mary's Canal Mineral Land Company, undated but endorsed 1864, signed by J. N. Denison: CP.

ning subscribed to 400 shares of Iron Cliffs stock.[34] Another sale by the Mineral Land Company, this one negotiated in 1865, was that of a quarter section of copper land to the Calumet & Hecla Company for $60,000. It was on this quarter section that that company's famous mine was later located.[35]

During the three years from March, 1863, to February, 1866, the Saint Mary's Canal Mineral Land Company paid its stockholders dividends amounting to at least 90 per cent of the par value of the stock, or $45 a share. A single dividend of 38 per cent, paid in 1864, probably represented the profits from the sale to the Iron Cliffs Company.[36] Corning's share of this was $33,075, and his dividends for the three years under discussion amounted to at least $82,000.[37]

While the mineral lands of the Saint Mary's Falls Ship Canal Company were being disposed of in the manner that has just been described, there was a movement afoot, seemingly spearheaded by Corning, to divide the company's timber lands among the stockholders. As early as February, 1860, Corning had written to a friend:

In my Judgement the Pine Lands of the Canal Co had best be divided and each one in interest take care of their own. . . . In doing so we save an expensive organization—and individuals can arrange with an Agent to sell the Lands for Commission on sales.[38]

[34] Samuel J. Tilden to Corning, New York, Oct. 18, 1864, CP; *Geological Survey of Michigan*, I, 24, 38. The Iron Cliffs Company later merged with the Cleveland Iron Mining Company to form the Cleveland-Cliffs Iron Company (*Robert D. Fisher Mining Manual*, I, in *Robert D. Fisher Manual of Valuable and Worthless Securities*, VII [1940]).

[35] *Geological Survey of Michigan*, I, 24; Anthony S. Wax, "Calumet and Hecla Copper Mines: An Episode in the Economic Development of Michigan," *Michigan History Magazine*, XVI (Winter, 1932), 16. In 1873 the Calumet and Hecla mine was estimated to be worth $13,000,000 (*Geological Survey of Michigan*, I, 24).

[36] Denison to Corning, Boston, March 14, 1863, undated letter (but endorsed 1864), Aug. 3, 1865, Feb. 20, 1866; John W. Brooks to Corning, Boston, April 20, 1863: CP.

[37] Corning remained a director of the Saint Mary's Canal Mineral Land Company until his death in 1872. In 1901 the company was succeeded by the Saint Mary's Mineral Land Company, which was subsequently sold to the Copper Range Company (*Robert D. Fisher Manual of Valuable and Worthless Securities*, VI [1938], 820).

[38] Corning to Schuyler Livingston, Albany, Feb. 14, 1860, CP.

In his wish for division Corning was seconded by Erastus Fairbanks, another of the company's directors, but he was opposed by at least three other directors—John Murray Forbes, John W. Brooks, and John N. A. Griswold.[39] It was not until 1862, after an abortive attempt had been made by the company to sell some of its timber land,[40] that these men withdrew their opposition and consented to a division, "provided a good scheme could be worked out for doing it." [41] At this time there remained in the possession of the Canal Company something in excess of 500,000 acres.

During the spring and summer of 1863 a method of dividing the lands was agreed on; the actual division was carried out by Cyrus Woodman, one of the most skillful land agents and speculators ever to operate in the Old Northwest. The lands of the Canal Company were broken up into 744 groups, ranging in size from forty to several thousand acres. A minimum valuation, based on the quality and quantity of its timber and the distance from floating water, was set upon each group. According to orders from the directors of the company the valuations were to average $2.10 an acre; as set by Woodman the actual average per acre was $2.20.[42]

The division was to take the form of an auction at Detroit on September 2, 1863. A catalogue issued in anticipation of the event, besides listing and describing each of the groups, set forth the method of sale:

[39] Livingston to Corning, New York, Feb. 11, 1860, CP. No expression of opinion from the Bostonians concerning their stand on this question has been found, but it is likely that they were reluctant to assume the personal management of their lands. When the canal lands were finally divided, the Boston stockholders pooled their holdings and formed themselves into the Michigan Pine Lands Association.

[40] *Catalogue of 125,000 Acres of Valuable Pine Lands in the State of Michigan, Belonging to the St. Mary's Falls Ship Canal Comp'y* (Detroit, 1862), 3; Fairbanks to Corning, St. Johnsbury, Vt., June 23, 1862, CP; Larry Gara, *Westernized Yankee: The Story of Cyrus Woodman* (Madison, Wis., 1956), 155.

[41] Pruyn to Corning, Albany, Nov. 29, 1862, CP.

[42] *Catalogue of 525,000 Acres . . . Belonging to the Saint Mary's Falls Ship Canal Company*, viii. Woodman's average has been compiled from the acreages and valuations as listed in the catalogue. On Woodman, see Gara, *Westernized Yankee*, and Irene D. Neu, "Land Credit in Frontier Wisconsin" (unpublished master's thesis, Cornell University, Ithaca, N.Y., 1945), 62–68.

The lands . . . will be offered as they have been arranged in groups, and will all be put up at the same time. . . . The person bidding the highest premium will be entitled to select a single group or more, or all of those offered as he may determine. . . .

If one is the highest bidder at five cents per acre, and buys 500 acres he will pay $25 as a premium above the minimum price of the group or groups which he may select.[43]

The sale was open both to stockholders in the Canal Company and to the general public. All premiums were payable immediately. Stockholders were required to pay 10 per cent of their purchases in cash or the bonds of the Canal Company, but the remaining 90 per cent might be paid in stock, at the option of the purchaser. The terms of purchase for those who were not stockholders were one-half down and the remainder in one year with interest at 7 per cent, payable either in money or in the bonds of the company. Both stock and bonds were to be accepted at par, and it was expected that the exchange of bonds for land, together with the cash payments, would meet all the company's outstanding obligations.[44]

In preparation for the sale Erastus Corning purchased additional Canal Company stock, obtaining 46 shares from John F. Winslow, his partner in the Troy ironworks; 179 shares from Gilbert C. Davidson, his Albany partner; 28 shares from his son, Erastus Corning, Jr., 112 shares from G. H. Thacher of Albany; and 100 shares from an unknown source.[45] Nor is it probable that the 465 shares listed here represent the full extent of his purchases at this time, for these added to the 1,080 shares which he held in June, 1863,[46] amounted to but 1,545 shares, whereas

[43] *Catalogue of 525,000 Acres . . . Belonging to the Saint Mary's Falls Ship Canal Company*, xi.

[44] *Ibid.*, viii; circular of Saint Mary's Falls Ship Canal Company, signed by Woodman, dated at Boston, Aug. 5, 1863, CP.

[45] John F. Winslow to Corning, Troy, Aug. 21, 1863; Corning to Brooks, Albany (?), Sept. 22, 1863; Gilbert C. Davidson to Corning, Albany, Sept. 1, 1863 (two letters): CP; Corning to Woodman, Albany, Aug. 24, 1863, Woodman Papers. All these shares were purchased at a discount, the value of Canal Company stock having fallen as a result of the company's inability to pay its debts (*New York Times*, Oct. 13, 1862).

[46] Woodman to Pruyn, Boston, June 11, 1863, CP.

a closer estimate of the actual number of shares which he held about the time of the land sale would be in the vicinity of 2,500.[47]

Corning, Forbes, Brooks, and Fairbanks all journeyed to Detroit for the auction, which was a great success. Lands valued at $900,000 were sold, the majority to stockholders, but some to outsiders. Sales to Corning accounted for at least one-quarter of the total, and perhaps more, for he obligated himself to pay $26,686.24 in cash. Since this represented one-tenth of the cost of the land which he purchased and since the average price per acre was $2.20, it seems safe to assume that he came into possession of an amount approaching 100,000 acres.[48]

Extensive as they were, the former Canal Company lands were not Corning's only holdings in Michigan. As early as 1836 he had acquired title to more than 5,500 acres in the Kalamazoo land district alone. In 1854 he owned no less than 1,000 acres in Branch County, 640 acres in Kalamazoo County, and 1,120 acres in Ottawa County—a total of 2,760 acres. In 1855 he was buying Michigan land on joint account with one of the Canal Company agents, the land being paid for in military warrants.[49] By December, 1859, he was represented in Michigan

[47] He subsequently exchanged some 2,400 shares for land and in Nov., 1863, remarked, "I find that I shall have some 8 or 9 thousand dollars stock [that is, 80 or 90 shares] over paying for the land purchased" (Corning to George S. Frost, Albany, Nov. 1, 1863, CP).

[48] Gara, *Westernized Yankee*, 157; Brooks to Corning, Boston, Feb. 16, 1864, CP. Brooks's letter simply states that Corning owes the Canal Company $26,686.24 on account of land purchased. Inasmuch as the whole of the purchase price could have been paid in cash, it can be argued that this figure may represent more than one-tenth of the cost of the land that was bought and therefore that the amount of land actually purchased was less than has been stated. But in March, 1864, Corning still held 80 shares of Canal Company stock (Corning to Woodman, Albany, March 12, 1864, Woodman Papers), so it hardly seems reasonable that he would have chosen to pay more than the required 10 per cent in cash. A distribution of Canal Company assets in Feb., 1864, reduced Corning's cash obligation for lands to $3,593.17 (Brooks to Corning, Boston, Feb. 16, 1864, CP).

[49] Abstracts of lands sold, Kalamazoo, 1836, in General Land Office, Washington, D.C. (I am indebted to Professor Paul Wallace Gates of Cornell University for this item); Corning to John F. King, Albany, April 21, 1854; to John Hall, Albany, April 26, 1854; to E. S. Swan, Albany, Nov. 9, 1854; Erastus Corning, Jr., to Corning, Albany, Nov. 19, 1855: CP.

by at least five land agents: Elias S. Swan of White Pigeon,
John Wells of Port Huron, Murphy and Baxter of Jonesville,
J. L. Whiting and Company of Detroit, and R. W. Landon of
Niles. The Jonesville, Detroit, and Niles agents managed a total
of 6,182 acres for him.[50] These were probably all farm lands,
for in June, 1859, Corning had remarked, "I am not the owner
of Pine Timbered Land to any extent." [51] This, of course, was
before the division of the Canal Company lands. Subsequent
to that division Corning continued his independent purchases.
In October, 1863, an agent was locating pinelands for him along
the line of "the new rail road." At the same time the Albany
capitalist was also interested in mineral lands and swamplands
in Michigan neither of which was a legacy from the Canal
Company.[52]

In the spring of 1864 Corning had an opportunity to dispose
of some of his Michigan land at a good profit. At that time
Cyrus Woodman, acting for Corning, E. and T. Fairbanks and
Company and the Michigan Pine Lands Association (which consisted of the Boston stockholders of the Canal Company), negotiated the sale of a 47,000-acre tract on the Pere Marquette
River. The land had been bought from the Canal Company
for $111,692.74. Corning's share of this was $45,151.10, about
40 per cent of the whole. Another 40 per cent had been purchased by E. and T. Fairbanks; the remaining 20 per cent had
been taken by the Bostonians. Woodman sold the entire acreage
to Captain Eber B. Ward of Detroit for $200,000.[53]

According to an agreement that had been made before the
sale, Woodman was to receive as a commission all that he could
get for the land over and above three dollars an acre. Therefore the amount to be divided among Corning, the Fairbankses,
and the Michigan Pine Lands associates was $141,000. Corn-

[50] Corning to Swan, to Murphy and Baxter, to J. L. Whiting and Company,
to R. W. Landon, to John Wells, to H. S. Sanford, all dated at Albany, Dec. 26,
1859, CP.

[51] Corning to James Davis, Albany, June 20, 1859, CP.

[52] Corning to Charles T. Harvey, Albany, Oct. 13, 1863; to Frost, Albany, Oct.
17, 1863, Nov. 19, 1869, Jan. 27, Feb. 1, 1870: CP.

[53] Woodman to Corning, Detroit, April 17, 1864, Woodman Papers.

ing's share of this was about $56,000—$11,000 more than he had invested in the land. Ward's payments were to be spread over a period of four years, and Corning accepted the Detroiter's notes for some $80,000—the sum of his own share and Woodman's commission on that share—at 7 per cent annually. When Ward refused to pay more than 6 per cent, Woodman had to make up the additional 1 per cent.[54]

After the sale of the Pere Marquette acreage, Corning continued to dispose of his canal lands as he disposed of his other holdings in Michigan—in piecemeal fashion whenever he found a buyer for a particular lot. In 1861 he had placed the management of his Michigan lands in the hands of George S. Frost, who at that time was land agent and treasurer of the Canal Company. Frost charged very low commissions, usually 2.5 per cent, sometimes even less than that.[55] But the services of Frost, although cheap, were something short of satisfactory. He was extremely careless, for instance, about keeping the taxes on the lands paid, so that on more than one occasion lots were sold for taxes. By the 1870's Corning was so exasperated with his agent that he hired another agent, Ralph C. Smith of Detroit, to check on Frost.[56]

During Corning's active career the bookkeeping details of his land business were handled by one of the clerks in the Albany hardware store. In the 1850's this person was a Mr. De Witt, who evidently kept a separate set of books in which he recorded deeds, mortgages, and sales. After Corning's retirement from active affairs he took care of his land business himself. If a letter book of this period is any criterion, he devoted much of his time to correspondence with his agents and with prospective buyers. Since his land books have not been pre-

[54] Woodman to Corning, to N. W. Bradley, to James Hinman, to Fairbanks, all dated at Detroit, April 17, 1864; to Corning, Boston, Oct. 28, 1865; to Corning, place illegible, July 13, 1868; Corning to Woodman, Albany, Aug. 24, 1868: Woodman Papers; Woodman to Corning, Cambridge, Mass., Oct. 7, 1868, CP.

[55] Corning to Frost, Albany, Nov. 26, 1861, Jan. 8, 1863 (should be 1864), CP. By contrast with Frost's fees, Woodman's contract with the Michigan Pine Lands Association allowed him 5 per cent commission on all sales, plus one-half of the proceeds over the valuation set upon the various tracts in 1863.

[56] Corning to Frost, Albany, Jan. 27, Feb. 1, 1870, CP.

served, it is impossible to know the extent of his holdings, the amount of his sales, or his profits. It is certain, however, that until the end of his life he regarded western lands as a good investment. At the time of his death it was remarked that "not a little of his property consists of Western lands." [57]

[57] *Albany Ev. Journal*, April 9, 1872.

· X ·

Corning of the Central

IN some respects the most important achievement of Erastus Corning, merchant and entrepreneur, was the creation of the New York Central Railroad. Formed by a merger of the lines between Albany and Troy on the east and Buffalo and Niagara Falls on the west, the Central, chartered in 1853 and capitalized for $23,000,000, was at the time of its founding the largest corporation in America. Corning was to serve as its president for almost a dozen years, and, deservedly or undeservedly, this was to be the phase of his career for which he would be longest remembered.

Neither the consolidation of the roads nor Corning's presidency of the new company was unexpected by his contemporaries. By the middle of the 1840's the first measures had been taken by the railroads of the Central Line toward operating as a unit, and after that time they quite regularly co-operated on such matters as passenger service, the prorating of fares, and immigrant travel. In 1847 the question of the roads' consolidation was before the legislature, and in September of that year a Senate committee reported that a union of the companies would be not only desirable but practicable. A preliminary step was taken in 1850 when the Auburn and Syracuse and the Auburn and Rochester united to form the Rochester and Syracuse. Later that same year the Tonawanda and the Attica and Syracuse were merged, the new company being known as the Buffalo and Rochester.[1] In the spring of 1853 the consolidation of all the roads was decided upon, and Matthew Vassar wrote to Corning: "I understand you are to be the Prest of the first Bord of Directors. This seems to be generaly conceded."[2]

The main factor in the decision to consolidate was the increasing competition for western traffic offered by the other east-west trunk lines: the New York and Erie, opened to Dunkirk in 1851; the Pennsylvania Central, completed to Pittsburgh in 1852; the Baltimore and Ohio, completed to Wheeling in 1853; and the Grand Trunk of Canada, opened between Montreal and Portland, Maine, in that same year. "To retain their control over the western trade and to prepare for the competition of their rivals, the Central roads drew up a plan to consolidate their lines into one system."[3]

Gathered into the New York Central were eight operating railroads and two "paper" roads—that is, roads projected but not built. These were the Mohawk Valley (planned to parallel the Utica and Schenectady on the south side of the Mohawk) and the Syracuse and Utica Direct. According to the terms of the consolidation agreement, the capital stock of the new corporation was set at $22,858,600, consisting of 228,586 shares of

[1] Harry H. Pierce, *Railroads of New York: A Study of Government Aid, 1826–1875* (Cambridge, Mass., 1953), 64–65; Frank W. Stevens, *The Beginnings of the New York Central Railroad* (New York, 1926), 198, 227, 317–330; *Documents of the Senate of the State of New York, Seventieth Session, 1847* (Albany, 1847), no. 149.

[2] Letter dated at Poughkeepsie, N.Y., March 28, 1853, CP.

[3] Pierce, *Railroads of New York*, 78–79; John Christie to Erastus Corning, New York, Jan. 21, 1850; Isaac Newton to Corning, New York, March 1, 1850; Dean Richmond to Corning, Buffalo, N.Y., Dec. 14, 1852: CP. The Central Line was always in a highly competitive situation where through traffic was concerned, but until the Erie was opened to Dunkirk, the Central roads' local traffic, the heaviest of any line in the United States, had been fairly secure. The main managerial problem, the lowering of costs while maintaining through rates, had been mitigated by the profits from the local business. The completion of the Erie menaced this desirable state of affairs. Not only did that road tap through eastbound traffic at a point west of the Central's Buffalo terminus, but "first by canals and later by branches to Buffalo and Rochester it could draw off the Central's longest-haul local traffic" (Thomas C. Cochran, *Railroad Leaders, 1845–1890: The Business Mind in Action* [Cambridge, Mass., 1953], 26).

$100 each.[4] This permitted a share-for-share exchange of stock in the old companies, including the merely projected roads, for stock in the new corporation.[5]

In addition to the exchange of their stock, shareholders in the old companies were paid a premium based on the value of the "estate, property and franchises of the said companies" and on the price at which the stocks of those companies had been selling in the market. These premiums, which were in the form of 30-year, 6 per cent bonds of the new company, ranged from 55 per cent in the case of the Utica and Schenectady and the Mohawk Valley to 17 per cent in the case of the Albany and Schenectady. No premium was paid the shareholders of the Schenectady and Troy, as the stock of that company "is not considered worth its nominal or par value, and its new stock is made subject to the further payment to the new company of $25 on each share." The convertible bonds and funded debts of the old companies were assumed by the new company; all other indebtedness and liabilities were to be paid by the old companies.[6]

In the events leading up to consolidation of the roads the president of the Utica and Schenectady played the leading part.[7] It was on motion of Corning at a meeting of the Central lines in Albany, on February 12, 1851, that it was resolved to

[4] *Agreement . . . Whereby the Said Companies Are Consolidated into . . . "The New York Central Railroad Company"* (Albany, 1854), 10. The capital might be increased by the conversion of bonds to $23,085,600 (*ibid.*).

[5] *Ibid.* An exception was made in the case of the Buffalo and Rochester. The shares of that road had a par value of but $50 each, so two of its shares were exchanged for one share of the new company.

[6] *Ibid.*, 12–13, 18–21. Other premiums were: Syracuse and Utica, 50 per cent; Syracuse and Utica Direct, 50 per cent; Buffalo and Rochester, 40 per cent; Rochester and Syracuse, 30 per cent; Rochester, Lockport and Niagara Falls, 25 per cent; and Buffalo and Lockport, 25 per cent (*ibid.*, 19–20). The most detailed account of the consolidation is to be found in Stevens, *Beginnings of the New York Central*, ch. xvii.

[7] Henry B. Gibson to Corning, Canandaigua, N.Y., Jan. 15, 1853; Azariah Boody to Corning, New York, Jan. 22, 1853; T. Tilston to Corning, New York, Feb. 21, 1853; Jacob Gould to Corning, Rochester, N.Y., April 1, 1853: CP. See also Edward Hungerford, *Men and Iron: The History of New York Central* (New York, 1938), 70; Stevens, *Beginnings of the New York Central*, 351.

apply to the legislature for a law authorizing "any two or more Companies on this Line to consolidate their stock and become one Company." [8] During the two years which passed before the legislature complied with the railroads' request, Corning placed himself in charge of the lines' Albany lobby and made a personal appeal to Thurlow Weed, whose Whig party was at that time in power. As in the case of the incorporation of the Saint Mary's Falls Ship Canal Company, Weed was able to meet the request of his old friend.[9] The New York Central Consolidation Bill became law on April 2, 1853.

Even before the law was passed, Corning was working out the terms of the merger, and it was well understood by all that his would be the decisive word.[10] On May 13, one week after a committee of the roads had reached final agreement as to terms and four days before the agreement was to be signed, John V. L. Pruyn, who was acting as secretary, felt free to "alter the rate of the Schdy & Troy Road," upon instructions from Corning.[11]

When the stockholders of the New York Central met for the first time on July 6, 1853, Corning held proxies for a large majority of the shares.[12] He therefore had the most important voice in choosing the first board of directors and in electing the first officers: himself as president, Dean Richmond of Buffalo as vice-president, and Pruyn as secretary and treasurer. Thus the Albany merchant placed himself at the head of a $23,000,000 corporation and, according to Russell Sage, earned a reputation as one of the greatest railroad men in the country.[13]

---

[8] Stevens, *Beginnings of the New York Central,* 351.

[9] Horace White to Corning, Syracuse, N.Y., Jan. 11, Jan. 18, 1853, CP; Glyndon G. Van Deusen, *Thurlow Weed, Wizard of the Lobby* (Boston, 1947), 225. For the role which Weed later played in influencing legislation favorable to the New York Central, see *ibid.,* 225–226, and Sidney D. Brummer, *Political History of New York State during the Period of the Civil War* (New York, 1911), 42–45.

[10] Boody to Corning, New York, Jan. 22, 1853; Matthew Vassar to Corning, Poughkeepsie, March 28, 1853; Gould to Corning, Rochester, April 4, 1853: CP.

[11] John V. L. Pruyn to Corning, Albany, May 13, 1853, CP.

[12] Stevens, *Beginnings of the New York Central,* 375.

[13] Russell Sage to Corning, Washington, Dec. 20, 1853, CP. Dean Richmond (1813–1866), a "prosperous dealer and shipper" of Buffalo, was connected with

At the time of consolidation Corning was listed as entitled to but 1,531 shares in the new company and $77,500 in consolidation bonds.[14] The last figure represents the premium that was paid to him as a stockholder in the old companies, but it does not represent the total of his profits from consolidation, as will be demonstrated. Furthermore, there is some doubt that 1,531 is the correct figure for his shareholdings in the new corporation. Is was his practice to carry stock in his various investments in the names of other persons, and in this instance he surely did so, for it would have been out of character for him to invite public censure by disclosing the true extent of his stake in the New York Central and therefore of his profits from the merger.

As it was, the new corporation and its directors did not escape editorial notice. The *New York Times* remarked upon "the very seductive terms of consolidation," implying that "the initiated managers" were probably profiting thereby. Henry V. Poor, editor of the *American Railroad Journal,* initially approved the consolidation itself but later condemned in explicit language what he called the excessive "watering" that accompanied the merger. The Central would be obliged repeatedly to borrow money, he pointed out, in order to meet the interest on the debt incurred for paying the premiums, and in the end the shipper would pay the bill.[15] After the election of the

---

the Buffalo and Rochester and the Buffalo and State Line railroads. He was also a politician. By 1860 he was the leader of the Regency and chairman of the Democratic State Committee. He was described by a contemporary as "destitute of all literary furnishment," but it was generally agreed that he was remarkably shrewd and able. See D. S. Alexander, *A Political History of the State of New York* (New York, 1906–1923), II, 271–272; Brummer, *Political History of New York during the Civil War,* 25; Cochran, *Railroad Leaders,* 24–25, 452–453; Henry B. Stanton, *Random Recollections,* 3d ed. (New York, 1887), 183.

[14] Record of New York Central Stockholders, 1853; Bond Account with Stockholders, 1853: both in Treasurer's Office, New York Central System, 466 Lexington Avenue, New York City. I am indebted to Professor Harry H. Pierce of Syracuse University for these items, as well as for the references in footnotes 32, 34, 62, and 66, below.

[15] *New York Times,* April 16, 1853; *American Railroad Journal,* IX (April 23, 1853), 266; X (May 27, 1854), 330–331.

first board of directors in early July, 1853, Horace Greeley's *Tribune* growled:

We find the dissatisfaction with the composition of the Board of Direction of the New-York Central Railroad is very general, and is not, it is intimated, confined to stockholders. An interest of many millions held in New-York and Boston is entirely unrepresented in the Board, while very small interests in other quarters were taken care of.[16]

Had the editors of the *Times,* the *American Railroad Journal,* and the *Tribune* known more details of the New York Central consolidation, their criticism might have been even more severe, for as a modern authority has pointed out, "the principal motives for consolidation of the New York Central were commercial, but the opportunity for large speculative profits was not lost on the parties to the agreement." [17]

Events leading to the inclusion of the Schenectady and Troy and the Mohawk Valley in the merger give an indication of the preconsolidation activities of those to whom the *Times* referred as "the initiated managers."

The Schenectady and Troy was a 20-mile road that had been built between 1840 and 1842 by the municipality of Troy. One of the best-constructed roads in the country, it had had to meet the almost ruinous competition of the much less efficient Mohawk and Hudson, which stretched from Schenectady to Albany and which enjoyed preferential treatment at the hands of the Utica and Schenectady, the management of which, dominated by Erastus Corning, had an interest in seeing western traffic flow to Albany rather than to Troy. As a consequence, by the early 1850's the Schenectady and Troy was in poor financial shape and was proving a drag on the taxpayers of Troy.[18]

On January 24, 1853, on the recommendation of a committee appointed by the common council and headed by Russell Sage, the municipality of Troy accepted for its railroad an offer of $200,000 from Edwin D. Morgan, then president of the Hudson River Railroad and later governor of New York. Another,

---

[16] *New York Tribune,* July 8, 1853.
[17] Pierce, *Railroads of New York,* 80.   [18] *Ibid.,* 61–63, 72, 75.

higher bid made by the New York and Harlem was passed over. Partners with Morgan in the purchase were Corning, Dean Richmond of Buffalo, Hamilton White of Syracuse, and John V. L. Pruyn. It is probable, too, that Russell Sage, James Boorman, and John Wilkinson received a cut of the profits. Nor did they have long to wait, for even before the sale of the Schenectady and Troy was definitely agreed upon, it had been decided that, if the transaction went through, the Troy road would be included in the New York Central consolidation.[19]

Corning held 1,200 shares in the Schenectady and Troy, for which he had paid about $31 a share.[20] According to the consolidation agreement, Schenectady and Troy stock was to be exchanged for New York Central stock at par upon the payment of $25 on each share.[21] Thus, for an outlay of less than $56 a share, totaling about $67,000, Corning received 1,200 shares in the newly consolidated road.[22] The par value of the shares was $120,000, but during the summer of 1853 New York Central stock was actually selling at 13 to 20 per cent above par.[23] If Corning sold the shares which he had acquired through the merger of the Troy road at that time (and perhaps he did, for as early as June 27 he was seeking a buyer for a large block of Central stock),[24] his profits from the Schenectady and Troy could have been increased by several thousand dollars, bringing the total almost to, if not over, the $70,000 mark.

Another road from which Corning reaped a large profit at the time of the New York Central consolidation was the Mohawk Valley. This was a "paper" road, for although the com-

[19] *Ibid.*, 77, 79. See also James A. Rawley, *Edwin D. Morgan, 1811–1883: Merchant in Politics* (New York, 1955), 25–27.

[20] Pierce, *Railroads of New York*, 149–150. The total number of shares was 6,500; the purchase price, $200,000. Corning's original allotment had been 1,537 shares, but he turned over 337 shares to John V. L. Pruyn (*ibid.*, 150).

[21] *Agreement . . . Whereby the Said Companies Are Consolidated into . . . "The New York Central Railroad Company,"* 20.

[22] These 1,200 shares were not included in the 1,531 shares of New York Central stock already mentioned. Morgan, who managed the purchase of the Troy road, did not make a settlement with Corning until August. At the time of the consolidation, therefore, these 1,200 shares stood in Morgan's name.

[23] *New York Times*, July 9—Aug. 31, 1853.

[24] Watts Sherman to Corning, New York, June 27, 1853, CP.

pany had been chartered in 1851 to build an extension of the Troy line from Schenectady to Utica, no progress had been made with its construction. Early in 1852 Corning, Pruyn, and other directors of the Utica and Schenectady, seeing the Mohawk Valley as a threat to their own line, hit upon a plan for gaining control of the rival road. Through the co-operation of the treasurer and one of the directors of the Mohawk Valley, the original subscribers to stock were induced to give up part of their subscriptions. The stock so surrendered was taken by Corning and Pruyn, who, in late July, 1852, were in a position to depose the old board of directors, elect a new one, and place Pruyn at its head. Now, a year later, the Mohawk Valley, still without a foot of track, was taken into the New York Central at a premium of 55 per cent. Corning, who held 403 shares in the Mohawk Valley, for which he had paid but par ($40,300), received in exchange 403 shares of New York Central stock, plus $22,165 in 6 per cent, 30-year bonds.[25]

The total profit which Corning derived from the New York Central consolidation could not have been short of $100,000, a handsome return for his admittedly important services in bringing about the merger. But this was not all. As president of the new company he was in a position to add greatly to his gains, for he continued to enjoy that source of profit which he had found so satisfactory in the case of the Utica and Schenectady, namely, the road's iron contracts. Hardly was consolidation a fact when the New York Central began the laying of a second track between Syracuse and Buffalo. Estimated cost of the iron for the project was placed by the engineer in charge at $1,568,030. Most, if not all of it, was bought through Erastus Corning & Co. of Albany. By the end of July, 1855, New York Central purchases on the Erastus Corning & Co. books stood at $1,098,407.30. Almost $700,000 of this sum was spent for rails, on which the Corning firm collected 2.5 per cent commission.[26]

[25] Pierce, *Railroads of New York*, 70–71. Pruyn, who held 337 shares in the Mohawk Valley, received $18,535 in bonds (*ibid.*).

[26] *American Railroad Journal*, X (June 17, 1854), 374–375; *Report of a Committee Appointed January 4th, 1855, by the Directors of the New York Central Railroad Company at the Request of the Stockholders* (Boston, 1855), 13–14. The

The bill for spikes amounted to $84,231.88.[27] On this article, which came from the Albany Iron Works, the president of the Central made a double profit, that of manufacturer and that of merchant. The same was true of the axles and tires, $71,-109.43 worth, which were purchased by the road during the two years from August, 1853, to July, 1855.[28]

The obvious connection between the New York Central and Erastus Corning & Co. was the primary cause of a demand from the stockholders late in 1854 for the appointment of a committee to look into the affairs of the Central. In addition to the iron contracts, the committee was also to inquire into other alleged irregularities, including those associated with the road's purchase of land in West Albany and in Buffalo and the monopoly enjoyed by George H. Thacher of Albany on sales of car wheels to the Central. The West Albany land, it was charged, had been bought at an exorbitant price, and the Buffalo land had been purchased from Dean Richmond, the company's vice-president. The Thacher car-wheel establishment, it was said, obtained its pig iron through Erastus Corning & Co., and Chauncey Vibbard, the Central's general superintendent, was one of the owners of the car-wheel patent.[29] The ensuing inquiry could have caused the president of the Central little anxiety, for on the investigating committee were Schuyler Livingston and John F. Seymour, his long-time friends, and Russell Sage, who had been so co-operative in the matter of the Schenectady and Troy.

Nonetheless, the report of the committee was at least mildly critical of Corning and of Erastus Corning & Co. In regard

---

rails were purchased in England through Baring Brothers, who extended to the Albany house credits totaling £100,000. When Erastus Corning & Co. was unable to meet its London obligations during "the stringency of 1854," the Barings permitted delay in remittances (Ralph M. Hidy, *The House of Baring in American Trade and Finance . . . 1763–1861* [Cambridge, Mass., 1949], 430, 454).

[27] *Report of a Committee Appointed January 4th, 1855, by the Directors of the New York Central,* 13.

[28] *Ibid.*

[29] *Ibid.,* 12–13; John F. Seymour to Corning, Utica, N.Y., Sept. 24, 1855, CP.

to the land purchases, the committee was of the opinion that the Buffalo property could have commanded a greater price than that actually paid for it, but the West Albany property, for the purchase of which Corning had been primarily responsible, had indeed been acquired at an exorbitant figure—$250 an acre. Further, the committee stated that although the prices charged the Central by Erastus Corning & Co. were not in general above market rates no large railroad company should "pay a commission to any one on this side of the Atlantic for importing railroad iron, there being in the large cities here agents of the principal manufacturers of rails ready to contract for delivery . . . without such commission." The allegations involving Thacher's car wheels were disposed of by Thacher's swearing to the committee that neither Corning nor Vibbard was in any way connected with his establishment.[30]

It was the consensus of the committee that "the practice of buying articles required for the use of the Railroad Company from its own officers might in time to come lead to abuses of great magnitude," and it was therefore recommended that "the system of purchases" be placed under such regulations and restrictions as might be best calculated to protect the interests of the company.[31] The report of the committee notwithstanding, the Central continued to buy iron through Corning's house. Between April 30, 1855, and January 19, 1856, purchases by the New York Central through Erastus Corning & Co. amounted to $588,744.31.[32] Eight years later, at the end of 1863, the *New York Times* charged that the privilege of supplying the Central with iron was worth at least $250,000 a year to its president.[33] Since the *Times* was always anti-Corning, its estimate may have been exaggerated, but it is a matter of record that between October, 1863, and September, 1864, the Central's

[30] *Report of a Committee Appointed January 4th, 1855, by the Directors of the New York Central*, 24, 27–28, 45–46.

[31] *Ibid.*, 22.

[32] General Ledger, no. 1, Comptroller's Office, New York Central System, 466 Lexington Avenue, New York City.

[33] *New York Times*, Dec. 2, 1863.

purchases from the Corning firm amounted to $701,027.46.[34]

Each year during Erastus Corning's tenure as president of the New York Central he appeared at the stockholders' meeting with a majority of votes at his command, either in the form of proxies or insured by the loyalty of the men who cast them.[35] Each year, of course, he chose the board of directors.

The board of directors convened every month at Albany [a contemporary of Corning wrote in 1872]. Here Mr. Corning sat at the head of the table, which was surrounded by Dean Richmond, General Gould, Alonzo C. Paige, John L. Schoolcraft and their associates in office. . . . The directors were all subject to Mr. Corning.[36]

Yet the Central was but little more than twelve months old when a rumor reached Corning that John Wilkinson, one of the road's directors and former president of the Syracuse and Utica, "is making interest for himself to take your place as President of the C. R. R." [37] It was also reported that Azariah Boody, another director, was "in concert of action with Wilkinson." [38] Probably as a result of their anti-Corning activities both men were dropped from the board at the next election, that is, in December, 1854. Meanwhile the New York and Boston stockholders were clamoring for representation, and Corning was quite willing to gratify them, for he had never felt strongly about the exclusion of directors from those places. He therefore caused the vacancies which had been created by the elimination of Wilkinson and Boody and the resignation of a third director, Henry B. Gibson of Canandaigua, to be filled

[34] "Money Paid to Individuals," record in Comptroller's Office, New York Central System. A drop in this figure in the two succeeding years (Oct., 1864, to Sept., 1865, and Oct., 1865, to Sept., 1866) to $171,438.14 and $145,590.04, respectively, coincided with Corning's lessening control of the Central.

[35] On Dec. 8, 1858, John V. L. Pruyn noted in his journal: "The Annual Election of Directors of the N.Y. Central Rail Road Coy took place today. . . . Most of the proxies were as usual in the names of Mr. Corning & Myself" (Pruyn Papers, New York State Library, Albany, N.Y.).

[36] *Rochester Democrat*, April 13, 1872.

[37] P. D. Michles to Corning, Syracuse, Aug. 28, 1854, CP.

[38] S. B. Jewett to Corning, Clarkston, N.Y., Dec. 1, 1854, CP.

by the election of two directors from New York City, Schuyler Livingston and Edward G. Faile, and one, Nathaniel Thayer, from Boston.[39] The loyalty of Thayer and Livingston, at least, to the Central's president was unquestioned, and both could be counted on to hold the proxies for large amounts of stock.[40]

In the New York Central election of 1858 Russell Sage of Troy and Joseph Field of Rochester were dropped from the board. On the basis of their vigorous written protests, it would seem that their names had been omitted for no other reason than that they had disagreed with the board's president.[41] In Sage's case summary dismissal seemed poor thanks for the assistance that he had rendered Corning and Morgan in the purchase of the Schenectady and Troy, but so great was Sage's respect for the New York Central's president that he continued to send him his proxy.[42]

During the latter part of 1855 and the early months of 1856 Corning was in Europe. From 1857 to 1869 and again from 1861 to 1863 he served in Congress. His long absences from Albany not only prevented his giving his various interests the personal attention he customarily lavished on them but also gave his opponents a clear field to intrigue against him. This perhaps explains why attempts to break his control of the Central made greater headway in the 1860's than in the first years after the consolidation.

For news of New York Central matters Corning was for months at a time dependent on his correspondents, primarily

---

[39] See list of directors in *Annual Report of the New York Central Rail-Road Company for the Year Ending September 30th, 1855, Made to the Board of Rail-Road Commissioners of the State of New York* (Albany, 1855); W. Sturgis to Corning, Boston, Dec. 4, 1854; Corning to Sturgis, Albany, Dec. 5, 1854; Corning to B. Carver, Albany, Dec. 7, 1854; Corning to Henry B. Gibson, Albany, Dec. 9, 1854: CP.

[40] Nathaniel Thayer was a partner in J. E. Thayer and Brother of Boston, large investors in the New York Central. Schuyler Livingston still commanded the proxy of Benjamin Ingham, who, by 1860, had invested $640,600 in stock and bonds of the New York Central (Pierce, *Railroads of New York*, 6).

[41] Hungerford, *Men and Iron*, 99–100.

[42] Sage to Corning, Troy, N.Y., Dec. 9, 1862, CP.

John V. L. Pruyn, who served as president pro tempore of the road in Corning's absence. But there were others who also kept him informed, especially, it would seem, of impending trouble. Toward the end of 1861 George H. Thacher, who was by this time mayor of Albany, wrote Corning of a rumor that there would be a demonstration against him at the December stockholders' meeting.[43] Early in 1862 both Erastus Corning, Jr., and Gilbert C. Davidson were warning the elder Corning of what they considered Pruyn's inordinate ambition, the former saying, "Pruyn injures your authority more than a little," and the latter stating that Pruyn had designs on the presidency of the road. Davidson also accused at least three other directors —Jacob Gould of Rochester, Hamilton White of Syracuse, and Livingston Spraker of Palatine Bridge—of being disloyal to Corning's policies. "Things are said & done," young Corning informed his father, "that would not be dreamed of if you were home." [44]

Although it is doubted that Corning ever seriously questioned the loyalty of Pruyn, recognizing as he probably did that both his son and Davidson were jealous of Pruyn's prerogatives, the reported widespread disaffection in the board must have given the president of the Central some uneasy moments in Washington. However, at the annual stockholders' meeting at the end of 1862, he was as usual in control of the majority of votes.

The following year real trouble developed. As early as August 5, 1863, Watts Sherman wrote to Corning from New York: "I am suspicious that their [*sic*] is a combination which will try to operate on the next election." [45] The combination, according to Pruyn, combined "all the elements of dissatisfaction of past years." Its figurehead was Thomas Olcott, president of the Mechanics and Farmers Bank of Albany and a long-time

---

[43] Thacher to Corning, Albany, Nov. 30, 1861, CP.

[44] Gilbert C. Davidson to Corning, Albany, March 4, March 19, 1862; Erastus Corning, Jr., to Corning, Albany, Feb. 6, March 23, 1862: CP.

[45] Sherman to Corning, New York, Aug. 5, 1862, CP.

acquaintance of Corning. Behind Olcott was Leonard W. Jerome, a well-known Wall Street operator, who is remembered today as the grandfather of Britain's Sir Winston Churchill.[46] It was rumored, also, that Salmon P. Chase, Lincoln's Secretary of the Treasury, was a member of the anti-Corning combination.[47]

The transfer books of the New York Central were at this time kept in the office of Duncan, Sherman and Company, the private banking house in New York City with which Watts Sherman, former cashier of the Albany City Bank, was then affiliated. Thus Sherman was in a position to keep Corning informed of the movements of "the combination."

The Jeromes have recently placed in their name over 5000 shares [he reported to the Central's president on October 27, 1863] & probably have a good deal not in their name—one of their friends has recently purchased 2000 shs. I have no doubt they hold together 10,000 shs at least & control a much larger amt.[48]

By November 6 Leonard Jerome controlled an estimated 16,000 shares; five days later the count stood at 30,000. All this information was passed along to Corning, but when Jerome presented himself at the transfer office and asked to see the New York Central's books, he was informed by Sherman or his partner or by an employee that no holdings but his own could be disclosed to him without an order "from each party requesting us to exhibit state of their a/c." Nor, Jerome was assured, would his account be shown to others without his consent.[49]

But if Jerome was at a disadvantage in the transfer office, the score was perhaps evened by the favorable publicity he received from the *New York Times,* a paper in which he had a large financial interest. The *New York Tribune* and the *New York Post* also came out for the Jerome party and for a change in

[46] Entry for Nov. 22, 1863, Pruyn Journal. For Jerome, see *National Cyclopedia of American Biography,* XXXII (New York, 1945), 448–449, and Anita Leslie, *The Remarkable Mr. Jerome* (New York, 1954).

[47] M. B. Spaulding to Corning, New York, Nov. 5, 1863, CP.

[48] Sherman to Corning, New York, Oct. 27, 1863, CP.

[49] Pruyn to Corning, New York, Nov. 6, 1863; Sherman to Corning, New York, Nov. 11, Nov. 14, 1863: CP.

the control of the Central. Of the metropolitan papers, only the *World* and the *Express* were on the side of Corning.[50]

Since both Corning and Dean Richmond, the Central's vice-president, were prominent Democrats (Richmond being chairman of the Democratic State Committee) and since the New York Central had long been accused, with justice, of tampering with state politics, newspaper discussion of the railroads' affairs almost inevitably took a political turn. The Republican organs, complained John V. L. Pruyn in late 1863, "assail the adm[inistration] of the Road & Mr. Corning's character and connection with it very severely." The *Times* charged that free trains had been provided for the use of electioneering Democrats, and the *Tribune* pointed out that Corning, Richmond, and Pruyn were all active and bitter opponents of Lincoln's administration. The *Tribune* also stated that a Republican assemblyman who was dependent upon the Central for a livelihood had been "manipulated" by Corning partisans and was obliged to vote steadily against his party. "Does not every Republican in our State," inquired the editor, ". . . *know* that the [Central's] support has been worth at least five thousand votes per annum to the Democratic party?"[51]

Corning, as usual, paid little attention to the tirades in the papers. Rather he concentrated his energies on the obtaining of proxies. As he had done twenty years before when Gideon Hawley had tried to challenge his position in the Utica and Schenectady, he now alerted his proxy gatherers and prepared to fight. To one Alexander Holland of New York City he sent lists of shareholders in New Jersey and Long Island, with instructions to his correspondent that at his earliest convenience he was "to take measures" to obtain the proxies of those whose names appeared on the lists. Nathaniel Thayer, the Boston director of the Central, was handed a list of New England stockholders whom it was expected that he would approach, while

[50] R. M. Blatchford to Corning, New York, Nov. 12, 1863; Sherman to Corning, New York, Nov. 13, 1863: CP; *New York Tribune*, Dec. 12, 1863; Hungerford, *Men and Iron*, 187–188.

[51] Entry for Nov. 22, 1863, Pruyn Journal; Sherman to Corning, New York, Nov. 13, 1863, CP; *New York Tribune*, Dec. 12, 1863.

John Butterfield of Utica and Jacob Gould of Rochester, both Central directors, were expected to obtain all available proxies in their respective cities. By November 25, two weeks before the scheduled election, proxies were arriving in Albany at a gratifying rate.[52]

In his struggle for continued mastery of the New York Central nothing escaped Corning's notice. When he learned that a Mr. Tallman of the Farmers Loan and Trust Company was collecting proxies for the Jerome party, he got in touch with Nathaniel Thayer, suggesting that John W. Brooks be sent to call on Tallman and point out to him the error of his ways.

It has occured to me [Corning wrote] that the Farmers Loan & Trust Co. are largely interested in the Michigan Central rail road, and if the Jerome party should succeed, I think Michigan Central interest would be interfeared [sic] with, as the Jerome party's interest is entirely on the South Shore.[53]

So assiduous was Corning in his quest for proxies that he wrote to at least one person, William M. Burr, who was reported by the *New York Times* to be in the enemy camp. By the beginning of December, moreover, Corning partisans were buying proxies. When it was found impossible to buy a proxy without buying stock as well, the stock was purchased also, at a premium of 40 per cent.[54]

As the day of the election drew near, Corning, Richmond, and Pruyn spent much of their time in New York City—attending to matters connected with the Central Railroad, in the language of Pruyn; buying stock, contracting for the use of

[52] Corning to Alexander Holland, to Nathaniel Thayer, to John Butterfield, all dated at Albany, Nov. 21, 1863; Gould to Corning, Rochester, Nov. 24, 1863; Robert L. Banks to Corning, Albany, Nov. 25, 1863: CP.

[53] Corning to Thayer, Albany, Nov. 21, 1863, CP.

[54] Corning to James H. Banker, Albany, Nov. 21, 1863; to W. M. Burr, Albany, Nov. 23, 1863; Sherman to Corning, New York, Dec. 2, 1863: CP. The transfer books had been closed a month before the scheduled election, but a person selling stock after the books were closed sold his proxy as well. The formal transfer was made after the election.

proxies at so much a vote, and in every possible way striving to perfect and perpetuate their tenure of office, in the language of the *New York Times*.[55] By December 6, three days before the election, the Corning camp was sure of victory.[56]

The New York Central stockholders' meeting of 1863 began in Albany on December 9. It continued for three days. On the evening of December 11 the old board was re-elected by a vote of approximately two to one. "No election of its kind in our Country," John V. L. Pruyn reported, "has ever produced such an extended and warm excitement." [57]

One of Corning's champions in the anxious weeks preceding the December meeting had been none other than Cornelius Vanderbilt. In mid-November the Commodore had sent his proxy to the Central's president, and at the December meeting Corning had voted on Vanderbilt's 5,250 shares of Central stock. This was approximately 3,200 shares more than the number which stood in Corning's own name. Nor had Vanderbilt limited his aid to his voting power. At his behest James H. Banker, one of his associates, had given considerable time to collecting proxies for Corning. Finally, on the eve of the election the Commodore himself had called on Leonard W. Jerome in a vain effort to persuade him to withdraw his support from Olcott.[58]

For all this Vanderbilt quite naturally expected compensation, and by November 21 it had apparently been decided that his reward was to be a board membership.[59] In the interests of strategy the stockholders were requested to vote for the old board, but early in January, 1864, Corning asked for and received the resignation of Jacob Gould of Rochester. Gould's place was filled by James H. Banker of New York City, who was

[55] Entry for Nov. 22, 1863, Pruyn Journal; *New York Times*, Dec. 2, 1863.
[56] Pruyn to Corning, New York, Dec. 6, 1863, CP.
[57] Entries for Dec. 9 and 11, 1863, Pruyn Journal.
[58] Cornelius Vanderbilt to Corning, New York, Nov. 12, 1863; Corning to James H. Banker, to Duncan, Sherman and Company, both dated at Albany, Nov. 21, 1863; Leonard W. Jerome to Vanderbilt, New York, Dec. 5, 1863: CP; *New York Times*, Dec. 14, 1863.
[59] Corning to Banker, Albany, Nov. 21, 1863, CP.

recognized by all as a Vanderbilt man.[60] This was Cornelius Vanderbilt's opening bid for control of the New York Central.

The year 1863 had been a hard one in Central affairs. Once again those critical of the close connection between the road's president and the Corning iron interests had made themselves heard. In June a workmen's strike at the railroad's West Albany shops had been marked by demonstrations against Corning personally and had resulted in the calling out of troops. In August the eastern trunk lines had broken an earlier agreement to keep up fares, with the result that there was a general reduction (led off by the Pennsylvania Central) and a consequent loss of revenue.[61] In August, too, the agitation over the coming December stockholders' meeting had begun. All this would have been trying enough for a man in vigorous health; for Corning, who had been unwell for years, it proved too much. Less than five months after his victory over Olcott and Jerome, at a meeting of the New York Central directors on April 28, 1864, he tendered his resignation from the presidency of the road. With expressions of regret, the resignation was accepted, and Dean Richmond was elected in his place. Corning remained a member of the board.[62]

Although the seventy-year-old Corning had given up his onerous duties as president of the Central, it was far from his intention to abandon either his interest in the company's affairs or his influence on its policy. He and Richmond had always worked in close co-operation, and he had always commanded Richmond's respect. On the occasions when Corning

---

[60] Gould to Corning, Rochester, Jan. 13, 1864, CP; *Documents of the Assembly of the State of New York, Ninetieth Session* (Albany, 1867), II, no. 19, p. 32. James H. Banker (1827–1885) was for many years vice-president of the Bank of New York and was associated with Vanderbilt "in a number of large enterprises" (*Rhodes' Journal of Banking*, XII [March, 1885], 254).

[61] John McBain Davidson to Corning, Albany, Feb. 18, 1863; Chauncey Vibbard to Corning, Albany, June 17, 1863; Corning to John W. Brooks, Albany (?), Aug. 8, 1863: CP; Joel Munsell, *Collections on the History of Albany*, II (Albany, 1867), 162–165.

[62] Minutes of the Meeting of the Directors of the New York Central Railroad Company, April 28, 1864, Secretary's Office, New York Central System, 230 Park Avenue, New York City.

had been absent from Albany and John V. L. Pruyn had presided at board meetings in the president's place, it had been Richmond's practice to stay away from the meetings. To a close friend of both himself and Corning he had confided his vow "never to set at the board" under any man but Corning.[63] It was with the outgoing president's blessing, then, that the new president took office, Corning doubtless believing that he would continue to enjoy Richmond's confidence and so continue to influence the Central's policy.

But almost immediately Richmond showed signs of his intention to pursue an independent course. Two days after he had taken over his new post, John V. L. Pruyn met him at dinner at the Cornings. With that touch of officiousness which some of his acquaintances found so annoying, Pruyn suggested to the new president that he "consult Mr. Corning as to the interest he felt disposed to take in the affairs of the Road, & how far he wished to be consulted about them." To this Richmond replied that Corning had told him some days before that he wished "to get rid of all care &c as to the Road." Richmond intimated, however, that he would talk further with Corning on the subject,[64] and perhaps he did, but by August, 1865, John F. Winslow was writing to Corning of the "alienation of feeling between Mr. Richmond and yourself." [65] At the annual stockholders' meeting in December of that year Corning's name was dropped from the board.[66] Since, prior to the meeting, he had been collecting proxies as usual,[67] it is reasonable to speculate that in his exasperation with Richmond the old creator of the Central erased his own name from the slate.

Meanwhile the influence of Vanderbilt in the affairs of the company was growing. In June, 1865, the Commodore joined

[63] G. C. Davidson to Corning, Albany, March 4, 1862, CP. It was possible, of course, that Richmond was not so much devoted to Corning as he was contemptuous of Pruyn—but that is not the way the episode was reported.

[64] Entry for April 29–30, 1864, Pruyn Journal.

[65] John F. Winslow to Corning, Aug. 8, 1865, CP.

[66] Minutes of the Meeting of the Stockholders of the New York Central Railroad Company, Dec. 13, 1865, Secretary's Office, New York Central System.

[67] Pruyn to Corning, London, Eng., Oct. 27, 1865, CP.

the directors in an inspection trip over the line. "He had not been West in thirty years," Pruyn noted in his journal, "& seemed to enjoy the trip very much." [68] By August it was reported that "Mr Richmond . . . & everybody else defers to Banker," [69] Vanderbilt's representative on the Central's board. In December, when Corning left the board, Horace F. Clark, Vanderbilt's son-in-law, was named a director of the road. Since Banker retained his place on the board, the Vanderbilt forces then had two representatives in the New York Central's directorate. Yet the Commodore made no attempt to control the Central's stock. On December 13, 1865, he held but 6,500 shares. By midsummer, 1866, he had sold every one.[70]

In the late spring of 1866 it was rumored in New York City that Henry Keep, a Wall Street broker, had bought control of the New York Central. About the same time it was being said that Richmond had broken with Vanderbilt.[71] The truth or falsity of the second rumor proved to be of small moment, however, for in late August, Richmond died. Even before this Vanderbilt had sold his interest in the Central, apparently leaving the field to Keep and his cohorts.

At the annual shareholders' meeting in December, 1866, Keep and his associates (the most important of whom were William G. Fargo, founder of Wells Fargo and Company, and Legrand Lockwood, a Wall Street broker) were found to control some $12,000,000 worth of the stock of the Central. This gave them control of the election. The result was that the two Vanderbilt men, Banker and Clark, were dropped from the board, and Corning, who had supported Keep, was reinstated as a director. Keep assumed the presidency,[72] and all doubtless congratulated themselves on the ease with which the Commodore had been dismissed. But jubilation came too soon. Vanderbilt was to win in the end, and for the outcome Erastus Corning cannot be absolved of responsibility.

[68] Entry for June 21, 1865, Pruyn Journal.
[69] Winslow to Corning, Troy, Aug. 12, 1865, CP.
[70] *New York Assembly Documents, 1867*, II, no. 19, pp. 102, 160.
[71] G. C. Davidson to Corning, New York, May 18, June 16, 1866, CP.
[72] Entry for Dec. 12, 1866, Pruyn Journal.

Corning, for all his astuteness, was a man with a blind spot. Beginning with the $4,500,000, 78-mile Utica and Schenectady, he had forged a $23,000,000, 300-mile railroad stretching from Buffalo to Albany. Yet the builder of the Central never understood the importance to his road of a dependable rail connection with New York City. Rather, he relied on the Hudson River as an entry into the metropolis. He saw transportation on the river as both cheaper and more convenient than transportation by rail. Since his days as a young merchant he had depended on the Hudson for his supplies. When he had business in Manhattan, he was in the habit of going down the river in comfort on the night boat. So far as the Central was concerned, it was to the immediate financial advantage of the company to favor water carriage south from Albany. If freight was interchanged at that city with the Hudson River Railroad, that road claimed one-third of the charges between Buffalo and New York, whereas goods could be moved by water from Albany to New York for only one-fifth of the charges between Buffalo and Manhattan.[73] It seems, too, that Corning owned an interest in the line of steamboats to which freight from the New York Central was usually consigned. In short, so far as the Hudson was concerned, Corning for a number of reasons never freed himself from what an American historian, in speaking of the people of the Empire State in 1853, has described as "the thralldom which waterways still held over the New York mind."[74]

When the Hudson River Railroad was completed from Manhattan to East Albany in 1851, Corning made no effort to enter into its control, although he was to serve on its board of directors for a number of years. He followed the same course in regard to the New York and Harlem, a second road which paralleled the Hudson and which was built through to Chatham, east of Albany, early in 1852. Nor did he, as president of the Central, attempt to make a working agreement with either of the roads, believing, as he did, that it was "best . . . for the

[73] *New York Assembly Documents, 1867*, II, no. 19, p. 61.
[74] Edward C. Kirkland, *A History of American Economic Life*, 3d ed. (New York, 1951), 250.

Central line to do their own business & leave all outsiders to fall in with them." [75]

In 1856 it was suggested to Corning by John F. Winslow that the control of the Hudson River Railroad should be in the hands of the Central and that half of all the shares of the former line could be purchased for some six or seven hundred thousand dollars,[76] but Corning apparently ignored the suggestion. Six years later, in August, 1862, Samuel Sloan, president of the Hudson River, estimated that control of the road might be purchased for a sum under a million dollars and urged that the Central take hold of it. In October of that same year Sloan referred to himself and Corning as being "the largest stockholders in the H. R. R. with perhaps one exception," but as late as June, 1863, Corning had apparently assured Sloan that he was "indifferent, indeed preferred not be re-elected" to the board of directors of the Hudson River.[77]

Corning clearly believed that the Central was less dependent on the Hudson River Railroad than was that road on the Central. During the years that he controlled the line from Buffalo to Albany, most of the freight from the West with a down-river destination was given to the Hudson River Railroad only in the winter months when the Hudson was frozen over. When the river was open, through shipments were consigned to the boat lines. Thus for much of the year the Hudson River's freight cars stood idle. This was a policy that suited the convenience of the Central, but it left that road extremely vulnerable at the season of the year when the river was impassable— a circumstance that was fully appreciated by Cornelius Vanderbilt.

Vanderbilt, who by the eve of the Civil War had made a fortune in ocean shipping, began to buy into railroads as early as the 1840's. In May, 1857, he purchased his first stock in the Harlem Railroad, a line which in subsequent years he came

[75] George Barnes to Corning, Syracuse, Feb. 11, 1852, CP: "I believe *as you do* that it would be best . . . for the Central line to do their own business," etc. (italics supplied).

[76] Winslow to Corning, Albany, Jan. 26, 1856, CP.

[77] Samuel Sloan to Corning, New York, Aug. 5, Oct. 11, 1862, June 10, 1863, CP.

to control through manipulation of the market. By 1862 he assumed the presidency of the Harlem. Three years later he became president of the Hudson River Railroad, the stock of which had also come into his control.[78] Thus he gathered in both railroads which might join Albany with New York City.

During Dean Richmond's regime as president of the New York Central there were attempts at co-operation between that road and the Vanderbilt lines. Once there was even talk of a consolidation, and Henry Keep was later to say that during the two years preceding his own incumbency Vanderbilt had managed the Central "through men in his interest." Certainly between the death of Richmond and the coming to power of Keep, the Commodore had things his own way. On October 18, 1866, about two months before Keep was to take over, the directors of the New York Central entered into a one-year agreement with the Hudson River Railroad by the terms of which freight revenues on goods interchanged by the two roads were to be prorated and in addition an annual bonus of $100,-000 was to be paid by the Central to the Hudson River road.[79] The bonus was to compensate the Hudson River for the idleness of its equipment during the months that the river was open.

When Keep took over the Central on December 12, 1866, Corning's policy with regard to eastbound freight was reinstated: that is, when the river was frozen, shipments arriving in Albany from the west over the tracks of the Central were to be offered to the Hudson River Railroad; when the river was open, such shipments were to be sent downstream by boat. At a meeting of the Central directors on December 20 a resolution was passed rescinding that part of the agreement with the Hudson River which entailed the payment of the $100,000 bonus. At this point Vanderbilt stepped in. Citing the Central's repudiation of the agreement, the Commodore, in his capacity

[78] Wheaton J. Lane, *Commodore Vanderbilt: An Epic of the Steam Age* (New York, 1942), 187–192, 208–211.

[79] *New York Assembly Documents, 1867*, II, no. 19, pp. 4, 28–29, 33, 60–61, 211–212.

as president of the Hudson River on January 17, 1867, ordered all traffic on that road halted at East Albany. Since the tracks on the bridge at Albany belonged to Vanderbilt's road, neither passengers nor freight could thereafter be interchanged with the Central.[80]

Ice had closed the river a month before, and the Central now found itself in an untenable position. Freight piled up in Albany, and passengers, forced to cross the river on foot or in sleighs, were none the happier for a heavy snowstorm. The officers of the Central held out for two days and then had to give in, Corning being one of the committee of directors that signed the capitulation. A new agreement, acceptable to Vanderbilt, was entered into between the Central and the Hudson River Railroad.[81]

An investigation of the incident by the railroad committee of the New York Assembly was to result in severe censure of Vanderbilt and his methods,[82] but the fact remained that the Commodore had won the battle and that Keep and his associates, including Corning, had gone down to defeat. On January 22, 23, and 24, 1867, Keep and Lockwood dumped their New York Central stock on the market.[83] Vanderbilt was probably a heavy purchaser at this time. In any case, by July he was advising his friends to buy Central, as he "thought" it would go up. By November it was generally recognized that the Commodore would control the coming election of Central directors.[84]

On December 11, 1867, at the annual shareholders' meeting in the Albany offices of the New York Central where Erastus

[80] *Ibid.*, 35, 193, 196–197.   [81] *Ibid.*, 78–80, 201.

[82] *Journal of the Assembly of the State of New York, Ninetieth Session* (Albany, 1867), I, 526.

[83] J. M. Davidson to Corning, New York, Jan. 24, 25, 1867, CP. Cf. *New York Times*, Jan. 23–25, 1867. It was this dumping of stock, rather than the interruption of traffic caused by the break at Albany, which depressed New York Central shares. Central fell only a little more than one point during the period of the break (from 108⅜ on Jan. 16 to 107¼ on Jan. 18), whereas between Jan. 21 and Jan. 24 it fell from 108½ to 99. See *New York Times* for these dates.

[84] Corning, Jr., to Corning, New York, July 27, 1867; G. C. Davidson to Corning, New York, Nov. 20, 30, 1867: CP.

Corning had so long presided, Cornelius Vanderbilt voted on $18,000,000 worth of Central stock.[85] The old board, including Corning, was turned out, and a new board of the Commodore's choosing came in. This marked the end of Corning's official connection with the Central. He continued to hold a small amount of the company's stock, and he was receptive to the gossip about Central affairs that John McBain Davidson picked up in the financial circles of New York City and passed along to him,[86] but during the half decade of life left to him he showed no interest in returning to a seat on the Central's board.

Although Corning and Vanderbilt were on opposite sides in the fight for control of the Central, there seems to have been no bitterness between the two men. In the course of his testimony before the railroad committee of the Assembly in February, 1867, the Commodore told of a conversation he had had with Corning a few weeks before, at the time when the Central and the Hudson River were attempting to negotiate prior to the breaking of connections at Albany. The two men had come out of the New York offices of the Hudson River Railroad Company together, and Vanderbilt had offered to take Corning to his hotel. As they jogged up Fifth Avenue, the Commodore said to his guest:

"Mr. Corning, I am very sorry we cannot get along together in this matter."

"I am, too," Corning replied. "If it was left to you and me we could fix it up in a little while."

---

[85] Lane, *Commodore Vanderbilt*, 224. Not all this stock was the Commodore's own. Something over $13,000,000 worth belonged to Edward Cunard, John Jacob Astor, Jr., John Steward, the firm of Bankard and Hutton, and others who had asked Vanderbilt to vote their shares, hoping, as they told him, "that such an organization will be effected as shall secure to the company the aid of your great and acknowledged abilities" (*ibid.*, 223).

[86] See, for instance, J. M. Davidson to Corning, New York, Jan. 3, 8, 14, Feb. 11, 27, Nov. 27, Dec. 4, 1868, Aug. 23, Sept. 23, 30, 1869, CP. In 1869 Vanderbilt forged a New York to Chicago railroad system by gaining control of the Lake Shore and Michigan Southern. The year after the Commodore's death, in 1877, his son, William H., was to take over the Canada Southern. By 1878 the Vanderbilt interests were also in control of the Michigan Central (Cochran, *Railroad Leaders*, 26).

"I believe we could," Vanderbilt acquiesced.[87]

The Commodore was later quoted as saying that although Keep was a "shyster" Corning was a man of business and a gentleman.[88] In speaking of Vanderbilt, Corning remarked to his brokers, H. T. Morgan and Company, in January, 1869: "I think Comdr Vanderbilt has watered the New York Central Rail Road stock a little more than it will bear in my judgement."[89] If his criticism of his successor was ever more severe than that, it is apparently not on record.

In assessing the railroad career of Erastus Corning, an authority on leadership in that field has stated that the first president of the Central "ran the best-equipped and most efficient road of the day." Moreover, he was a man of "broad interests and imagination."[90] Although Corning used his connection with the Central to promote his mercantile, banking, and manufacturing activities, the scope of those activities reflected benefit on the railroad. He failed to secure for the Central a rail line to New York City, but fifteen years before Vanderbilt took over, Corning had provided his road with western connections that gave it access to Chicago. In every important sense he was the architect of the New York Central.

[87] *New York Assembly Documents, 1867*, II, no. 19, p. 197.

[88] J. M. Davidson to Corning, Feb. 1, 1867, CP. Cornelius Vanderbilt's attitude toward Corning was not shared by his son, William H. Vanderbilt. According to John McBain Davidson, the younger Vanderbilt made it a point to attack in some "dirty, contemptible manner" everyone who had ever been directly or indirectly associated with the Central's first president (Davidson to Corning, New York, June 3, 1868, CP).

[89] Letter dated at Albany, Jan. 5, 1869, CP.

[90] Cochran, *Railroad Leaders*, 25.

· XI ·

The Last Chapter

AS was true in the earlier period when Corning was head of the Utica and Schenectady, so during his later career he continued to be interested in a number of railroads in addition to the one of which he was president. Although he resigned his directorship in the Great Western of Canada in 1854, he remained on the boards of the Michigan Central and the Chicago, Burlington & Quincy throughout his life. He also served for a time in the directorate of the Ohio and Mississippi and the Keokuk and St. Paul railroads and of the Burlington and Missouri River Railroad in Iowa.[1]

Corning's railroad investments were so widespread that it would have been possible for a traveler at the end of the 1860's to span the continent riding exclusively on lines in which the Albany capitalist had a large interest. Besides the New York Central, the Michigan Central, and the Chicago, Burlington & Quincy, these included the Erie and North East, the Detroit and Pontiac, the New Albany and Salem, the Lake Erie, Wabash and St. Louis, the Chicago and Great Eastern, the Green Bay and Lake Pepin, the Hannibal and St. Joseph, the Burlington and Missouri River railroads in Iowa and Nebraska, the Union Pacific, and the California Central.[2]

[1] C. J. Brydges to Erastus Corning, Hamilton, Canada West, Oct. 3, 1854; Corning to S. S. M. Barlow, New York, Oct. 20, 1863; J. N. Denison to Corning, Boston, June 1, 1869: CP.

[2] John M. Forbes to D. D. Williamson and J. C. Green, Boston, Dec. 23, 1853; Corning to Winslow, Lanier and Company, Albany, May 23, 1854; to Marie and

187

During the years that he was investing heavily in railroad stocks and bonds, Corning was also placing large sums in federal, state, and municipal securities. In June, 1845, he was one of the purchasers of "the New York State 6 pr cent Loan." In September, 1849, Camman and Whitehouse of New York City acknowledged his check for $44,669.50 "in payment for U.S. stock purchased for your a/c." At the same time the New York house was endeavoring to sell for him at a profit some Detroit city bonds that had been purchased at an earlier date. In January, 1851, De Launay, Iselin and Clark, another Manhattan firm, was trying to buy Albany city water bonds for Corning's account. Throughout his life Corning continued to invest in this class of securities. In March, 1864, he bought $50,000 worth of Michigan state bonds. Two years later he received word from Michigan that arrangements had been completed for the purchase of an additional $50,000 worth. In the years just after the Civil War he was buying widely of the stocks of express and telegraph companies.[3]

The sums which Corning had at his command for investment were large. As early as the mayoralty campaign of 1833 his wealth was being commented upon. By 1850 he was Albany's richest citizen. On the eve of the Civil War he was said to be worth $3,000,000.[4] His reported income for the year 1863 was $101,300—far more than that attributed to any other

Hunz, Albany, Sept. 1, 1854; to H. E. Robinson, Albany, Oct. 27, 1864; to U. N. Murdock, Albany, Feb. 1, 1869; to Denison, Albany, June 20, 1870; T. M. Sother to Corning, New York, Sept. 26, 1870; Samuel Marsh to Corning, New York, Nov. 14, 1870: CP.

[3] James Walker to Corning, Schenectady, June 12, 1845; Camman and Whitehouse to Corning, New York, Sept. 22, Oct. 4, 1849; De Launay, Iselin and Clark to Corning, New York, Jan. 1, 1851; J. Owen to Corning, Detroit, March 23, 1864, Jan. 6, 1866; John McBain Davidson to Corning, New York (?), April 26, Nov. 23, 1865; Corning to George E. Cook, Albany, Feb. 1, 1869; Hiram Barney to Corning, New York, July 28, 1870: CP. Corning held shares in Western Union and the National Telegraph Company and in Wells Fargo and Company and American Express.

[4] Thurlow Weed Barnes, *Memoir of Thurlow Weed*, in Thurlow Weed, *Life of Thurlow Weed, Including His Autobiography and a Memoir* (Boston, 1884), II, 189; *New York Herald*, April 10, 1872.

resident of Albany and considerably less than the actual figure.[5] Nine years later his fortune was placed at $8,000,000.[6]

By the 1860's many of Corning's earlier investments were paying large returns, and this accounts in part for the probable doubling of his wealth in those years; but it was also the case that he profited greatly because of the Civil War. During the conflict the ironworks at Troy operated at the peak of their capacity, and the volume of business of the Albany hardware house was very great. Additional income was derived from other war-generated activities.

On the outbreak of hostilities Corning's Albany partner, Gilbert C. Davidson, established himself temporarily in New York City, where, by early May, 1861, he was confident of obtaining important government contracts for himself and Corning.[7] By November he could report that he had "control of a large amount of work for Government." In that month he was dealing in such articles as blankets, muskets, and sabers on a large scale. "Out of these things," he wrote to Corning, "I hope we shall get something handsome." On one transaction concerned with the sale of blankets to the army he anticipated a profit of $37,500.[8] In June, 1862, Corning, who was serving in Congress at the time, was buying pepper in the expectation of an increased tariff on that commodity. In 1863 he was dealing in tobacco in the New Orleans market.[9]

Despite his great wealth, Corning continued to give careful attention to the many details of his various interests. As in the 1840's, so in the fifties and sixties the iron contracts of the

[5] Joel Munsell, *Collections on the History of Albany*, II (Albany, 1867), 180; Rufus S. Tucker, "The Distribution of Income among Income Taxpayers in the United States, 1863–1935," *Quarterly Journal of Economics*, LII (Aug., 1938), 561.

[6] *Albany Ev. Journal*, April 9, 1872.

[7] Gilbert C. Davidson to Corning, New York, May 5, May 7, 1861, CP.

[8] Davidson to Corning, New York, Nov. 8, Nov. 21, 1861, CP. Davidson buttressed his optimistic predictions by relating that A. T. Steward, who was vying with him for certain contracts, had remarked that "he had never made so much money as he has since the war broke out" (*ibid.*).

[9] Watts Sherman to Corning, New York, June 20, 1862; H. A. Tilden to Corning, New York, May 9, May 12 (?), 1863: CP.

railroads in which he was interested remained a matter of
moment to him. In the later years the Burlington lines especially were valued customers of the house of Corning. Sometimes the roads settled their iron bills in cash; sometimes the
bills canceled assessments on stock for which Corning had subscribed; sometimes Erastus Corning & Co. accepted mortgage
bonds in lieu of payment. After 1866, when he withdrew from
his Albany iron and hardware house, Corning expended considerable effort on obtaining orders for the Troy ironworks.
In doing so he depended, as he always had, on personal con-
tacts. As late as October, 1869, he was writing to James F. Joy,
who was then president of the Michigan Central Railroad and
influential in a number of western lines:

My object in troubling you is to say that the "Albany Iron Works"
at Troy will be much pleased to furnish you and Rail Roads which
you may be interested in with Spikes, Rivits [sic], Fish Plates,
Axels, Bar Iron, all of the best quality—you can order direct from
the Works at Troy—and they will give prompt attention to your
wishes—I shall be much pleased if you should find it consistent to
give them orders.[10]

In his retirement the elderly Corning devoted much time
to the writing of letters in his careful, copybook hand. In
addition to soliciting orders for iron, he kept in close touch
with his western land agents. He also wrote frequently to his
New York brokers and to Nathaniel Thayer in Boston.
Through Thayer he kept himself informed of western railroad matters.

In buying and selling securities Corning in his last years
made use of the services of both Duncan, Sherman and Company and H. T. Morgan and Company. But his approach to
other investments remained highly personal. In the late 1860's,
for instance, through his former Albany associate, James
Horner, he became interested in the Pompton Steel Works of
Passaic County, New Jersey. Horner was then one of the
proprietors of the New Jersey works. At the beginning of
November, 1868, Horner and his partner, James Ludlum, were

---

[10] Letter dated at Albany, Oct. 21, 1869, CP.

in debt to Corning some $130,000, on which they paid semi-annual interest of $4,550.[11] Through Charles T. Harvey, who had been one of the construction engineers on the Sault Canal, Corning, about 1870, became an investor in New York City's first elevated railway.[12]

So long as he was able, Corning spent part of each day in the office of the Albany City Bank, the presidency of which he retained until his death. In 1850 the Albany City had been responsible for the establishment of the Albany City Savings Institution, a bank of deposit for "tradesmen, clerks, mechanics, laborers, minors, servants and others," which was "open daily to receive deposits, and on Wednesday evenings for females." [13] Corning headed this as well. After 1869 he was president of yet a third bank, for in that year the National Savings Bank of Albany was founded and he consented to serve as executive officer.[14]

Throughout the 1860's Corning was often far from well. As early as 1861, at the age of sixty-seven, he expressed the wish to sell the Albany hardware and iron business to someone "who has less years on them." [15] In October, 1863, when the struggle with Olcott and Jerome for control of the New York Central was coming to a head, Corning resigned his seat in Congress,[16] giving the poor state of his health as his reason. In November and December of that year the veteran president of the Central showed some of his former vigor, but in the spring of 1864 he voluntarily surrendered to Dean Richmond the post that he had struggled so hard to hold. For the next two years he lived

[11] James Ludlum to Corning, New York, April 18, 1866; Corning to James Horner and Company, Albany, Nov. 2, 1869; James Horner and Company to Erastus Corning, Jr., Pompton, N.J., April 23, 1872: CP.

[12] Charles T. Harvey to Corning, New York, May 24, 1870; Tarrytown, N.Y., Dec. 10, Dec. 21, 1870: CP.

[13] Joel Munsell, *The Annals of Albany*, 2d ed., II (Albany, 1870), 339; *Laws of the State of New York, Seventy-third Session* (Albany, 1850), 180. For the history of savings banks, see Fritz Redlich, *History of American Business Leaders: A Series of Studies* (Ann Arbor, Mich., 1940–1951), II, pt. II, *passim.*

[14] Amasa J. Parker, *Landmarks of Albany County, New York* (Syracuse, N.Y., 1879), pt. I, 375.

[15] Corning to S. A. Goddard, Albany, Nov. 17, 1861, CP.

[16] Joel Munsell, *Collections on the History of Albany*, II (Albany, 1870), 173.

quietly, seemingly making an effort to cut himself off from at least some business cares, but by the fall of 1866 he was again taking a hand in New York Central affairs. The following summer he was a delegate to the New York State constitutional convention.

During the winter of 1868–1869 he spent a number of months in bed, unable even to write but sometimes well enough to dictate to a clerk. Doubtless there were those who thought the old gentleman, now halfway through his seventies, was in his last illness, but the following winter he was driving back and forth to Troy, concerned with ironworks affairs. A traveler, seeing him on the road one December day, remarked that he seemed "of late . . . to have gained a new lease of life." [17]

Corning's old age was not a lonely one. His wife, who survived him, shared his gregariousness, and the Corning home seems seldom to have been without guests. To the sorrow of the aunt and uncle, three of the nieces whom Harriet and Erastus had reared died in their young womanhood. The fourth lived in Canada. But John V. L. Pruyn and his second wife were frequent visitors at the house on State Street, as were Erastus, Jr., his wife, and their son, a third Erastus.[18] In the summer of 1866 Edwin, the elder Cornings' other son, married Mary De Camp, an outstandingly beautiful if somewhat shallow young woman who apparently lived quite amicably for long periods in the home of her parents-in-law.[19]

Each summer the Cornings left Albany during the warmer months. In the early years of their marriage, Harriet had established herself with the children at their farm in Canaan, New York, and Erastus joined them when his business affairs

[17] *Ibid.*, IV (Albany, 1871), 78.

[18] Erastus Corning, Jr., married Gertrude Tibbets, daughter of Benjamin Tibbets of Albany, in 1850. She died in 1869. In 1873 Corning, Jr., married Mary Parker, daughter of Amasa J. Parker, a distinguished jurist of the capital city.

[19] Erastus Corning was to bequeath Mary the income from a $150,000 trust fund "during her natural life" (copy of will in Surrogate's Court, Albany). After the death of Edwin Corning, his widow married General Robert Lenox Banks, whose first wife had been Emma Turner, one of the nieces reared by the Cornings.

permitted. By the 1840's they had acquired a summer house at Sachem's Head, Connecticut. In the fifties they had gone to Saratoga. By the sixties the parents were members of the summer colony at Newport, although their sons continued to prefer the upstate New York spa.

Corning's "new lease of life" which had been remarked upon in the early winter of 1869–1870 lasted just two years. His son, Edwin, died in the fall of 1871, and after that the father became bedridden. He was never to resume an active life. He died on April 9, 1872, in his seventy-eighth year. A long line of the great and humble walked in his funeral procession and thronged St. Peter's Church, where final tribute was paid to Albany's outstanding citizen.[20] Almost sixty years had passed since young Erastus Corning made his first appearance on Hardware Row.

When Erastus Corning died, the country stood at the beginning of a new era—the era of the giant corporation and the "nationalization of business." It was to be an era which the old capitalist, Albany oriented as he was and accustomed to the simpler business organizations of an earlier day, would not have liked and perhaps would not have understood, but it was one which he had done much to help create.

[20] Born a Presbyterian, Corning died an Episcopalian. For an account of his funeral see *Albany Argus*, April 15, 1872.

Bibliography

THE Corning Papers in the Albany Institute of History and Art in Albany, New York, are the chief source of information about Erastus Corning. These papers consist of some 30,000 pieces, most of which pertain to the business and political careers of the Corning with whom this work is concerned. There is a relatively small amount of social correspondence, and possibly one-fifth of the collection relates to the activities of Erastus Corning, Jr. (1827–1897), son of the elder Erastus. There are also a few papers which belonged to later Cornings. The material is uncatalogued and unarranged, but is tied in bundles, in rough chronological order, just as its owners left it.

For the most part, the papers concerned with the elder Corning consist of letters received. There are but three thin volumes containing letter-press copies of outgoing correspondence, and a very few miscellaneous, loose copies of individual letters. It is also to be regretted that, with the exception of two little account books which Corning kept when he was a boy in Troy, no accounts or ledgers associated with any of his various enterprises are extant. The letters received, however, are in an excellent state of preservation. Communications from Edward C. Delavan, John Murray Forbes, Erastus Fairbanks, John Seymour, Hiram Barney, Watts Sherman, John V. L. Pruyn, Henry B. Gibson, and Jacob Gould are especially numerous; letters from such men as Horatio Seymour, William H. Seward, Edwin D. Morgan, and Thurlow Weed are fewer in volume, but perhaps no less worthy of note.

Of other manuscript sources, those found to be most valuable for purposes of this study were the John V. L. Pruyn Papers in the New York State Library, the Seymour Family Papers in the Collection of Regional History at Cornell University, the Seymour Papers in the Wisconsin Historical Society Library, in Madison, Wisconsin, and the Joy Papers in the Michigan Historical Collections at the University of Michigan.

I. MANUSCRIPTS AND RECORDS

Chicago, Burlington & Quincy Railroad Company Papers. Newberry Library, Chicago, Ill.

Erastus Corning Papers. Albany Institute of History and Art, Albany, N.Y.

Farmers Loan and Trust Company Letter Books, 1831–1854. 5 vols. Microfilm copies, Collection of Regional History, Cornell University, Ithaca, N.Y.

James F. Joy Papers. Burton Historical Collection, Detroit Public Library, Detroit, Mich.

Miscellaneous Autographs no. 120. Collection of Regional History, Cornell University, Ithaca, N.Y.

Miscellaneous Papers no. 58. Collection of Regional History, Cornell University, Ithaca, N.Y.

Miscellaneous records concerning the Albany City Bank, the Albany City Savings Institution, and the National Savings Bank of Albany. Banking Department, State of New York, State Office Building, Albany, N.Y.

Edwin D. Morgan Papers. New York State Library, Albany, N.Y.

John V. L. Pruyn Papers. New York State Library, Albany, N.Y.

Seymour Family Papers. Collection of Regional History, Cornell University, Ithaca, N.Y.

Seymour Papers. Wisconsin Historical Society, Madison, Wis.

Cyrus Woodman Papers. Wisconsin Historical Society, Madison, Wis.

Silas Wright Papers. New York State Library, Albany, N.Y.

II. NEWSPAPERS AND CONTEMPORARY PERIODICALS

Albany Argus, 1814–1872. (References previous to Nov. 1, 1836, are to the semiweekly edition; subsequent to that date, all references are to the daily edition.)

Albany Evening Journal, 1830–1872.

Albany Evening Times, April 9, 1872.

American Railroad Journal (title varies), 1850–1870.
Bankers' Magazine and Statistical Register, 1857.
Chicago American, Aug. 12, 1839.
Corning (N.Y.) Journal, 1851–1872.
Daily Knickerbocker (Albany), April 13, 1872.
Havana (N.Y.) Republican, Nov. 27, 1839.
Indiana Journal (Indianapolis), July 23, 1836.
Iowa Advocate and Half-Breed Journal (Nashville, Iowa), Aug. 16,
    Sept. 1, Sept. 22, Dec. 15, 1847 (only known copies), reprinted in
    Annals of Iowa, 3d ser., X (July, 1912), 450–466.
Merchants' Magazine and Commercial Review, 1849–1867.
New York Times, 1851–1872.
New York Tribune, 1850–1872.

III. GOVERNMENT DOCUMENTS

Iowa
"Decree in Partition of the Half Breed Tract in Lee County,
    Iowa," reprinted in *Annals of Iowa*, 3d ser., XIV (Oct., 1924),
    424–460.
Laws of the Territory of Iowa, 1839.

Michigan
House of Representatives, Documents, 1855, no. 12; *1861*, no. 33.
Laws of Michigan, 1834–1865.

New York (State)
Assembly Documents, 1841, no. 15, no. 147; *1867*, II, no. 19.
Laws of New York, 1800–1870.
Senate Documents, 1847, IV, no. 149.

New York (Cayuga County)
Register of Deeds, 1835–1872. Office of the Clerk of Cayuga
    County, Auburn, N.Y.
Register of Mortgages, 1835. Office of the Clerk of Cayuga
    County, Auburn, N.Y.

New York (Steuben County)
Register of Deeds, 1835–1872. Office of the Clerk of Steuben
    County, Bath, N.Y.

Wisconsin
Laws of the Territory of Wisconsin, 1838.
Laws of the State of Wisconsin, 1861.

United States
  Bureau of the Census. *Manufactures of the United States in 1860; Compiled from the Original Returns of the Eighth Census.* Washington, 1865.
  Interstate Commerce Commission. *Valuation Reports,* XXVII (New York Central Railroad), 1930.
  Reports of Cases Argued and Adjudged in the Supreme Court, 1843–1854. By Benjamin C. Howard; ed. with notes and references to later decisions by Stewart Rapalje. 2d ed. 17 vols. Albany and New York, 1883–1903.
  United States Statutes-at-Large, vols. IV, VII, XII, XIII. Boston, 1850–1866.

IV. OTHER PRIMARY SOURCES

Albany (N.Y.). *City Directory,* 1819–1891.
American Land Company. *Catalogue of Lands in the North-western States Belonging to the American Land Company.* New York, 1847.
——. *Catalogue of 96,046 Acres of Land Belonging to the American Land Company.* New York, 1844.
——. *First Annual Report of the Trustees of the American Land Company.* New York, 1836.
Bigelow, John. *Retrospections of an Active Life.* 5 vols. New York, 1913.
Browning, Orville Hickman. *Diary.* Ed. with introduction and notes by Theodore Calvin Pease and James G. Randall. 2 vols. Springfield, Ill. 1925–1933.
Buffalo (N.Y.). *City Directory, 1836.*
Cunningham, Edith P. *C. E. P. and E. F. P.: Family Letters, 1861–1869.* Boston, 1949.
The Federal Cases; Comprising Cases Argued and Determined in the Circuit and District Courts of the United States from the Earliest Times to the Beginning of the Federal Reporter. 30 vols. St. Paul, Minn., 1894–1897.
Fernow, Berthold, ed. *Calendar of Wills on File and Recorded in the Offices of the Clerk of the Court of Appeals, of the County Clerk at Albany, and of the Secretary of State, 1626–1836.* New York, 1896.

Hill, John J. *Reminiscences of Albany.* New York, 1884.

Holland Land Company's Papers. (Buffalo Historical Society *Publications,* vols. XXXII, XXXIII.) Buffalo, 1937, 1941.

Martin, Morgan L. "Narrative of Morgan L. Martin," *Collections of the State Historical Society of Wisconsin,* XI (1888), 385–415.

The Merchant's and Banker's Almanac. New York, 1854, 1856.

New York Central Railroad Company. *Agreement between the Albany and Schenectady Rail Road Company, the Schenectady and Troy Rail Road Company, the Utica and Schenectady Rail Road Company, the Mohawk Valley Rail Road Company, the Syracuse and Utica Rail Road Company, the Syracuse and Utica Direct Rail Road Company, the Rochester and Syracuse Rail Road Company, the Buffalo and Rochester Rail Road Company, the Rochester, Lockport, and Niagara Falls Rail Road Company, and the Buffalo and Lockport Rail Road Company; Whereby the Said Companies Are Consolidated into One Corporation under the Name of "The New York Central Railroad Company."* Albany, 1854.

——. *Annual Report,* 1853–1870.

——. *Report of a Committee Appointed January 4th, 1855, by the Directors of the New York Central Railroad Company at the Request of the Stockholders.* Boston, 1855.

——. *Report of the Committee of Stockholders of the New York Central Railroad Company, to Whom Was Referred the Annual Report of the Company for the Year Ending September 30th, 1863.* Albany, 1864.

New York Land Company. "Articles of Association of the New York Land Company," *Annals of Iowa,* 3d ser., XIV (Oct., 1924), 437–438.

Saint Mary's Falls Ship Canal Company. *Catalogue of 525,000 Acres of Pine Timber Lands Belonging to the Saint Mary's Falls Ship Canal Company.* Detroit, 1863 (?).

——. *A Catalogue of 125,000 Acres of Valuable Pine Lands in the State of Michigan, Belonging to the St. Mary's Falls Ship Canal Comp'y.* Detroit, 1862.

Scholte, Henry P. *Eene Stem uit Pella* (Amsterdam, Holland, 1848?), trans. by Jacob Van der Zee as "The Coming of the Hollanders to Iowa," *Iowa Journal of History and Politics,* IX (Oct., 1911), 528–574.

Sigourney, Lydia H. *Letters of Life.* New York, 1866.

Stanton, Henry B. *Random Recollections.* 3d ed. New York, 1887.

Troy (N.Y.). *City Directory, 1844.*

Weed, Thurlow. *Life of Thurlow Weed, Including His Autobiography and a Memoir.* 2 vols. Boston, 1884.

Woodworth, John. *Reminiscences of Troy.* Albany, 1860.

Worth, Gorham S. *Random Recollections of Albany from 1800 to 1808.* 3d ed. Albany, 1866.

V. SECONDARY SOURCES

Alexander, De Alva Stanwood. *A Political History of the State of New York.* 4 vols. New York, 1906–1923.

Anderson, George B. *Landmarks of Rensselaer County, New York.* Syracuse, N.Y., 1897.

Atherton, Lewis E. *The Pioneer Merchant in Mid-America.* Columbia, Mo., 1939.

Baxter, James P., 3rd. *The Introduction of the Ironclad Warship.* Cambridge, Mass., 1933.

Bishop, John L. *A History of American Manufactures from 1608 to 1860.* 2 vols. Philadelphia, 1864.

Boyer, Charles S. *Early Forges and Furnaces in New Jersey.* Philadelphia, 1931.

Brown, John H., ed. *The Cyclopedia of American Biographies.* 7 vols. Boston, 1897–1903.

——. *Lamb's Biographical Dictionary of the United States.* 7 vols. Boston, 1900–1903.

Brummer, Sidney D. *Political History of New York State during the Period of the Civil War.* New York, 1911.

Buck, Norman S. *The Development of the Organization of Anglo-American Trade.* New Haven, Conn., 1925.

The Centennial History of Chautauqua County. 2 vols. Jamestown, N.Y., 1904.

Chaddock, Robert E. *The Safety Fund Banking System in New York, 1829–1866.* (Senate Document no. 581, 61 Cong., 2 Sess.) Washington, 1910.

Chandler, Alfred D., Jr. *Henry Varnum Poor, Business Editor, Analyst, and Reformer.* Cambridge, Mass., 1956.

Chandler, William. *History of the St. Mary's Falls Ship Canal.* Lansing, Mich., 1878.

Chase, Franklin H. *Syracuse and Its Environs: A History.* New York, 1924.

Clark, Victor S. *History of Manufactures in the United States.* 3 vols. New York, 1929.

Clayton, W. W. *History of Steuben County, New York.* Philadelphia, 1879.

Cochran, Thomas C. *Railroad Leaders, 1845–1890: The Business Mind in Action.* Cambridge, Mass., 1953.

Corning, N.Y., Junior Chamber of Commerce. *Focus on Corning.* Corning (?), 1948 (?).

Currie, Archibald W. *The Grand Trunk Railway of Canada.* Toronto, 1957.

Dewey, Davis R. *State Banking before the Civil War.* (Senate Document no. 581, 61 Cong., 2 Sess.) Washington, 1910.

Dilliston, William H. *Historical Directory of the Banks of the State of New York.* New York, 1946.

Doty, William J., ed. *The Historic Annals of Southwestern New York.* 3 vols. New York, 1940.

Downs, John P., and Fenwick Y. Hedley, eds. *History of Chautauqua County, New York, and Its People.* 3 vols. Boston, 1921.

Ellis, David M. "Rivalry between the New York Central and the Erie Canal," *New York History,* XXIX (July, 1948), 268–300.

Encyclopedia of Contemporary Biography of New York. 3 vols. New York, 1878–1884.

Erwin, Charles H. *History of the Town and Village of Painted Post and of the Town of Erwin.* Painted Post, N.Y., 1874.

Evans, Paul Demund. *The Holland Land Company.* (Buffalo Historical Society *Publications,* XXVIII.) Buffalo, 1924.

Ferris, Tracy. "Railways of British North America," *Ontario Historical Society Papers and Records,* XXXVIII (Toronto, 1946), 31–42.

Fitch, Charles E. *Memorial Encyclopedia of the State of New York.* 3 vols. Boston, 1916.

Flagg, Azariah C. *Banks and Banking in the State of New York, 1777–1864.* Brooklyn, 1868.

Flick, Alexander C. *History of the State of New York.* 10 vols. New York, 1933–1937.

Gara, Larry. *Westernized Yankee: The Story of Cyrus Woodman.* Madison, Wis., 1956.

Gates, Paul Wallace. *The Wisconsin Pine Lands of Cornell University.* Ithaca, N.Y., 1943.

Geological Survey of Michigan, vol. I: *Upper Peninsula, 1869–1873.* New York, 1873.

Gordon, Thomas F. *Gazetteer of the State of New York.* Philadelphia, 1836.

Hakes, Harlo, ed. *Landmarks of Steuben County, New York.* Syracuse, N.Y., 1896.

Hall, Henry, ed. *America's Successful Men of Affairs.* 2 vols. New York, 1895–1896.

Hammond, Bray. *Banks and Politics in America from the Revolution to the Civil War.* Princeton, N.J., 1957.

——. "Public Policy and National Banks," a review of Arthur M. Schlesinger, Jr., *Age of Jackson,* in *Journal of Economic History,* VI (May, 1946), pp. 79–84.

Harlow, Alvin F. *The Road of the Century: The Story of the New York Central.* New York, 1947.

Hidy, Muriel. "George Peabody, Merchant and Financier, 1829–1854." Unpublished Ph.D. dissertation, Radcliffe College, 1939.

Hidy, Ralph M. *The House of Baring in American Trade and Finance . . . 1763–1861.* Cambridge, Mass., 1949.

Hill, Henry Wayland, ed. *Municipality of Buffalo, New York: A History, 1720–1923.* 4 vols. New York, 1923.

History of Cayuga County, New York. Auburn, N.Y., 1908.

The History of Lee County, Iowa, Containing a History of the County, Its Cities, Towns, &c. Chicago, 1879.

History of Tioga County, Pennsylvania. Harrisburg, 1897.

Holton, David P. and Francis K. *Winslow Memorial: Family Records of the Winslows and Their Descendants in America, with the English Ancestry as Far as Known.* 2 vols. New York, 1877–1888.

Howell, George R., and Jonathan Tenney, eds. *Bi-centennial History of Albany: History of the County of Albany, N.Y., from 1609 to 1886.* 2 vols. New York, 1886.

Hughes, Sarah F., ed. *Letters and Recollections of John Murray Forbes.* 2 vols. Boston, 1899.

Hughes, Thomas P. *American Ancestry, I: The City of Albany.* Albany, 1887.

Hungerford, Edward. *Men and Iron: The History of New York Central.* New York, 1938.

———. *Men of Erie.* New York, 1946.

Jenks, Leland H. *The Migration of British Capital to 1875.* New York, 1927.

Jones, Fred M. *Middlemen in the Domestic Trade of the United States, 1800–1860.* Urbana, Ill., 1937.

Kilburn, Frederich D. *New York's State Banking Institution: A Historical Sketch with a Digest of the Banking Law.* Albany (?), 1900 (?).

Lane, Wheaton J. *Commodore Vanderbilt: An Epic of the Steam Age.* New York, 1942.

McConkey, M. C. "James F. Joy." Manuscript biography consisting of four loose-leaf volumes, Michigan Historical Collections, University of Michigan, Ann Arbor, Mich.

McMaster, Guy H. *History of the Settlement of Steuben County, New York.* Bath, N.Y., 1853.

Malone, Dumas, ed. *Dictionary of American Biography.* 20 vols. New York, 1928–1936.

Memorial and Family History of Erie County, New York. 2 vols. New York, 1906–1908.

Miller, William, ed. *Men in Business: Essays in the History of Entrepreneurship.* Cambridge, Mass., 1952.

Munsell, Joel. *The Annals of Albany.* 10 vols., Albany, 1850–1859; 2d ed., 4 vols., 1869–1871.

———. *Collections on the History of Albany.* 4 vols. Albany, 1865–1871.

Nason, Henry B. *Biographical Record: Officers and Graduates of the Rensselaer Polytechnic Institute, 1824–1886.* Troy, N.Y., 1887.

Neu, Irene D. "The Building of the Sault Canal: 1852–1855," *Mississippi Valley Historical Review,* XL (June, 1953), 25–46.

———. "An English Businessman in Sicily, 1806–1861," *Business History Review,* XXXI (Winter, 1957), 355–374.

———. "Land Credit in Frontier Wisconsin." Unpublished master's thesis, Cornell University, Ithaca, N.Y., 1945.

Nevins, Allan. *Abram S. Hewitt, with Some Account of Peter Cooper.* New York, 1935.

Newton, A. W. "The Chicago and Aurora Railroad," *Railway and Locomotive Historical Society Bulletin,* no. 76 (March, 1949).

"Notes on the Service of Israel T. Hatch in Behalf of New York's

Canals," Buffalo Historical Society *Publications,* XIV (1910), 389–396.

Overton, Richard C. *Burlington West: A Colonization History of the Burlington Railroad.* Cambridge, Mass., 1941.

Parker, Amasa J. *Landmarks of Albany County, New York.* Syracuse, N.Y., 1897.

Pearson, Henry G. *An American Railroad Builder, John Murray Forbes.* Boston, 1911.

Pierce, Harry H. *Railroads of New York: A Study of Government Aid, 1826–1875.* Cambridge, Mass., 1953.

Prentiss, G. L. *The Union Theological Seminary in the City of New York: Its Design and Another Decade of Its History, with a Sketch of the Life and Public Services of Charles Butler, LL.D.* Asbury Park, N.J., 1899.

Rawley, James A. *Edwin D. Morgan, 1811–1883: Merchant in Politics.* New York, 1955.

Redlich, Fritz. *History of American Business Leaders: A Series of Studies.* 2 vols. in 3. Ann Arbor, Mich., 1940–1951.

Remey, Charles M., ed. "Life and Letters of Judge Charles Mason of Iowa, Middle Western Pioneer, 1804–1882." 17 vols. Typescript, Cornell University Library, Ithaca, N.Y.

Reynolds, Cuyler. *Albany Chronicles.* Albany, 1906.

——. *Hudson-Mohawk Genealogical and Family Memoirs.* 4 vols. New York, 1911.

Rice, Harriet L. P. *Harmanus Bleecker, an Albany Dutchman, 1779–1849.* Albany, 1924.

Robert D. Fisher Manual of Valuable and Worthless Securities, VI (1938). New York, 1938.

Robert D. Fisher Mining Manual, I, in *Robert D. Fisher Manual of Valuable and Worthless Securities,* VII (1940). New York, 1940.

Roberts, Millard F., comp. *Historical Gazetteer of Steuben County, New York.* Syracuse, N.Y., 1891.

Robinson, Charles F. *Weld Collections.* Ann Arbor, Mich., 1938.

Schafer, Joseph. *The Winnebago-Horicon Basin.* Madison, Wis., 1937.

Scoville, Joseph. *The Old Merchants of New York City.* 4 vols. New York, 1863–1866.

Sexton, John L. "Coal Mines and Mining," *Papers and Proceedings of the Tioga County Historical Society,* I (1906), 171–175.

Singewald, Joseph T., Jr. "Report on the Iron Ores of Maryland, with an Account of the Iron Industry," *Maryland Geological Survey*, IX (Baltimore, 1911), 121–325.

Spafford, Horatio Gates. *A Gazetteer of the State of New-York*. Albany, 1813.

——. *A Gazetteer of the State of New-York*. Albany, 1824.

Spriggs, W. M. "Great Western Railway of Canada," *Railway and Locomotive Historical Society Bulletin*, no. 51 (Feb., 1940).

Stevens, Frank W. *The Beginnings of the New York Central Railroad*. New York, 1926.

Swank, James M. *History of the Manufacture of Iron in All Ages*. Philadelphia, 1892.

Taussig, F. W. *The Tariff History of the United States*. New York, 1931.

Towner, Ausburn. *Our County and Its People: A History of the Valley and County of Chemung*. Syracuse, N.Y., 1892.

Tucker, Rufus S. "The Distribution of Income among Income Taxpayers in the United States, 1863–1935," *Quarterly Journal of Economics*, LII (Aug., 1938), 547–587.

Van der Zee, Jacob. "The Half-Breed Tract," *Iowa Journal of History and Politics*, XIII (April, 1915), 151–164.

Van Deusen, Glyndon G. *Thurlow Weed, Wizard of the Lobby*. Boston, 1947.

Wax, Anthony S. "Calumet and Hecla Copper Mines: An Episode in the Economic Development of Michigan," *Michigan History Magazine*, XVI (Winter, 1932), 5–41.

Weise, Arthur J. *History of the City of Albany, New York*. Albany, 1884.

——. *History of the City of Troy*. Troy, N.Y., 1876.

——. *Troy's One Hundred Years, 1789–1889*. Troy, N.Y., 1891.

Wheeler, Francis B. *John F. Winslow, LL.D. and the Monitor*. Poughkeepsie, N.Y., 1893.

Wick, B. L. "The Struggle for the Half-Breed Tract," *Annals of Iowa*, 3d ser., VII (April, 1905), 16–29.

Writers' Program of the Works Projects Administration. *Maryland: A Guide to the Old Line State*. New York, 1940.

Young, Andrew W. *History of Chautauqua County, New York*. Buffalo, 1875.

Index